LOGIC, LANGUAGE-GAMES
AND INFORMATION

Logic, Language-Games and Information

KANTIAN THEMES IN THE PHILOSOPHY OF LOGIC

BY

JAAKKO HINTIKKA

OXFORD
AT THE CLARENDON PRESS

Oxford University Press, Walton Street, Oxford OX2 6DP

OXFORD LONDON GLASGOW
NEW YORK TORONTO MELBOURNE WELLINGTON
KUALA LUMPUR SINGAPORE JAKARTA HONG KONG TOKYO
DELHI BOMBAY CALCUTTA MADRAS KARACHI
NAIROBI DAR ES SALAAM CAPE TOWN

ISBN 0 19 824364 2

© *Oxford University Press 1973*

First published 1973
Reprinted 1973, 1979

Printed in Great Britain
at the University Press, Oxford
by Eric Buckley
Printer to the University

PREFACE

THIS book is addressed to two interrelated questions: what is the relevance of formal logic to those numerous activities in which language is used for some non-linguistic purpose? What kind of information (if any) can deduction (logical inference) give to us? Attempts to answer the former question will lead us to examine some of the connecting links between language and reality postulated by logicians and philosophers. The latter question prompts us to discuss the notions of analyticity and information. In order to keep the scope of the enterprise manageable, I have restricted virtually the whole discussion in this book to languages whose logical apparatus is that of first-order logic (quantification theory). Some extensions are in fact obvious, but in this work I shall not try to extend the discussion further to any other part of logic, be it set theory, infinitary logic, type theory, modal logic, or inductive logic.

My answers to both the questions just mentioned turn out to be closely connected—through convergence as well as by contrast—with some of the main ideas of Kant's philosophy of logic and mathematics. The intrinsic interest of these Kantian views has led me to keep an eye on them as the argument of this book proceeds, and even to examine briefly some aspects of their historical background. In a sense, a revival of certain characteristically Kantian themes is thus taking place as a consequence of my observations, though in a considerably modified form.

This book is based on the John Locke Lectures I delivered at Oxford University in 1964. Much of the material, however, has since been modified and expanded; and several of the original lectures have been published on different occasions and in different parts of the world. They are reprinted here, often with considerable revisions. The earlier publications as well as the editors and publishers who have kindly consented to the reprinting of these lectures are listed in the note, 'On the Origin of the Different Essays', elsewhere in this volume.

The separate publication has naturally resulted in some amount of repetition. I have not tried to eliminate it completely, for I see some merit in the possibility of studying the several chapters independently of each other. Nor have I tried to eliminate all the minor differences in notation and usage between the different chapters.

Since much of my argument has as its technical basis the theory of distributive normal forms, it seems to me appropriate to include as a kind of technical appendix to this volume a final chapter which contains a systematic discussion of these normal forms, in spite of the fact that its original address was somewhat different from that of the other lectures and papers appearing here. The methods used are also put into a perspective in the opening chapter 'Logic in Philosophy—Philosophy of Logic' in more informal terms. (This chapter was not originally part of my John Locke Lectures.) Several of the points argued for in the rest of the book are touched on there.

My debts in connection with this book are to more people than I can list here. I am especially grateful to those numerous colleagues and students with whom I have had the opportunity to discuss over the years the topics dealt with here. I am also greatly indebted to Oxford University for the invitation to give the John Locke Lectures out of which this book has grown, and to the University as well as to several of its members for their splendid hospitality during my stay in Oxford. The Center for Advanced Study in the Behavioral Sciences (Stanford, California) has provided much of the leisure (and of the facilities) needed for the final editing. I also want to register my thanks to the Clarendon Press for its patient interest in my John Locke Lectures.

I dedicate this volume to my wife Soili without whom it would not have been written.

JAAKKO HINTIKKA

California and Helsinki
Summer 1971

CONTENTS

ON THE ORIGIN OF THE
DIFFERENT ESSAYS

THE different chapters of this book have somewhat different histories.

Chapter I first appeared under the title 'A Program and a Set of Concepts for Philosophical Logic' in *The Monist*, vol. 51 (1967), pp. 69–92. It is reprinted here, with numerous small changes, with the permission of the publisher, Open Court Publishing Company, La Salle, Illinois.

An early version of Chapter II was originally the second of my John Locke Lectures. It first appeared (under its present title) in *The Monist*, vol. 53 (1969), pp. 204–30, and is reprinted with the permission of the publisher.

A considerably shorter version of Chapter III was likewise a part of my Lectures. It first appeared in American Philosophical Quarterly Monograph Series, no. 2: *Studies in Logical Theory*, ed. by Nicholas Rescher (Basil Blackwell, Oxford, 1968), pp. 46–72.

Chapter IV first appeared in the Quine issue of *Synthese*, vol. 19 (1968–9), nos. 1–2, pp. 69–81, and was reprinted together with the rest of this issue in *Words and Objections: Essays on the Work of W. V. Quine*, ed. by Donald Davidson and Jaakko Hintikka (D. Reidel Publishing Company, Dordrecht, 1969), pp. 69–81. It appears here with a number of small changes and three somewhat longer additions. I have not tried to answer Quine's objections to this paper, however, although they seem to me based on a misunderstanding.

Chapter V is based on my last John Locke Lecture. Its present version was presented at the Metaphysics Colloquium of New York University on 4 January 1971, and it will also appear in the *Proceedings* of the Colloquium.*

Chapters VI–IX originally formed the central part of my Lectures in Oxford. Subsequently they were also presented at a symposium which met in August 1964 at the Internationales Forschungszentrum Salzburg. This explains their earlier publication in *Deskription, Analytizität und Existenz: 3–4*

Forschungsgespräch des internationalen Forschungszentrums für Grund-fragen der Wissenschaften Salzburg, ed. by Paul Weingartner (Pustet, Salzburg and Munich, 1966), pp. 193–214, 215–33, 234–53, and 254–72, respectively. They are reprinted here with several small changes and some minor cuts. 'An Analysis of Analyticity' was also read before the Finnish Academy of Science and Letters and appeared in its *Proceedings* for 1964 (Helsinki, 1966), pp. 101–22.

Chapter X was originally the oral version of my contribution to the symposium on the theme 'Are Mathematical Truths Synthetic *A Priori*?' at the annual meeting of the American Philosophical Association, Eastern Division, in 1968. It first appeared in *Noûs*, vol. 4 (1970), pp. 131–52, and is reprinted by permission of the Wayne State University Press.

Chapter XI first appeared in *Formal Systems and Recursive Functions: Proceedings of the Eighth Logic Colloquium, Oxford, July 1963*, ed. by J. N. Crossley and M. A. E. Dummett (North-Holland Publishing Company, Amsterdam, 1965), pp. 48–91. It is a greatly expanded version of my contribution to the Oxford Colloquium.

All previously published material appears here with the permission of the earlier editors and publishers. Those not already mentioned are: Professor Eugene Freeman (for *The Monist*); D. Reidel Publishing Company (for *Synthese*); Professor Milton Munitz (for the New York University Metaphysics Colloquium); Professor Hector-Neri Castañeda (for *Noûs*).

I

LOGIC IN PHILOSOPHY—PHILOSOPHY OF LOGIC

1. *On the relation of logic to philosophy*

In this book, the consequences of certain logical insights for philosophical problems will be studied. This kind of enterprise has been given different names: philosophy of logic, philosophical logic, logical analysis in philosophy, and so on. In order to find our bearings among such designations, among the ideas on which they are based, and among the conceptual tools which are at our disposal for such an enterprise, a brief survey of some aspects of the interrelations between logic and philosophy is in order. We shall begin with the question: Is there a branch of logical studies especially relevant to applications to philosophy? Is there such a thing as 'philosophical logic'? Basically, my answer is 'no'. There does not seem to be much intrinsic difference in philosophical interest between the different conventional compartments of logic. Much of the recent work in the more esoteric parts of mathematical logic possesses, it seems to me, a great deal of relevance to philosophical inquiry. It is true that most of this work has not caught the eye of philosophers, or has done so only in those relatively rare cases in which logicians have themselves called philosophers' attention to their problems.[1] However, much of the work that has been done in such areas as recursive function theory, model theory, and metamathematics is concerned with the explication and development of concepts and conceptual problems which

[1] Typically, they have done this when a problem they face is thought of as having philosophical significance. A frequent case in point is the problem of choosing the axioms of one's set-theory. Important as this problem, and others like it, are likely to be, they do not exhaust the philosophical interest of recent developments in logic and in the foundational studies. For a survey of these, see Andrzej Mostowski, *Thirty Years of Foundational Studies* (Acta Philosophica Fennica, vol. 17, Basil Blackwell, Oxford, 1966), or Joseph R. Shoenfield, *Mathematical Logic* (Addison-Wesley Publishing Company, Reading, Mass., 1967).

are of the greatest interest and relevance to a philosopher's pursuits.[2]

This lack of interest of the philosophical community in some of the most truly philosophical parts of logic is of course partly inevitable. It is due to the difficulty of mastering a rapidly growing and in many cases highly technical field. What is really disconcerting is not so much the undiluted ignorance of some philosophers' comments on such old subjects as Gödel's results as their failure (or reluctance) to follow Socrates and recognize the extent of their ignorance.

In a rough and ready way, one can nevertheless make a distinction between problems which are studied, at the present moment at least, primarily because of their significance for mathematical logic itself or for the foundations of mathematics, and problems which do not have much of this kind of interest (or not as much as some other subjects) but which are nevertheless of a genuine philosophical interest. Again this division is not hard-and-fast; some problems of the latter kind may later become interesting even to a technically minded logician or may have technical results among their by-products. However, in many cases one may make a distinction here. For instance, not very much of the work that has been done or is being done in modal logic seems to augur new insights into important technical problems in logic or in foundational studies. Nevertheless, modal logic promises much by way of clarification of a great many of the most central philosophical concepts and problems, although apparently less by way of illuminating the concepts of logical necessity and possibility than by illuminating, e.g., the nature of the different propositional attitudes.[3]

[2] Fascinating glimpses of the philosophical implications of this work are given in recent papers by Georg Kreisel. See 'Mathematical Logic', in *Lectures on Modern Mathematics*, vol. 3, ed. by T. L. Saaty (John Wiley & Sons, New York, 1965); 'Mathematical Logic: What Has It Done for the Philosophy of Mathematics?', in *Bertrand Russell: Philosopher of the Century*, ed. by R. Schoenman (Allen & Unwin Ltd., London, and Atlantic-Little, Brown & Co., Boston, 1967), pp. 201–72; 'Informal Rigour and Completeness Proofs', in *Problems in the Philosophy of Mathematics*, ed. by Imre Lakatos (North-Holland Publishing Company, Amsterdam, 1967), pp. 138–57.

[3] This has been made possible by the development of a satisfactory semantical (model-theoretic) treatment of modal logic, due largely to Stig Kanger and Saul Kripke. See Stig Kanger, *Provability in Logic* (Stockholm Studies in Philosophy, vol. 1, Almqvist & Wiksell, Stockholm, 1957); Stig Kanger, 'The Morning Star Paradox', *Theoria*, vol. 23 (1957), pp. 1–11; Stig Kanger, 'A Note on Quantification and Modalities', ibid., pp. 133–4; Stig Kanger, 'On the Characterization of

If one wants to label such parts of logic as modal logic 'philosophical logic' and to distinguish them from others, I have no objections. However, it should be understood that this will not be then an honorific title: on this terminology many of the non-philosophical parts of logic will undoubtedly turn out to have as much philosophical relevance as the so-called philosophical ones. In so far as there is a deeper distinction here, it concerns the nature of the concepts one is trying to understand and to make precise in the different parts of logic. Although many concepts studied in the more technical parts of present-day logic have a clear-cut intuitive content,[4] they are often fairly complicated and soon lead to considerable technical problems. For instance, an attempt to formulate the intuitive notion of arithmetical truth which we seem to have will at once face the fact that the class of these truths cannot be axiomatized. Nevertheless there are, it seems to me, certain concepts which have a great deal of philosophical interest but which can be explicated without too great technical difficulties. In this book, our attention will be focused on a few such relatively non-technical concepts. They belong to the metatheory (syntax, semantics, and pragmatics) of first-order logic (quantification theory). Although these concepts are much less technical than those belonging to many other parts of logic, they frequently lead to problems that have not been dealt with in literature.

In this introductory chapter, I shall try to indicate how these

Modalities', ibid., pp. 152–5; Saul Kripke, 'A Completeness Theorem in Modal Logic', *Journal of Symbolic Logic*, vol. 24 (1959), pp. 1–14; Saul Kripke, 'Semantical Considerations on Modal Logic', *Acta Philosophica Fennica*, vol. 16 (1963), pp. 83–94; Saul Kripke, 'The Undecidability of Monadic Modal Quantification Theory', *Zeitschrift für mathematische Logik und Grundlagen der Mathematik*, vol. 8 (1962), pp. 113–16; Saul Kripke, 'Semantical Analysis of Modal Logic I', ibid., vol. 9 (1963), pp. 67–96; Saul Kripke, 'Semantical Analysis of Modal Logic II', in *The Theory of Models*, ed. by J. W. Addison, L. Henkin, and A. Tarski (North-Holland Publishing Company, Amsterdam, 1965). Cf. also my papers, 'Modality and Quantification', *Theoria*, vol. 27 (1961), pp. 119–28, and 'The Modes of Modality', *Acta Philosophica Fennica*, vol. 16 (1963), pp. 65–82. These two essays have been reprinted in Jaakko Hintikka, *Models for Modalities: Selected Essays* (Synthese Library, D. Reidel Publishing Company, Dordrecht, 1969).

For applications, cf. Jaakko Hintikka, *Knowledge and Belief: An Introduction to the Logic of the Two Notions* (Contemporary Philosophy Series, Cornell University Press, Ithaca, N.Y., 1962); Jaakko Hintikka, *Models for Modalities* (above), and recent papers by Richard Montague.

4 An interesting candidate here is the concept of *second-order* consequence whose importance has recently been emphasized by Kreisel.

concepts can be assigned a natural place in a somewhat more extensive framework of notions which in my tentative and qualified sense are typical of 'philosophical logic'. I shall also indicate, by way of anticipation of the later chapters of this book, some of the applications and problems to which they easily give rise.

2. *Descriptive* v. *modal concepts*

The crucial notion here is that of 'possible world'. Usually it may be interpreted either in the sense of a possible state of affairs or in the sense of a possible course of events; the difference is not relevant to most of my discussion. The importance of this notion derives partly from an idea which has come up a few times in philosophical discussion but which has scarcely ever been elaborated or discussed extensively. In the use of many important concepts, one can distinguish what might be called the descriptive component from the non-descriptive or modal component.[5] This distinction may be characterized as follows: very often what one does by means of a given concept can be analysed by saying that one first describes a possible state of affairs (possible course of events), or several of them, and then comments on it or on them. For instance, one might express one's approval or disapproval of the state of affairs in question, label it as being physically impossible to realize, say that someone knows that it obtains, etc. (Richard Hare, who has made similar remarks in his *Language of Morals*, speaks here of the phrastic and the neustic of a sentence.) This suggests a programme for the logical analysis of a great many important concepts. In order to analyse them, we must first study the concept of a 'possible world' or, if we indulge in what W. V. Quine has called 'semantic ascent', of a 'description of a possible world'. Once this has been accomplished, many other concepts may be studied as operators or functions on such possible worlds or descriptions thereof. In other words, this suggests approaching the ordinary non-modal logic as the logic of world-descriptions, and approaching modal logic (in the wide sense in which it

---

[5] The best and the most extensive discussion of this distinction is given by Erik Stenius in *Wittgenstein's 'Tractatus': A Critical Exposition of Its Main Lines of Thought* (Basil Blackwell, Oxford, 1960), ch. ix. Cf. also Richard Hare, *The Language of Morals* (Clarendon Press, Oxford, 1952), especially pp. 17 ff.

includes not only the study of the concepts of possibility and necessity but also the study of all the other concepts with a similar behaviour) as a study of the properties and interrelations of different possible worlds.[6] It is obvious that these two tasks are in many ways interrelated with each other.

This programme may sound vague and schematic when presented in general terms. Enough work has been done along these lines, however, to show what it amounts to in practice. Its significance is based partly on the fact that we have much more to say about the relatively commonplace notion of truth in a possible world than about such rarefied notions as *logical* truth, *logical* consequence, etc.

But does not this approach involve right from the beginning philosophically suspect entities? It may involve entities other than those philosophers often deal with, but I want to insist that these 'entities' are constantly being relied on by the man in the .street. Anyone who has ever considered, say, the probability of the different possibilities regarding tomorrow's weather has considered several 'possible states of affairs'. Anyone who has ever discussed what he perceives or does not perceive in some particular situation has implicitly classified possible states of affairs into those which are compatible with what he perceives and those which are incompatible with it, for this is just what is involved in the description of what one perceives. (These examples also illustrate the large scope of this kind of conceptual analysis.)[7] The philosophical analysis of what is involved in such

---

[6] This is essentially just what has been done in the work referred to in note 3 above. An especially interesting possibility here is an analysis of the difficulties which Quine and others have found in the idea of a quantified modal logic. I have commented on these difficulties elsewhere, especially in 'Existential Presuppositions and Uniqueness Presuppositions', in *Models for Modalities* (note 3 above), pp. 112–47, and in 'The Semantics of Modal Notions and the Indeterminacy of Ontology', *Synthese*, vol. 21 (1970), pp. 408–24.

[7] In particular, they illustrate the possibility of treating perceptual terms ('perceives', 'sees', etc.) as modal notions. This possibility is foreshadowed in Miss G. E. M. Anscombe's suggestive Howison Lecture 'The Intentionality of Sensation: a Grammatical Feature', in *Analytical Philosophy: Second Series*, ed. by R. J. Butler (Basil Blackwell, Oxford, 1965), pp. 158–80. I have tried to explore this possibility in 'On the Logic of Perception', in *Perception and Personal Identity*, ed. by Norman S. Care and Robert H. Grimm (The Press of Case Western Reserve University, Cleveland, Ohio, 1969), pp. 140–73 (with a reply to comments, pp. 188–96), reprinted in *Models for Modalities* (note 3 above), pp. 151–83. Cf. also my paper, 'Objects of Knowledge and Belief: Acquaintances and Public Figures', *Journal of Philosophy*, vol. 67 (1970), pp. 869–83.

situations may ultimately discover hidden 'intensional entities' or other sorts of philosophically debatable assumptions. At the present stage of the discussion, I want to insist only that my 'possible states of affairs' are entities such as ordinary people normally have no qualms about trafficking with. Whatever difficulties they may give rise to, they cannot be rejected at the outset for philosophical reasons.

A major qualification has to be made here, however. The interplay of the modal and the descriptive component is more involved than my remarks have perhaps suggested. Let us call those modalities (in the wide sense of the word which was explained above and which we shall presuppose in the sequel) which serve to express or to describe the state or attitude (in the widest sense of these words) of some individual *personal* modalities. They are sometimes known as *propositional attitudes*. Examples are offered by such concepts as hope, knowledge, belief, expectation, striving, etc. In considering them as operators, we must make them relative to some individual. Now Wittgenstein has made some very interesting observations on concepts of this sort. If I have understood them correctly, part of what he has emphasized is that the use of such personal modalities has always to be connected with certain public criteria.[8] Statements like 'John hopes that Mary would come' must be intelligible to others besides John, and others must sometimes be said to be in the position to know that they are true. Logically speaking, we could express a similar point by saying that statements ascribing such propositional attitudes to others must be able to occur as a part of the description of a possible state of affairs. This establishes the possibility of the iterated use of personal modalities whenever they pertain to different persons. But pushing this idea further, it may also be argued that even operators related to the same person must be amenable to iteration in a certain sense. If there are public criteria for saying of someone else 'he believes that p', then we can in a sense define what it strictly speaking ought to mean for me to say 'I believe that p': it would mean that exactly those conditions are satisfied that would

---

[8] Ludwig Wittgenstein, *Philosophische Untersuchungen* (*Philosophical Investigations* (Basil Blackwell, Oxford, 1953)), *passim*. See, e.g., § 580: 'An "inner process" stands in need of outward criteria.' Cf. Norman Malcolm, 'Wittgenstein's *Philosophical Investigations*', *Philosophical Review*, vol. 63 (1954), pp. 530–59; reprinted in *Knowledge and Certainty* (Prentice-Hall, Englewood Cliffs, N.J., 1963), pp. 96–129.

enable someone else to say of me, truly: 'He believes that *p*.' By the symmetry between the different pronouns it could be argued that this is logically speaking the basic meaning of the personal modalities as used in the first person singular.[9] Of course this is not what first-person statements are ordinarily used for, since it is obvious that they normally convey much more than this. However, their additional meanings should be analysed by starting from this basic sense. In this sense, which ought to suffice as the only unanalysable sense for the purpose of philosophical discussion, personal modalities can be iterated even when they pertain to one and the same person.

All this shows that the interplay between description and modality is a more complicated matter than my initial remarks perhaps suggested, for it shows that modal concepts can occur within the 'description' to which a modal operator is applied. (This is just what the possibility of the iterated use of modalities means.) Hence the two components cannot be distinguished from each other as simply as might seem. How exactly it is that a modal concept can contribute to the description of a state of affairs cannot be discussed here.

3. *Different kinds of descriptions of possible worlds*

Subject to this qualification, however, we can hope to distinguish the two elements, the descriptive one and the modal one, in the use of many philosophically important concepts. This suggests a two-part programme for philosophical logic. It suggests that we study the descriptive functions of our language from the vantage point of the idea of a possible world; and it suggests that we also study that great variety of concepts which we have labelled 'modal' from the point of view of the way in which one in using them classifies or relates to each other different possible worlds. In this chapter, it is in order to discuss the first part of this programme only. As a consequence, I shall not say here anything about the way in which one can from this point of view put the foundations of modal logic into a new perspective.

[9] A related point has been argued by Bruce Aune in his paper, 'The Complexity of Avowals', in *Philosophy in America*, ed. by Max Black (Muirhead Library of Philosophy, George Allen & Unwin, London, 1965), pp. 35–57. Aune emphasizes the univocity of personal modalities (*inter alia*) as used in the first and the third person.

In a way, my emphasis on the idea of possible world is not at all new. A less picturesque name for a notion closely related to our 'possible world' is 'model'. My plea for the importance of the idea of 'possible world' is therefore partly a plea for the philosophical significance of the model theory of first-order logic.[10] However, it seems to me that the ideas of this model theory have to be developed in suitable directions in order to bring out fully their philosophical significance. A few such developments will be indicated here. Some of them will be discussed in detail in the rest of this book.

One way of seeing the desirability of these developments is to start from the somewhat old-fashioned way of developing the semantics of quantification theory (first-order logic) in terms of what Carnap dubbed state-descriptions.[11] These are just what the name promises: they are as full descriptions of possible states of affairs as one can give by means of negated or unnegated atomic sentences of some fixed first-order language, which may be thought of as an applied language. (These atomic sentences are allowed to contain names for the members of a given domain of individuals and predicates from a given finite set of predicates.) Formally speaking, a state-description is a set of sentences which for each atomic sentence S of the kind just described contains either S itself or its negation $\sim S$.

Because of their close connection with the important idea of a 'description of a possible world' Carnapian state-descriptions are highly interesting philosophically. They have served as the basis of much of Carnap's work in semantics, including his pioneering work in the semantics of modal logic, and in the theory of inductive probability.[12] This work already supports

[10] See, e.g., Abraham Robinson, *Introduction to Model Theory and to the Meta-mathematics of Algebra* (North-Holland Publishing Company, Amsterdam, 1963), or *The Theory of Models: Proceedings of the 1963 International Symposium in Berkeley*, ed. by J. W. Addison, Leon Henkin, and Alfred Tarski (North-Holland Publishing Company, Amsterdam, 1965).

[11] Rudolf Carnap, *Meaning and Necessity*, second edition (The University of Chicago Press, Chicago, 1955), p. 9 and *passim*. Cf. also my paper, 'Carnap's Semantics in Retrospect' (forthcoming).

[12] Rudolf Carnap, *The Logical Foundations of Probability*, second edition (The University of Chicago Press, Chicago, 1962); Rudolf Carnap, *The Continuum of Inductive Methods* (The University of Chicago Press, Chicago, 1952); Rudolf Carnap and Wolfgang Stegmüller, *Induktive Logik und Wahrscheinlichkeit* (Springer-Verlag, Vienna, 1959); Rudolf Carnap, 'The Philosopher Replies: V. Probability and Induction', in *The Philosophy of Rudolf Carnap*, ed. by P. A. Schilpp (The

my claim for the philosophical importance of the idea of a possible world.

However, state-descriptions have definite disadvantages for the purposes of philosophical logic. When we are dealing with an infinite domain, they are infinite, and hence difficult to deal with without strong set-theoretical methods. This disadvantage is connected with another, more basic flaw in this notion of Carnap's: In order to be able to specify a state-description we must have at our disposal a name for each member of the universe of discourse. In order to do anything specific by means of state-descriptions, we must therefore know the whole universe in the sense of being able to name all its members. This is undesirable for many of the applications of the notion of state-description, and has caused Carnap's approach to be subjected to criticism.[13]

One way of viewing the situation is to surmise that the disadvantages of the notion of state-description are due to the fact that it is an *exhaustive* description of a possible world. It is only natural that we cannot give an exhaustive description of a universe without knowing all its members, or of an infinite universe without using an infinity of sentences.

In order to rid our approach of the disadvantages of Carnap's notion, we may try to do two different things. On the one hand, we may try to give up any attempt to give an exhaustive description of our universe of discourse, and to be content with *partial* descriptions. They must of course be still complete enough to show that the described state of affairs is logically possible; but it may be hoped that a notion less demanding than that of a state-description serves this purpose. Pursuing this idea, we can arrive at the notion of *model set*.[14]

Since model sets are only partial descriptions of possible states

Library of Living Philosophers, Open Court, La Salle, Illinois, 1963), pp. 966–98.
[13] See, e.g., Max Black, 'The Semantic Definition of Truth', *Analysis*, vol. 8 (1947–8), reprinted in *Philosophy and Analysis*, ed. by Margaret Macdonald (Basil Blackwell, Oxford, 1954), pp. 235–60, and my papers referred to below in note 30. Some criticisms are also presented in the chapter 'Are Logical Truths Tautologies?' below.

[14] See 'Form and Content in Quantification Theory', *Acta Philosophica Fennica*, vol. 8 (1955), pp. 11–55; 'Notes on Quantification Theory', *Societas Scientiarum Fennica, Commentationes Physico-Mathematicae*, vol. 17, no. 2 (1955). Model sets are discussed and used extensively (under the name 'Hintikka Sets') in Raymond Smullyan, *First-Order Logic* (Springer, Berlin, Heidelberg, and New York, 1968).

of affairs, they are not mutually exclusive. This is a disadvantage for all the purposes that involve the number of mutually exclusive alternatives—the number of different possible worlds, as we may say. For instance, these numbers may be expected to play a crucial role in any reasonable inductive logic. In order to serve these purposes, we must try to do something else. One possible course is to try to give as exhaustive descriptions of the different states of affairs as we can but to restrict our resources of expression in some suitable way. In order to avoid the reliance of one's list of individuals that bothers the notion of state-description, we have to make these exhaustive descriptions independent of the names that we have at our disposal. They contain quantifiers and bound variables, but they must not contain any names (besides those that occur explicitly in the sentences which we want to study). As a result, these descriptions are not any longer descriptions of possible worlds: they are descriptions of possible *kinds* of worlds. This restriction is not enough, however; something further is needed. A restriction which serves us here may be explained as imposing a limit on the number of individuals one is allowed to consider in their relation to each other in the sentences we are using.[15] This parameter may be called the degree of the sentences in question. I shall indicate later how it may be defined. The resulting descriptions of different kinds of possible world I have called constituents. Each sentence F of degree d may be represented as a disjunction of constituents of the same degree. This is called the distributive normal form of F.

4. *Model sets*

Both these ideas have applications of some interest. Let me explain first the idea of a model set in some more detail. One way of arriving at it is as follows: consider the set μ of all sentences that are true in the world described by some state-description. It can be characterized by a number of conditions that are essentially reformulations of the truth-conditions of the

---

[15] The number of individuals which we are considering in their relation to each other in the sense intended has nothing to do with the number of individuals in our universe of discourse. If I say, 'every man has a father', I am considering only two men at one and the same time (as it were) in their relation to each other, namely an arbitrary man and *his* father, although I am making a statement about all the men in my universe of discourse.

sentential connectives and of quantifiers. For instance, we have to require the following:

If $(F \& G) \in \mu$, then $F \in \mu$ and $G \in \mu$, and vice versa.

Furthermore, we have to require that the original state-description is a part of μ.

Now it is easily seen that exactly one half of these conditions is in a sense redundant. For instance, in the condition just quoted we may omit the vice versa part. In general, we need only closure conditions which go 'downwards' in the sense that they say that *if* certain more complicated sentences occur in μ, *then* certain simpler ones must also occur there. (See the list of conditions below.) Instead of requiring that some state-description is included in μ, it suffices to require that an atomic sentence never occurs in μ together with its negation.

The resulting conditions define a model set. They may be formulated as follows:

(C.$\sim$) If F is atomic and $F \in \mu$, then not $\sim F \in \mu$.
(C.&) If $(F \& G) \in \mu$, then $F \in \mu$ and $G \in \mu$.
(C.v) If $(F \vee G) \in \mu$, then $F \in \mu$ or $G \in \mu$.
(C.E) If $(Ex)F \in \mu$, then $F(a/x) \in \mu$ for at least one free singular term a.
(C.U) If $(Ux)F \in \mu$, then $F(b/x) \in \mu$ for each free singular term b which occurs in the sentences of μ.

Here $F(a/x)$ is the result of substituting a everywhere for x in F. It has been assumed for simplicity that negation-signs are allowed to occur only immediately before atomic sentences. This does not essentially restrict the applicability of our concepts.

The sense in which model sets perform the same function as state-descriptions has already been hinted at. Previously, we could say that a sentence is true in some possible world (is *satisfiable*) if it is true in the world described by some state-description. Now we can say the same of model sets: a sentence is satisfiable if and only if it occurs as a member of some model set, or, as we can also express the same idea, if and only if it can be *imbedded in* a model set. Proofs of this fact have been given elsewhere.[16] In terms of satisfiability, we can define in the

---

[16] See the works mentioned in note 14 above.

usual way all the other central metalogical notions: A sentence is inconsistent if and only if it is not satisfiable; it is logically true if and only if its negation is not satisfiable; a sentence F follows logically from G if and only if F & $\sim G$ is not satisfiable; and so on.

It is seen at once that model sets are easier to deal with than state-descriptions in many respects. For instance, they may be finite, and in fact very small, whereas state-descriptions are extremely large even when we have a relatively small universe and a relatively meagre set of basic predicates.

More important than this are the systematic uses of the notion of a model set. By its means, we obtain an interesting way of looking at the usual rules of proof in first-order logic (quantification theory). A proof of F can be conceived of as a disproof of $\sim F$; hence it suffices to consider disproofs only. A disproof of G can now be thought of as a way of showing that G cannot be imbedded in a model set. The conditions defining a model set show us at once one way in which we may try to show this: we may start from the unit set $\{G\}$ of G and try to extend it into a model set by adjoining to it one by one the members which it does not have but which it ought to have if it were a model set. Each application of this idea to a disjunction splits the attempted model set construction into two. If all these ways of trying to imbed G into a model set lead to a violation of the condition (C. $\sim$), it is easy to show that G is inconsistent (not satisfiable). It is not much more difficult to show that every sentence that is not satisfiable can be shown to be inconsistent in this very way. In fact, this result amounts to a completeness proof of quantification theory, and is about as simple a proof as we can hope for.[17]

Thus we have a simple and intuitive way of looking at a certain set of rules of disproof in quantification theory: They are nothing but step-by-step rules for building model sets. By duality (by taking negations everywhere and by turning round the direction of the procedure) we obtain a set of rules of proof for quantification theory. In effect, a proof of F in terms of these rules is nothing but a frustrated attempt to describe a *counterexample* to F (i.e., to construct a model set for $\sim F$). These rules

---

[17] Cf. 'Notes on Quantification Theory' (note 14 above). A set of rules for building model sets is also given in an appendix to this chapter.

turn out to have an especially simple and important form; they are essentially a version of Herbrand-type rules for quantification theory.[18] (For this reason, virtually all the points one makes in terms of model sets can be formulated in terms of Herbrand-type methods. Technically, model sets therefore do not offer much that is new over and above what can be done in terms of Herbrand-type considerations.)

In this way, we obtain a simple and systematic way of building the central parts of the metatheory of first-order logic. Further results are easily obtained. For instance, one easily proves the following result:

If $\mu + \lambda$ is disprovable while neither μ nor λ is, there is a sentence F satisfying the following conditions: (i) F contains only such predicates and individual constants as occur both in the members of μ and in the members of λ; (ii) $\mu + \{F\}$ and $\lambda + \{\sim F\}$ are disprovable.

The proof proceeds by a straightforward induction on the length of the disproof in question.[19] This is essentially a form of Craig's famous interpolation lemma.[20] The proof one obtains for it in this way enables us to tell a number of further facts about F on

[18] See J. Herbrand, 'Recherches sur la théorie de la démonstration', *Travaux de la Société des sciences et des lettres de Varsovie*, classe III, vol. 33 (1928), pp. 33–160, reprinted (with other material) in J. Herbrand, *Écrits logiques*, ed. by J. van Heijenoort (Presses Universitaires de France, Paris, 1968) and translated (by Warren D. Goldfarb) in J. Herbrand, *The Logical Writings of Jacques Herbrand*, ed. by Warren D. Goldfarb (translation of the preceding volume; D. Reidel Publishing Company, Dordrecht, 1971).

[19] If this length is zero, i.e., if $\mu + \lambda$ can be disproved by showing that it violates (C. $\sim$), there must be an atomic formula G such that either $G \in \mu$, $\sim G \in \lambda$ or $G \in \lambda$, $\sim G \in \mu$, for otherwise one of the two sets μ, λ would be disprovable. In the former case, put $F = \sim G$, in the latter, $F = G$.

In the general case, the inductive hypothesis says that one can find F for *any* shorter disproof. The proof splits here into several cases depending on what the first step of the disproof of $\mu + \lambda$ is. For instance, suppose we first adjoined to $\mu + \lambda$ a formula of the form $G(b/x)$ where $(Ux)G \in \mu$ and where b occurs in the formulas of μ. Then by the inductive hypothesis (as applied to $\mu + \{G(b/x)\}$ and λ) we can find H with the required symbols such that $\mu + \{G(b/x)\} + \{H\}$ and $\lambda + \{\sim H\}$ are disprovable. But then so is $\mu + \{H\}$, as one may easily show.

The other cases are not much more difficult; the most intricate is the case which is like the one just treated but in which b occurs in the members of λ but not in those of μ. The reader can supply the details without much trouble.

This argument also provides us with an effective method of constructing F on the basis of the given disproof of $\mu + \lambda$.

[20] In the form in which we have formulated it, it is a separation lemma rather than an interpolation result. In order to see the connection, consider the case in which $\lambda = \{G_1\}$, $\mu = \{\sim G_2\}$. Then our result says that whenever $G_1 \supset G_2$ is

the basis of μ, λ, and of the disproof of $\mu + \lambda$.[21] This simple result illustrates the power of the theory one can build in this way.

More important than this for our present purposes are the philosophical virtues of the concept of a model set. It facilitates greatly the formulation and the solution of several conceptual problems. In an earlier article, I used it to show how a quantification theory without existential presuppositions (i.e., with possibly empty singular terms) can be formulated—and how it *must* be formulated.[22] Another (unpublished) example illustrates the same point. In another article, I have pointed out that the bound variables of quantification admit of two different sorts of interpretation. I have called them exclusive and inclusive interpretations.[23] The inclusive interpretation is the usual one; exclusive interpretations are the ones we have to wean the students away from in teaching elementary logic courses. The exclusive interpretations are explications of such interpretations of quantifiers as the natural reading of 'John hates everyone' as 'really' meaning 'John hates everyone, except possibly John himself', or the equally natural reading of 'Charles admires someone' as 'Charles admires someone else'. In brief, on the

---

provable while neither $\sim G_1$ nor G_2 is, there is an 'interpolation formula' F whose free symbols all occur both in G_1 and in G_2 such that $G_1 \supset F$ and $F \supset G_2$ are provable.

For Craig's proof, see 'Linear Reasoning: A New Form of the Herbrand–Gentzen Theorem', *Journal of Symbolic Logic*, vol. 22 (1957), pp. 250–68; 'Three Uses of the Herbrand–Gentzen Theorem in Relating Model Theory and Proof Theory', ibid., pp. 269–85. For an evaluation of its significance, see J. W. Addison, 'The Theory of Hierarchies', in *Logic, Methodology, and Philosophy of Science, Proceedings of the 1960 International Congress*, ed. by Ernest Nagel, Patrick Suppes, and Alfred Tarski (Stanford University Press, Stanford, California, 1962), pp. 26–37, especially p. 31.

[21] For a number of ways of strengthening Craig's lemma in this direction, see Leon Henkin, 'An Extension of the Craig–Lyndon Interpolation Theorem', *Journal of Symbolic Logic*, vol. 28 (1963), pp. 201–16. Some of Henkin's results may be obtained in the way we have indicated here.

[22] Jaakko Hintikka, 'Studies in the Logic of Existence and Necessity. Part I, Existence', *The Monist*, vol. 50 (1966), pp. 55–76, reprinted in *Models for Modalities* (note 3 above), pp. 23–44.

[23] Jaakko Hintikka, 'Identity, Variables, and Impredicative Definitions', *Journal of Symbolic Logic*, vol. 21 (1956), pp. 225–45. There are really two variants of an exclusive interpretation, one strongly exclusive and the other weakly exclusive. They are distinguished from each other by the question whether we want to exclude coincidences of bound variables whose scopes have a common part *always* or merely whenever the two variables actually occur with the scope of both the quantifiers to which they are bound.

(weakly) exclusive interpretation a bound variable is allowed to range over all individuals except those whose names occur within the scope of the variable. Even this is not a full explanation, but a full one is readily obtained by means of model sets. In order to impose an exclusive interpretation in the quantifiers occurring in them, we clearly have to change the last two conditions to read:

$(C.E)_{excl}$ If $(Ex)F \in \mu$, then $F(a/x) \in \mu$ for at least one free singular term a which does not occur in F;

$(C.U)_{excl}$ If $(Ux)F \in \mu$, then $F(b/x) \in \mu$ for each free singular term b which occurs in the members of μ but not in F.

This at once gives us a full formalization of an exclusive interpretation, thus illustrating the flexibility and power of model sets for the purposes of conceptual analysis.

5. *Model sets as models and as 'pictures'*

Model sets have certain important further virtues, moreover. One way of showing that all the members of each given model set μ can be true in one and the same possible world is to give them an interpretation which may appear artificial but which has a genuine philosophical interest. We can in a certain sense interpret all the members of μ as speaking of themselves. (This dodge is an old hat for logicians, for it goes back at least to Henkin's important completeness proofs of 1949–50.)[24] Roughly speaking, we choose as our universe of discourse the set of all the free singular terms occurring in the members of μ (the symbols themselves, not what they stand for) and let each atomic sentence say that it occurs itself in μ. For the definition of the model one obtains in this way, we thus need essentially only the atomic sentences of μ. The details are obvious, and do not matter much anyway. What is important is the following consequence of the success of this kind of proof: if we have succeeded in building a model set for the purpose of showing that a certain sentence or set of sentences can be true in some possible world, we have

[24] Leon Henkin, 'The Completeness of the First-Order Functional Calculus', *Journal of Symbolic Logic*, vol. 14 (1949), pp. 159–66, and 'Completeness in the Theory of Types', ibid., vol. 15 (1950), pp. 81–91. They are reprinted in *The Philosophy of Mathematics*, ed. by Jaakko Hintikka (Oxford Readings in Philosophy, Oxford University Press, 1969), pp. 42–50 and 51–63, respectively.

done more than to show this in the abstract. By producing the model set μ, we have produced an actual model of the kind of world in which all the members of μ would be true; all we need in order to demonstrate the satisfiability is to interpret the members of μ as referring to this model which is of course a part of this actual world of ours. (It is essentially a set of written symbols.) This may help to allay to some extent the fears of those philosophers who find a 'possible world' too eerie an entity. They can see that for a wide range of logical purposes these possible worlds may simply be taken to be suitably restricted parts of our actual world.

The observation that model sets can serve as their own models can be developed further. Earlier, we saw that suitably formulated proofs in quantification theory can all be viewed as frustrated attempts to build descriptions of counter-examples to the sentence F to be proved (that is, to build model sets which would include $\sim F$). Now we can say more than this: we can say that these proofs are abortive attempts to build such counter-examples themselves, not just verbal descriptions of them. This gives us an even more striking interpretation of quantificational proofs, especially of the important Herbrand-type proofs.

This point of view can be developed further in several directions, one of which might be especially interesting philosophically. (It will be elaborated and defended in the chapter 'Quantification and the Picture Theory of Language' below.) It is well known that in his *Tractatus* Wittgenstein wanted to view all sentences as logical pictures (isomorphic representations) of such states of affairs as would make them true.[25] This 'picture theory of language' has its limitations, and cannot in my opinion give us a full theory of the workings of any logically very interesting language, real or ideal. However, it is a much more powerful and interesting theory than its recent detractors apparently realize. Among other things it is interesting to explore the limits of its applicability. As far as logic is concerned,

[25] Cf. Stenius, op. cit., Chs. vi–vii; Max Black, *A Companion to Wittgenstein's 'Tractatus'* (Cambridge University Press, 1964), especially pp. 72–88, 118–22, 161–4; James Griffin, *Wittgenstein's Logical Atomism* (Clarendon Press, Oxford, 1964), Ch. viii; George Pitcher, *The Philosophy of Wittgenstein* (Prentice-Hall, Englewood Cliffs, N.J., 1964), Ch. iv; Wolfgang Stegmüller, 'Eine Modelltheoretische Präzisierung der Wittgensteinschen Bildtheorie', *Notre Dame Journal of Formal Logic*, vol. 7 (1966), pp. 181–95.

:his theory works most happily as a partial explanation of how ιtomic sentences are understood. In my view it has never been extended in a natural way to quantified sentences.[26] One way of doing so now results from our observations. If atomic sentences can be interpreted as (logical) pictures, then so can consistent sets of such sentences. In particular, we can interpret model sets (strictly speaking, those subsets of model sets which consist of atomic sentences only) in this way. This gives us an interesting extension of the orthodox picture theory to quantification theory. In this modified theory (or model), quantificational sentences are not themselves 'pictures' of states of affairs such as they would be if these sentences were true. Rather, they must be viewed as recipes for the construction of such pictures, namely, such model sets as include them. This connects the picture theory (or, as I prefer to call it, the picture view) for the first time in a clear-cut way with the rules of proof in quantification theory, for we have seen that one particularly important complete set of such rules can be viewed as a set of rules of attempting to construct model sets, i.e., pictures, for the negations of the sentences to be proved. Thus the picture model becomes related in an interesting way with the metatheory of first-order logic.

This extension of the picture theory is commented on further in the chapter 'Quantification and the Picture Theory of Language' later in this volume. One thing that soon emerges from such a study is a vivid sense of limitations of the picture theory as a putative model of the way our language works. Although the extension we sketched has several interesting aspects, many attractive features of the original picture theory break down when it is extended in this way. For instance, infinite or even very large 'pictures' such as model sets cannot simply be 'compared with reality' in the way Wittgenstein apparently assumes that his pictures can be compared without any further ado.[27]

---

[26] Cf. Black, *Companion*, pp. 280–90. The unsatisfactoriness of considering quantified statements as possibly infinite conjunctions and disjunctions scarcely needs to be argued here. What is more interesting is the fact that the idea of a 'proto-picture' does not seem to help us much more. Part of the reason for this may be seen from what follows. If quantified sentences are recipes for the constructions of pictures, but are not themselves pictures, there is no hope of finding 'proto-pictures' imbedded in them.

[27] Cf. *Tractatus* 4.05 'Reality is compared with propositions.'

We have not understood the way our language functions before we have said much of the logic of the processes by means of which these infinite pictures are shown to match or to fail to match the part of the world they refer to. All this makes the relation of the extended picture theory to the use of language much more complicated than in Wittgenstein's original theory, and calls for further investigation.

Thus the concept of a model set, which was essentially that of a partial description of a possible world, turns out to be a useful tool in philosophical logic. Not only does it help us to formulate old problems and solve them; it also leads us to interesting new tasks and problems.

6. *Descriptions of possible worlds with restricted resources of expression*

The other direction which I indicated for the further development of the notion of state-description gives rise to equally interesting problems and results. The basic task in this direction is to make sense of the idea of 'considering so many individuals together in their relation to each other' in a sentence. This idea is clear as long as we are considering only individuals by means of their names; they are readily counted. What is perhaps not as obvious is that each quantifier also invites us to consider an individual, however indefinite it may be. A good approximation toward the number of individuals we are considering together in a given quantificational sentence F (i.e., the degree of F) is therefore the sum of the number of its free singular terms and the length of the longest sequence of nested quantifiers occurring in F (i.e., the number of the different layers of quantifiers in F at its deepest). This approximation serves many purposes quite well. However, it can be made sharper in various ways. First of all, it only serves its purpose satisfactorily if an exclusive interpretation of quantifiers is assumed (and a similar qualification made about the free singular terms of a sentence). Secondly, it is obvious that the individuals that two quantifiers with overlapping scopes invite us to consider are not always related to each other in the sentence. When are they in fact related to each other? In order to answer this question, let us consider two quantifiers occurring in F such that the latter occurs within the scope of the former and that the bound variables occurring in them are x and y, respectively. Then one case is clear: we have related to each other the individuals introduced by these two quantifiers if x and y occur (bound to the quantifiers in question) in one and the same atomic part in F. In this case we shall say that the quantifiers (and the variables bound to them) are *immediately related* to each other in F. However, these variables can also be related to each other mediately. This is the case if there is within the scope of the outer quantifier a sequence of quantifiers with the bound variables $z_1, z_2,..., z_k$ such that x is immediately related to z_1, z_i to z_{i+1} ($i = 1, 2,..., k-1$), and z_k to y. In these circumstances, we shall say that the quantifiers containing x and y are *related* to each other. (In other words, the relation of being related to is the ancestral of the relation of being immediately related to.) Then instead of the longest sequence of nested quantifiers in F we can consider the longest sequence of nested *and related* quantifiers (each quantifier related to its successor). We shall call its length (the number of quantifiers in it) the *depth* of F.

When the degree of F is defined as the sum of this number and the number of free individual symbols in F, the convertibility of F into a disjunction of constituents with the same degree and with the same free symbols still remains valid.

The full definition of a constituent is too complicated to be given here.[28] The basic idea is simple enough, however. It suffices to indicate it for constituents without free singular terms. Such a constituent (say one of degree d) is as full a description of a possible world as one can give without ever speaking of more than d individuals at the same time and without mentioning any particular individuals. In a way, constituents may be considered as a way of building up a theory of 'finitary' or 'approximative' semantics of the kind Herbrand seems to have had in mind.[29]

---

[28] Constituents and distributive normal forms are discussed systematically in the last chapter of this book, which originally appeared in *Formal Systems and Recursive Functions, Proceedings of the Eighth Logic Colloquium, Oxford, July 1963*, ed. by J. N. Crossley and M. A. E. Dummett (North-Holland Publishing Company, Amsterdam, 1965), pp. 47–90. Cf. also Jaakko Hintikka, *Distributive Normal Forms in the Calculus of Predicates* (Acta Philosophica Fennica, vol. 6, Societas Philosophica Fennica, Helsinki, 1953); 'Distributive Normal Forms and Deductive Interpolation', *Zeitschrift für mathematische Logik und Grundlagen der Mathematik*, vol. 10 (1964), pp. 185–91.

[29] Cf. Herbrand, op. cit., and Burton Dreben and John Denton, 'Herbrand-Style Consistency Proofs', in *Intuitionism and Proof Theory*, ed. by A. Kino, J. Myhill,

The basic reason why they are philosophically interesting is very intuitive, and closely related to their basic meaning according to which they are as nearly exhaustive descriptions of possible worlds as our limited resources allow us to give. Constituents of degree d (with certain fixed predicates and free singular terms) represent all the alternatives that we can describe by the resources that have been employed in them. Each sentence of degree d or less which is also restricted to these predicates and singular terms admits some of these alternatives, and excludes the rest. Everything that can be done in terms of such admitted or excluded alternatives can be done by means of the constituents. For instance, a sentence is in some sense the more probable the more alternatives it admits. This gives rise to a new theory of inductive probability in the same way as Carnap's notion of a state-description led him to his theory of inductive probability. Although parts of the new theory of inductive probability remain to be worked out, it has already proved to be highly suggestive of interesting further concepts and results.[30] Not surprisingly, its major advantage seems to be its capability of handling inductive generalizations, that is to say, quantified sentences arrived at on inductive grounds. This seems to me to be highly encouraging in several respects. For one thing, it means that for the first time we can hope to find in inductive logic exact methods for discussing the learning of general laws. Also, the problem of testing truly general non-probabilistic hypotheses, which is admittedly a very poorly understood subject, can perhaps now be approached in ordinary probabilistic terms.[31]

and R. Vesley (North-Holland Publishing Company, Amsterdam, 1970), pp. 419–33.

[30] Cf. my papers 'Towards a Theory of Inductive Generalization', in *Proceedings of the 1964 International Congress for Logic, Methodology, and Philosophy of Science*, ed. by Yehoshua Bar-Hillel (North-Holland Publishing Company, Amsterdam, 1965), pp. 274–88; 'On a Combined System of Inductive Logic', *Acta Philosophica Fennica*, vol. 18 (1965), pp. 21–30; 'Induction by Enumeration and Induction by Elimination', in *The Problem of Inductive Logic, Proceedings of the International Colloquium in the Philosophy of Science, London, 1965*, vol. 2, ed. by Imre Lakatos (North-Holland Publishing Company, Amsterdam, 1968), pp. 191–216; 'A Two-Dimensional Continuum of Inductive Methods', in *Aspects of Inductive Logic*, ed. by Jaakko Hintikka and Patrick Suppes (North-Holland Publishing Company, Amsterdam, 1966), pp. 113–32. Cf. also Jaakko Hintikka and Risto Hilpinen, 'Knowledge, Acceptance, and Inductive Logic', *Aspects of Inductive Logic*, pp. 1–20.

[31] Concerning the insufficiency of accepted statistical practices to clarify this

Conversely, there is a sense in which a sentence is the more informative the more alternatives it rules out. (This sense has been strongly emphasized by Sir Karl Popper[32] and partly formalized by Carnap and Bar-Hillel.)[33] This notion of information can also be spelled out in terms of the theory of distributive normal forms.[34] As a special case, we obtain the notion of a sentence with zero information, that is to say, the notion of tautology, which can in this way be partly vindicated.

This concept of information can be given a new twist, however. In order to see what it is, it is necessary to go back to the notion of constituent. The distributive normal forms, which are disjunctions of constituents, constitute a direct generalization of the complete disjunctive normal form of propositional logic. Unlike this propositional normal form, the distributive normal forms do not give us a decision method. Why not? The reason is that some of the constituents of degree two or more are, unlike the disjuncts of the propositional normal form, inconsistent. Moreover, there is no recursive way of finding out which constituents are inconsistent, although there is a very natural mechanical way of weeding out certain trivially inconsistent ones.

Thus we face a choice in trying to define concepts like information in terms of constituents. Shall we consider consistent (satisfiable) constituents only, or shall we include non-trivially

problem, cf. Leonard J. Savage, *The Foundations of Statistics* (John Wiley & Sons, New York, 1954), pp. 254–6.

[32] See Sir Karl R. Popper, *The Logic of Scientific Discovery* (Hutchinson's, London, 1959), secs. 23, 31, appendix *ix, and *passim*.

[33] Yehoshua Bar-Hillel and Rudolf Carnap, 'Semantic Information', *British Journal of the Philosophy of Science*, vol. 4 (1953–4), pp. 147–57; *An Outline of a Theory of Semantic Information* (Technical Report No. 247 of the Research Laboratory of Electronics, Massachusetts Institute of Technology; Cambridge, Mass., 1952), reprinted as Ch. xv of Yehoshua Bar-Hillel, *Language and Information: Selected Essays on Their Theory and Application* (Addison-Wesley Series in Logic; Addison-Wesley Publishing Company, Reading, Mass., Palo Alto, Calif., and London, 1964). Cf. also J. G. Kemeny, 'A Logical Measure Function', *Journal of Symbolic Logic*, vol. 18 (1953), pp. 298–308.

[34] In addition to papers mentioned in note 28 above, see 'Are Logical Truths Analytic?', *Philosophical Review*, vol. 74 (1965), pp. 178–203; Jaakko Hintikka and Juhani Pietarinen, 'Semantic Information and Inductive Logic', in *Aspects of Inductive Logic* (note 30 above), pp. 96–112, 'On Semantic Information', in *Information and Inference*, ed. by Jaakko Hintikka and Patrick Suppes (D. Reidel Publishing Company, Dordrecht, 1970), pp. 3–27; and Chapters VII, VIII, and X of the present volume.

inconsistent constituents also? In some cases we obviously must choose one of these alternatives. For instance, in the theory of inductive probability we can only consider consistent ones. (Incidentally, this makes the resulting degrees of confirmation non-recursive in general, a fact not altogether lacking philosophical interest, for it suggests an interesting answer to Black's question, 'How difficult might induction be?')[35] In the case of information theory, however, the decision seems to be much more difficult. Fortunately, we are spared the task of making a decision here, for *both* choices (i.e., either disregarding non-trivially inconsistent constituents or handling them on a par with consistent ones) result in interesting theories of information, although of course theories of an entirely different character.[36] The concepts they deal with might be called depth information and surface information, respectively.[37] (As a special case, we obtain the concepts of depth tautology and surface tautology.) Their character might be explained, albeit somewhat roughly, as follows: depth information is the totality of information we can extract from a sentence by all the means that logic puts to our disposal. Surface information, on the contrary, is only that part of the total information which the sentence gives us explicitly. It may be increased by logical operations. In fact, this notion of surface information seems to give us for the first time a clear-cut sense in which a valid logical or mathematical argument is not tautological but may increase the information we have. In first-order logic, valid logical inferences must be depth tautologies, but they are not all surface tautologies.

[35] Max Black, 'How Difficult Might Induction Be?', in Max Black, *Problems of Analysis* (Cornell University Press, Ithaca, N.Y., 1954), pp. 209–25. In my terms, the answer turns out to be this: the general problem of induction in a universe governed by a certain complex of laws L is as difficult as the decision problem for the theory whose only non-logical axiom is L.

[36] Concerning the desirability of developing a theory of information based on the second alternative, cf. Rulon Wells, 'A Measure of Subjective Information', in *Structure of Language and Its Mathematical Aspects* (Proceedings of Symposia in Applied Mathematics, vol. 12, American Mathematical Society, Providence, R.I., 1961), pp. 237–44. I cannot agree with Wells, however, in his suggestion that two sentences which are both of the explicit form $F \lor \sim F$ could have different subjective information.

[37] The highly interesting 'surface' notions will be studied in somewhat greater detail in Chapters VII, VIII, and X below. See also my papers, 'Surface Information and Depth Information' in *Information and Inference* (note 34 above), pp. 263–97, 'Are Mathematical Truths Synthetic *A Priori*?', *Journal of Philosophy*, vol. 65 (1968), pp. 640–51, and 'Surface Semantics: Definition and Its Motivation' (forthcoming).

This alone would lend a great deal of interest to these conceptual developments. As an extra bonus, it turns out that the notion of surface tautology is closely related to certain classical issues in the philosophy of logic, notably to Kant's doctrine of the synthetic character of mathematical reasoning.[38] From our point of view this doctrine may be considered essentially as saying that much of the non-trivial reasoning codified in mathematical logic is not tautologous in the sense of surface tautology.

The connection is mediated by the idea of 'considering so many individuals in their relation to each other'. On the one hand, this idea is related to Kant's notion of a construction. On the other hand, it is connected with non-trivial provability as follows: all the non-trivially inconsistent constituents can be discovered by a systematic procedure which consists essentially in raising the degree of our constituents more and more. The element of undecidability is due to the fact that we often do not know how deep we have to go to uncover whatever hidden inconsistencies there may be in a given constituent. The length of this process seems to be a good rough index of the non-triviality of the disproof in question, and various sharper measures of the same kind of non-triviality are easily characterized.[39] Since all the other important kinds of logical argument (proofs of logical truth, proofs from premises, equivalence proofs) can likewise be shown to turn on the elimination of inconsistent constituents, we obtain in the same way interesting indexes of their non-triviality (syntheticity). Non-trivial proofs thus turn out to be exactly those in which surface information grows, and also exactly those in which new individuals are 'constructed' in the sense of being brought into the argument. The surface information grows the more the more individuals we have to consider in their relation to each other.

There also seem to be interesting connections between the notion of surface information and such concepts as 'meaning'

---

[38] In addition to Chapters V, VII, VIII, and X of the present book, see also my papers 'On Kant's Notion of Intuition (*Anschauung*)', in *The First Critique: Reflections on Kant's Critique of Pure Reason*, ed. by Terence Penelhum and J. J. MacIntosh (Wadsworth Studies in Philosophical Criticism, Wadsworth Publishing Company, Belmont, Cal., 1969), pp. 38–53, 'Kant on the Mathematical Method', *The Monist*, vol. 51 (1967), pp. 352–75, and 'Kantian Intuitions', *Inquiry*, vol. 15 (1972).

[39] In addition to the last chapter of the present book, see 'Surface Information and Depth Information' (note 37 above).

and 'saying'. When we discuss what a statement *means* or *says* or what someone *means* or *asserts* (apart from psychological factors) by it, we are often unwilling to include within this meaning something that follows logically from what he says only by a complicated logical argument. If someone should assert the axioms of elementary geometry, he does not thereby *assert* all their consequences, nor are they part of what his assertion *means* in what seems to me the most obvious and ordinary senses of assertion and meaning. The notion of surface information is therefore likely to turn out important also for the purpose of understanding these senses, a task which largely remains to be accomplished.

APPENDIX

Rules for Model Set Construction

Assume that λ is an approximation to a model set. Then a new approximation can be obtained by means of an application of one of the following rules:

(A.&)   If $(F_1 \& F_2) \in \lambda$, add F_1 and F_2 to λ.

(A.v)   If $(F_1 \vee F_2) \in \lambda$, and if neither F_1 nor F_2 occurs in λ, add F_1 or F_2 to λ.

(A.E)   If $(Ex)F \in \lambda$ and if λ contains no sentences of the form $F(b/x)$, add $F(a/x)$ to λ, where a is an arbitrary *new* singular term.

(A.U)   If $(Ux)F \in \lambda$ and if b occurs in the members of λ, add $F(b/x)$ to λ.

When (A.v) is used, both of the two alternative outcomes will have to be considered, i.e., our construction tree branches always when (A.v) is applied.

If one of the approximations to a model set we reach in this way fails to satisfy (C.$\sim$), we have come to a dead end, for no further applications of our rules can remove this violation of the defining conditions of a model set.

If this happens to *all* branches of some construction tree, the initial set of sentences was inconsistent. Showing this in general means of course proving the soundness of our rules. Likewise, showing that the inconsistency of each inconsistent set of sentences can be brought out in this way means proving the completeness of our set of rules. For proofs, see the works listed in note 14 above.

In order to make sure that an inconsistent set of sentences will eventually be shown to be inconsistent in this way, it suffices to give the other rules a priority over (A.E) from some stage on.

II

QUANTIFICATION AND THE PICTURE THEORY OF LANGUAGE

1. *The picture view of language*

IN the first chapter of this book, I sketched some aspects of a semantical theory of quantification, developed in terms of the concept of model set.[1] I also indicated a method of relating this semantical, or half-semantical, theory to the usual deductive (syntactical) methods. This method turned on considering proofs of logical truth as frustrated attempts to describe a counter-example to the sentence to be proved.[2] In this chapter, I propose to relate some of the observations that can be made along these lines to the doctrines which are generally known as picture theories of language.[3] My main thesis is that these theories can be related rather closely to the logic of quantification by developing them in a suitable direction, and by using the concept of model set as a mediating link.

Since I do not think that these 'theories' really amount to a general theory of language I shall often speak of a picture *view* instead of a picture *theory*. But even though a view of this kind does not go very far towards providing a full account of what really happens when language is used, it may nevertheless serve

---

[1] Above, pp. 9–15. See also the literature mentioned there in note 14. The definition of model set is given above, p. 11.

[2] A model set (of an interpreted first-order language) can be thought of as a partial description of a 'possible world' in which all its members are true. This is shown (*inter alia*) by the fact that a set of sentences of our language (say λ) is satisfiable if and only if there is a model set μ, $\mu \supseteq \lambda$. A method of trying to prove a sentence F is obtained by considering the step-by-step procedures by means of which we might try to construct a counter-example to it, i.e., a model set μ, $\sim F \in \mu$. If these procedures are frustrated in all directions, then F can be shown to be logically true. For details see the preceding chapter and the literature referred to there. Rules for trying to construct a model set in which a given set λ of first-order sentences can be embedded are given in the Appendix to Chapter I above.

[3] The best-known version of these theories is the one developed in Ludwig Wittgenstein's *Tractatus Logico-Philosophicus* (Routledge & Kegan Paul, London, 1921).

as an instructive model to which we can compare our observations of how language actually functions, rather like the language games Wittgenstein envisages in his later writings.[4]

The best-known example of what I just referred to as a picture theory was put forward by Wittgenstein in the *Tractatus Logico-Philosophicus*. I cannot here enter the thorny thickets of Wittgensteinian exegesis, however.[5] What I shall do is take (with some modifications) one particular interpretation of Wittgenstein's theory, and show how it can be developed further so as to become very closely related to our methods of dealing with quantification theory. This interpretation is the one given by Erik Stenius in his book *Wittgenstein's Tractatus*.[6] Although I think that Stenius is right on most of the important problems of interpretation, it does not matter for my present purpose even if his interpretation should turn out not to be a faithful reproduction of the contents of *Tractatus* as much as a further development and a modification of Wittgenstein's ideas. I can always say with another philosopher, in view of the intrinsic interest of Stenius's views: 'Se non e vero, e ben trovato.'

2. *The basic ideas*

What I shall try to say is basically very simple. It is complicated, however, by the necessity of explaining fairly carefully

[4] See especially *Preliminary Studies for the Philosophical Investigations, Generally Known as the Blue and Brown Books* (Basil Blackwell, Oxford, 1958); and *Philosophische Untersuchungen—Philosophical Investigations* (Basil Blackwell, Oxford, 1953).

[5] The extensive secondary literature on the *Tractatus* seems to me especially inconclusive concerning the motives and the precise character of the picture theory. Representative samples of this literature are Max Black, *A Companion to Wittgenstein's Tractatus* (Cambridge University Press, 1964); G. E. M. Anscombe, *An Introduction to Wittgenstein's Tractatus* (Hutchinson, London, 1959; 2nd ed., with changes, 1965); James Griffin, *Wittgenstein's Logical Atomism* (Clarendon Press, Oxford, 1964); George Pitcher, *The Philosophy of Wittgenstein* (Prentice-Hall, Englewood Cliffs, N.J., 1964); and the essays reprinted in *Essays on Wittgenstein's Tractatus*, ed. by I. M. Copi and R. W. Beard (Macmillan, London and New York, 1966). The best discussions of Wittgenstein's picture theory are (in my judgement) those given by Erik Stenius and Wolfgang Stegmüller; see Erik Stenius, *Wittgenstein's Tractatus: A Critical Exposition of Its Main Lines of Thought* (Basil Blackwell, Oxford, 1960); cf. also his papers, 'Linguistic Structure and the Structure of Experience', *Theoria*, vol. 20 (1954), pp. 153–72, and 'Mood and Language-Game', *Synthese*, vol. 17 (1967), pp. 254–74; and Wolfgang Stegmüller, 'Eine Modelltheoretische Präzisierung der Wittgensteinschen Bildtheorie', *Notre Dame Journal of Formal Logic*, vol. 7 (1966), pp. 181–95.

[6] See the preceding footnote for references to Stenius's book and to some of the discussion it has provoked.

the basic ideas of my version of the picture view in order to avoid at least some of the misinterpretations that have befallen Wittgenstein's picture theory. The following seem to me some of the most salient features of the version of picture view I want to consider:

(i) When a sentence is said to be a picture of a fact, the force of the term 'picture' is that of 'isomorphic representation'.

(ii) In order for anything to be an isomorphic representation of anything else, they must both have a certain structure. In the terminology of Stenius, they must both be 'articulate fields'. This means that they must both be structured into a number of *individuals* (Stenius calls them objects), and a number of properties which these individuals may have, and a number of relations (each with a fixed number of terms) which may obtain between these individuals. We shall call both properties and relations *predicates*, and we shall refer to predicates and individuals as the *elements* of the field in question. (Properties are one-place predicates while relations are predicates with more than one argument.)

(iii) Two articulate fields R and S can be said to be isomorphic only with respect to what Stenius calls a *key*. A key is one-to-one correlation of the elements of R with the elements of S. The only further requirement is that the key must correlate each element of R with an element of S which is of the same *category*. That is to say, it must correlate individuals with individuals, properties with properties, and in general n-place predicates with n-place predicates.

(iv) Let ϕ be such a key correlating each element s of S with an element $\phi(s)$ of R. This key is said to establish an isomorphism if and only if the following condition is satisfied:

(1) If s is an n-term predicate of S and if $a_1, a_2,..., a_n$ are individuals of S, then this predicate belongs to the individuals $a_1, a_2,..., a_n$ (in this order) if and only if the correlated predicate $\phi(S)$ belongs to the correlated individuals $\phi(a_1), \phi(a_2),..., \phi(a_n)$.

This explains, however briefly, the notion of an isomorphism on which the variant of the picture theory which I am considering depends. But how does it apply to languages? The following points will go some way towards answering this question:

(i) The key can still be selected in a great variety of ways. Sometimes the picture theory has been misunderstood because this liberty has not been appreciated; it has been thought that the key should somehow correlate with each other elements which are 'similar' in some everyday sense of the word, e.g., spatial relations with spatial relations.[7] This, however, is a serious misunderstanding of the picture theory.[8] It seems to me that this misunderstanding is due to a source which has also caused certain other difficulties in understanding the nature of the picture theory. This common source of difficulty is a failure to understand, or to accept, the very general and abstract sense in which such crucial concepts as that of a correlation and a relation have to be understood in the picture theory.

(ii) Nevertheless, the key remains the same for all the sentences of one and the same language. It is what characterizes a given language from the point of the picture view. The key is what one must know in order to understand the sentences of the language.

(iii) When we are given a sentence of a language, we are not given a number of individuals plus a number of predicates. We are, rather, given a number of words or comparable symbols, of which the sentence in question is put together according to certain grammatical rules.[9] Now words are not individuals in the sense in which we are using the term. In the most common sense of the word, a word is a type of word-tokens. This necessitates a minor modification of one original picture view. What is to be correlated one-to-one with the elements of reality are not word-tokens but word-types. Unlike word-types, word-tokens are correlated many–one with the elements of reality. In what follows, by 'word' we shall normally mean a word-type.

(iv) We seem to be involved in a much more serious violation of the category requirement, however. When the nature of an isomorphic representation was explained, we considered

---

[7] See, e.g., Edna Daitz, 'The Picture Theory of Meaning', *Mind*, vol. 62 (1953), pp. 184–201.

[8] *Tractatus* 4.011, 4.014, and 4.016 should be enough to discourage this idea; cf. also Wittgenstein's subsequent distinction between 'pictures by similarity' and pictures in a wider sense in *The Blue Book* (note 4 above), pp. 36–8.

[9] In this post-Chomsky era it is scarcely necessary to point out the extent to which this statement is an oversimplification. This oversimplification does not matter for my present purposes, however.

correlations of individuals with individuals and of predicates with predicates with as many arguments. However, in describing the relation of a language (whether natural or formalized) to reality, it is natural to say that each of the different elements of reality is in the language represented by a word or by some comparable symbol referring to it. This apparently violates the category requirement, for it seems to mean that the individuals of the sentence (i.e., the words it contains) are correlated not only with the individuals of the reality but also with its predicates.

One of the most important distinguishing marks of the variant of the picture theory which we are considering is the solution it offers to this difficulty. According to this solution, what really corresponds to (say) a relation in a sentence is not the word which is usually said to refer to the relation in question. For instance, what in the English language (considered from the vantage point of our picture view) corresponds to the relation of loving is not the word 'loves' but rather a relation which in the simplest case could be described as the relation of filling the two gaps of the sentence-frame '. . . loves . . .', i.e., the relation of standing respectively on the left-hand side and on the right-hand side of the word 'loves'. Of course, this is strictly true of very simple sentences only. But in so far as the picture theory applies to the English language, there must be a similar relation obtaining between certain linguistic expressions in all the English sentences in which someone is said to love someone else (by using the verb 'to love'). Given any such sentence, there must be purely linguistic criteria for distinguishing who is said in it to love whom (in the sense of criteria for picking out the expressions which refer to these two individuals).

3. *Logical symbolism as a pictorial language*

The question of the applicability of our picture view to ordinary language may also be approached from a different direction. It seems to me that the version of the picture view which I have just sketched is in certain respects very congenial to a logician. In a way, the usual logical notation (e.g., that of *Principia Mathematica*) is the perfect answer to a picture theorist's prayers. For what corresponds (say) to a two-place relation in the current logical symbolism is not just a predicate symbol (letter), e.g., 'P', but a letter with two argument-places attached to it:

'*P* (..., ...)'. And this is nothing but a relation which obtains between two expressions whenever (and only when) they happen to fill the appropriate argument-places in '*P* (..., ...)'. Thus the usual logical notation of predicate logic (Quine's 'canonical notation') is just what a picture theorist needs.

This success carries over to a natural language just to the extent to which this language can be translated into the usual logical symbolism which Frege and Russell already used. (Cf. *Tractatus* 3.325.) It is usually said that, e.g., an English sentence in which a certain person is said to love some other person is of the logical form '$P(a, b)$', i.e., of the form of a two-place predicate ascribed to a pair of individuals, referred to by '*a*' and '*b*'. In order to say this, however, we must be able to tell which English expressions correspond to '*a*' and '*b*'. And in so far as there is a purely linguistic rule for doing this, there exists in a sufficiently abstract sense of the word a purely linguistic relation which obtains between these English expressions. (On the notion of a general rule, cf. *Tractatus* 4.0141.)

Thus there is a very close connection between the picture theory of language and the idea that everything we say in a natural language must be translatable into a logical symbolism. This fact can (and should) serve to elucidate Wittgenstein's remarks in the *Tractatus* much further than his commentators have realized. It is not for nothing that Wittgenstein points out that in the case of a sentence in a logical notation it is 'obvious' that it can be conceived of as a picture (4.012) and that he uses a sentence in the same notation to illustrate one of the crucial features of his picture theory (3.1432; cf. also 3.143). It seems to me that Wittgenstein approaches in the *Tractatus* the idea that a key has to preserve categories (i.e., the idea of a 'true key' in Stenius's sense) largely through the idea that the logical symbolism of Frege and Russell brings out the actual roles of the different kinds of symbols.[10]

[10] From this point of view, we can also understand at once why Wittgenstein found it so easy to believe that all language is basically pictorial. The *Principia* symbolism did seem to be a universal notation for everything that can be expressed clearly ('kann klar gesagt werden'). Hence the 'pictorial' character of this particular symbolism was easily taken to show the pictorial character of all logically satisfactory language.

This point has probably been obscured by the fact that Wittgenstein spends a great deal of time and space to criticize what he took to be the divergencies of the *Principia* symbolism from an explicit and consistently developed picture view. These

Since the picture view of language is thus applicable to natural languages to the extent in which they can be translated into a suitable logical symbolism, we may in discussing this view simply restrict our remarks to sentences which are already in such a symbolism. In the sequel, it is assumed that 'a', 'b', 'c',... are symbols referring to individuals—we shall call them free singular terms—and that 'P', 'Q',... are predicate symbols (each with a fixed number of argument-places). The letters 'x', 'y', 'z',... are used to indicate the argument-places of predicate symbols and to serve as bound variables. From these symbols, atomic sentences are built in the usual way. For instance, if '$P(x, y)$' is a predicate symbol with two argument-places and if 'a' and 'b' are free singular terms, '$P(a, b)$' is an atomic sentence.

4. *Picture view and truth-conditions*

Finally, it may be noted that in a sense the term 'picture theory of language' is a misnomer. This theory does not hold that all the sentences of a language are pictures of actual facts. Indeed, in the different grammatically correct sentences of a language the different elements of the language appear in many different combinations. What the 'picture theory' suggests is not that every sentence is a picture of a fact but that *true* sentences are isomorphic representations of the reality of which they speak. (A false sentence is a picture of the world such as it would be *if* the sentence *were true*.) It is interesting to see that Wittgenstein's picture theory was from the very beginning calculated to explain the nature of truth. One of his earliest notebook entries on the subject contains the remark: 'This must yield the nature of truth straight away.'[11]

For an atomic sentence in our logical symbolism it is easy to formulate the condition on which it is true. Each predicate symbol 'P' with (say) n argument-places stands for a predicate.

criticisms are directed largely against certain features of those parts of the *Principia* symbolism, however, which we are not here directly concerned with, especially against Russell's theory of types and against his treatment of identity. Although they point to serious discrepancies between the *Principia* symbolism and what Wittgenstein took to be the implications of the picture view, they nevertheless should not obscure the great extent to which the usual logical notation (including that of the *Principia Mathematica*) is pictorial in what I take to be the sense intended in the *Tractatus* and hence tends to encourage a picture view of language.

[11] Ludwig Wittgenstein, *Notebooks 1914–1916*, ed. by G. E. M. Anscombe (Basil Blackwell, Oxford, 1961), p. 7.

It was pointed out, however, that what really represents this predicate is not the predicate symbol 'P' itself, but rather the relation which obtains between n expressions of the right sort if and only if they fill the appropriate argument-places in the expression '$P(x_1, x_2,..., x_n)$'. In our sense of the term, a key correlates this relation with the predicate for which 'P' stands. In doing so, it of course also correlates the predicate symbol 'P' with the same predicate. In what follows, we shall consider this correlation rather than the one of the original kind. The new correlation will be called an *interpretation* rather than a key. It correlates each predicate symbol 'P' with n argument-places with a predicate $\phi(P)$, with the same number of arguments. Free singular terms are correlated with individuals, as before. An interpretation will not establish an isomorphism, although the associated key which correlates '$P(x_1, x_2,..., x_n)$' with $\phi(P)$ will establish one.

Using these conventions, a truth-condition for atomic sentences can be easily formulated:

(2) The sentence '$P(a_1, a_2,..., a_n)$' where 'P' is a predicate symbol with n argument-places and 'a_1', 'a_2',..., 'a_n' are free singular terms (not necessarily different from one another) is true if and only if the predicate $\phi(P)$ belongs to the individuals $\phi(a_1), \phi(a_2),..., \phi(a_n)$ (in this order).

This concludes our brief survey of one particular variant of the picture theory of language. This survey has to some extent been idiosyncratic, omitting some of the most important aspects of Wittgenstein's picture theory.

5. *Model sets and satisfiability*

This survey is nevertheless hoped to serve two purposes. First, it prepares ground for an extension of the picture view to quantification theory. Second, it brings out the close relation which there obtains between some aspects of the picture view of language and symbolic logic. Certain connections between them were already pointed out. What is more important, the truth-condition for atomic sentences which was just formulated on the basis of our version of the picture view of language is to all practical purposes also the basis of a semantical theory of quantification (predicate logic). There is thus at least one

important point of contact between the picture view of language
and a semantical approach to logic. In fact, it is in many ways
interesting and useful to compare the two. Some of the apparent
differences are largely differences in emphasis and in point of
view rather than in substance. For instance, in a picture theory
one often assumes that one is given a fixed interpretation, and
studies how the different sentences of a language fare on this
interpretation. In semantics, one typically has in mind a given
fixed sentence or set of sentences. By varying the interpretation
of its predicate symbols and free singular terms one studies
its basic logical properties, such as satisfiability on the truth-
condition (2) of atomic sentences. We call a set of sentences
(say λ) satisfiable if and only if there is an articulate field R and
an interpretation of all the free singular terms and predicate
symbols of λ with respect to R which makes all the members of λ
true. The truth of atomic sentences is determined by (2) and
the truth of other quantificational sentences is determined in the
usual way.[12] Such a pair of an articulate field and an interpretation with respect to it will be called a *model* of λ.

How is this characterization of satisfiability related to the
definition which I have given elsewhere in terms of model
sets?[13] It is easy to show that the two definitions are equivalent.
In other words, we can prove the following result:

(3) A set of sentences λ is embeddable in a model set if and only if
it has a model.

More explicitly, we may say: λ is embeddable in a model set
if and only if there is an articulate field R and a mapping ϕ
which maps a set of free singular terms (which includes all the
free singular terms occurring in the members of λ) on to the set
of individuals of R and which also maps all the predicate

---

[12] For propositional connectives, we can use the usual truth-table characterizations: $(F_1 \& F_2)$ is true if and only if F_1 and F_2 are both true; $(F_1 \vee F_2)$ is true if
and only if at least one of the two sentences F_1 and F_2 is true; etc. For quantified
sentences, we can use the truth-conditions (truth in a model) defined in any introduction to the model theory of first-order languages. They take an especially simple
form if we make the simplifying assumption that there is at least one free singular
term referring to each individual i of the 'field' R, i.e., singular term 't' such that
$\phi(t) = i$. (They need not all occur in the members of λ.) Then we can say, e.g.,
that $(Ex)F$ is true if and only if, there is an individual i of R such that if 't' is
mapped by ϕ on i, the result of substituting 't' for 'x' in F is true. If this simplifying
assumption is not made, we have to use the more complicated method due to Tarski.

[13] See the references given above in note 1 and Chapter I of the present book.

symbols occurring in the members of λ into the predicates of R such that R and ϕ together make all the members of λ true.

Proof: The 'if' part is very easy. Given R and ϕ of the desired kind, we may consider the set μ of all the sentences which are made true by R and ϕ. This set is easily seen to be a model set which includes all the members of λ.

In order to prove the 'only if' part, assume that $\lambda \subseteq \mu$ where μ is a model set. It suffices to find R and ϕ which make all the members of μ true.

In order to find them, we shall use a method which may first seem surprising but which in reality harks back to the very basic ideas of the picture view. In a sense, we use μ as its own model. We let the free singular terms occurring in the sentences of μ be the individuals R. (They are, of course, really types of symbols, not tokens, but we have already decided to widen the picture view so as to allow this.) For each such term 'b', we set $\phi(b) = $ 'b'. Given (by way of example) a two-place predicate symbol '$P(x, y)$', occurring in the sentences of μ, we define the interpretation $\phi(P)$ of 'P' by requiring that $\phi(P)$ is to obtain between $\phi(a)$ and $\phi(b)$ if and only if '$P(a, b)$' $\in \mu$. For other predicate symbols, the interpretation ϕ is defined similarly.

On this interpretation, every atomic sentence occurring in μ is true by definition. Every negation of an atomic sentence which occurs in μ is true in virtue of $(C. \sim)$. The truth of all the other members of μ on this interpretation can be proved by a simple inductive argument (induction on the number of connectives and quantifiers in the sentence in question). This inductive argument, the details of which are omitted here, completes the proof.[14]

Thus the study of satisfiability may be considered as a study of the different interpretations (with respect to different models) which can be given to a set of quantificational sentences.

The proof I just outlined is worth commenting on more fully.

[14] Arguments of the (general) type just sketched go back essentially to Leon Henkin's important completeness proofs; see his papers 'The Completeness of the First-Order Functional Calculus', *Journal of Symbolic Logic*, vol. 14 (1949), pp. 159–66, and 'Completeness in the Theory of Types', *Journal of Symbolic Logic*, vol. 15 (1950), pp. 81–91, reprinted in *The Philosophy of Mathematics*, ed. by Jaakko Hintikka (Oxford Readings in Philosophy, Oxford University Press, 1969), pp. 42–50 and 51–63, respectively. Henkin, too, shows how to construct certain sets of sentences that can serve as their own models. But the kind of set he uses (maximal consistent sets) are normally much larger and much more complicated than model sets.

What happened in the second part of this proof can be described as follows: We were given a set of sentences μ. First, we gave this set a structure. We defined certain individuals and predicates in terms of membership in μ. (The individuals were the free singular terms occurring in the sentences of μ, and the predicates were the predicates $\phi(P)$ mentioned in the proof.) This converted μ into an articulate field R. Then we interpreted the sentences of μ as speaking of the articulate field (hence, in the sense just defined, as speaking of themselves). Finally, I indicated a way of showing that all the members of μ are true on this interpretation.

Here we are primarily interested in the first step. The articulate field (structure) which we associated with μ is very closely connected with the structure which it must have from the point of view of our picture theory. This structure in effect is just what will later enable us to consider model sets as pictures in the sense of our picture theory. For instance, I said that according to the version of the picture theory I am considering, the predicates of which a sentence speaks must be represented in the sentence by certain predicates (with equally many argument-places). These predicates may be taken to be exactly the predicates $\phi(P)$ which we defined in the proof.

The situation is slightly complicated by the fact that model sets are only *partial* descriptions of the world they speak of.[15] This fact leads us to expect that there will usually be more than one structure that can be naturally associated with a given model set μ. This expectation turns out to be justified. In fact, we may relax the way in which we defined $\phi(P)$ above. In defining it, we stipulated that $\phi(P)$ is to hold between 'a' and 'b' if *and only if* '$P(a, b)$' $\in \mu$. Only part of this requirement is needed in the argument which I sketched. It suffices to replace this definition by a weaker requirement—let us call it (w)—which says only that $\phi(P)$ holds between 'a' and 'b' whenever '$P(a, b)$' $\in \mu$ and that $\phi(P)$ fails to hold between 'a' and 'b' whenever '$\sim P(a, b)$' $\in \mu$. This leaves at large the case in which neither '$P(a, b)$' nor '$\sim P(a, b)$' occurs in μ.

(Notice that if a predicate symbol P or an individual symbol a does not occur in the members of μ at all, we can define $\phi(P)$ or

---

[15] This partiality is what makes it possible for model sets to be much smaller than, e.g., the maximal consistent sets employed by Henkin. Cf. the preceding note.

$\phi(a)$ completely arbitrarily, and still obtain a model in which all the members of μ are true. In the sequel, I shall assume that this possibility may be used.) Any articulate field which we can in this way obtain from a given model set μ will be said to be *associated with* μ. The relation $\phi(P)$ which helps to define this field is likewise said to be *associated with P.*

6. *Model sets as pictures*

The question remains: Can the picture view be extended from atomic sentences to sentences containing quantifiers?

It is obvious that some changes are needed already for the purpose of accommodating propositional connectives. Consider, for instance, a disjunction of two atomic sentences. It does not present us with a unique picture of reality; rather, it gives us two alternative pictures. In general, a truth-function of atomic sentences does not present us with a single picture of the world. Such a truth-function admits certain possibilities concerning the world and excludes the rest. In extending the picture view to truth-functions of atomic sentences we therefore cannot hope to conceive of the truth-function as a single picture. The best we can hope is that it supplies us with a method of constructing a number of alternative pictures of the world, namely, pictures of those states of affairs which it admits and which make it true. We cannot hope to do more than this in quantification theory, either.

Subject to this limitation, however, the picture view can be naturally and simply extended so as to apply to quantified sentences. Some methods of extension have been discussed or suggested before.[16] I shall not comment on them here. Instead, I shall outline an extension of my own. Expressed very briefly, it amounts to considering model sets as 'logical pictures of the world' in the sense of our version of the picture theory. A model set is an isomorphic representation of a part of the world such as it would be if all the members of the model set were true. Many things Wittgenstein and other picture theorists have said of atomic sentences as pictures will apply equally well to model sets.

---

[16] One such method was already adumbrated in the *Tractatus* itself; others have been suggested later. See, e.g., G. E. M. Anscombe, *An Introduction* (see note 5 above), Ch. II; Erik Stenius, *Wittgenstein's Tractatus* (see note 5 above), pp. 153-4; John Wisdom, 'Logical Constructions I', reprinted in Copi and Beard.

Speaking more explicitly, the different model sets in which a given set λ of quantificational sentences can be embedded are (partial) pictures of the different states of affairs which would make all the members of λ true.[17] They are the alternative pictures of the world which we can construct by starting from λ.

The sense in which model sets are pictures may be explained by saying that they become isomorphic representations of states of affairs which would make all their members true if they are given a structure in the way we did in the proof of the second half of (3). In other words, all the members of a model set μ are true if and only if the reality is isomorphic with one of the structures (articulate fields) associated with it.[18] This isomorphism (which is of course relative to a fixed key, i.e., relative to a given interpretation of the language) yields a dramatic consequence when we begin to vary the key. In the simplest conceivable case, isomorphism degenerates into identity. What this means in the case at hand is that if the sentences of a model set are interpreted so as to refer to themselves, the model set in question becomes its own model. This explains the choice of the term 'model set'. The possibility of considering model sets as their own models was what the second part of the proof of (3) hinged on.

It is easily seen that model sets are not the only sets of sentences which can serve as their own models. The same is true of state-descriptions and of certain maximal consistent sets of sentences.[19] Many sets of this sort seem to have very interesting properties and uses. However, model sets appear to be the simplest sets which have this property and whose members are allowed to contain quantifiers.

In order to spell out the exact sense in which this is true we

[17] This is of course strictly true only if we are willing to countenance languages with uncountably many symbols. (Sufficiently large partial descriptions of worlds with uncountably many individuals cannot be embedded in countable model sets.) I do not see any harm in this assumption, however. The same warning is needed in the sequel, too.

[18] If, in defining the sets of structures associated with a model set μ, I had not allowed for the introduction of new singular terms, we should have to say instead that the relevant part of reality has to be isomorphic with one of the structures associated with μ, thus complicating the discussion somewhat.

[19] State-descriptions have been used widely by Rudolf Carnap; see, e.g., *Meaning and Necessity* (University of Chicago Press, Chicago, Ill., 1948; 2nd ed., 1956). Certain kinds of maximal consistent sets of which this is true have been employed, e.g., by Henkin in his completeness proofs; cf. note 14 above.

have to remember that model sets are not intended to be complete pictures of reality. Keeping this in mind, we can see that the following pair of results is what can be reasonably expected to constitute the pictorial nature of model sets:

(4) If an articulate field R and an interpretation Ψ make all the sentences of a model set μ true, then there is an articulate field associated with μ which is isomorphic with R. This isomorphism is established by a key which correlates $\Psi(P)$ with some predicate $\phi(P)$ which satisfies the requirement (w) mentioned above with respect to μ.

(5) If an articulate field associated with μ is isomorphic with some arbitrary articulate field R with respect to a key which correlates $\Psi(P)$ with the predicate $\phi(P)$ associated with P, then all the members of μ are made true by R and by an interpretation which correlates $\Psi(P)$ with each predicate symbol P.

I shall not prove these two results here. They are easy enough to prove on the basis of what has already been said. I have mentioned them simply to bring out the exact sense in which model sets are pictures. This sense can be brought out in a more striking way by introducing a new locution. Instead of saying that a structure R is isomorphic with one of the structures associated with a model set μ, we can say that μ is isomorphic with a *part of R*. Then the results (3)–(5) may be summed up as follows:

(6) All the members of a set of sentences λ are made true by a model R, and an interpretation Ψ if and only if there is a model set $\mu \supseteq \lambda$ which is isomorphic with a part of R with respect to the key which with each $\Psi(P)$ correlates the predicate $\phi(P)$ associated with P.

In this sense, a number of quantificational sentences are true if and only if they can be embedded in a model set which is a 'picture' (an isomorphic representation) of a part of reality.

In (4)–(6), the most important situation is of course the one in which Ψ is the key characteristic of some given *interpreted* first-order language, for instance natural language partly translated into quantificational 'canonical notation'. (See point (ii) above on p. 29.) Then (6) says that in such a language a model set can be turned into an isomorph ('picture') of a part of a world in which all its members are true by simply obeying the category requirement precisely in the way adumbrated above.

(See (iv) on pp. 29–30.) This perhaps illustrates the naturalness of the present extension of the picture view. Virtually the only change as compared with the original Wittgenstein–Stenius version is that we are considering model sets as pictures instead of individual sentences.

What we have thus obtained is an extension and a modification of the picture theory. According to this extension, quantificational sentences are not themselves 'pictures' of reality. The workings of quantificational discourse, including the logical laws which govern quantifiers, can nevertheless be understood on the basis of the picture theory. Although individual sentences are not attempted pictures of reality, certain sets of sentences, to wit, model sets, are such pictures. As was indicated above in Chapter I, for the purposes of the most natural proof procedures (Herbrand methods) in first-order logic, model sets can be considered verbal *descriptions* of certain logically possible states of affairs. Now we can say more of them; they are also (partial) *pictures* of the same states of affairs, in the sense of our version of the picture theory.

7. *Logical proofs as frustrated picture constructions: basic ideas and their anticipations by earlier logicians*

The central role which model sets have, or may be given, in the systematic development of quantification theory therefore reflects the naturalness of the picture view. In Chapter I it was mentioned that all logical proofs and disproofs that can be carried out in quantification theory can be viewed as frustrated attempts to construct model sets in which to embed certain sentences.[20] Now we can see that all these constructions are nothing but picture constructions in the sense of our picture theory. The fact that the rules of model set construction are but inverted forms of certain rules of natural deduction shows that our version of the picture view is not only connected with the semantics of quantification theory but also with natural deduction methods.

These connections have several different kinds of interest, the least of which is not historical. The picture view of language has a longer history than the followers and commentators of Wittgenstein's usually recognize. A reason why this history is seldom

[20] See above, Chapter I, section 4.

discussed in connection with Wittgenstein's *Tractatus* is not very hard to perceive, whether we accept it or not. Some of the most interesting earlier expositions of the idea that our linguistic symbolism in some sense mirrors (or that it ought to mirror) the interrelations of the objects to which our symbols refer differ markedly from the version of the picture theory expounded in the *Tractatus*. In the earlier versions, the idea was often applied to the role of language or some other kind of symbolism in logical and mathematical demonstration and in other forms of logical and mathematical reasoning. This might perhaps be called a dynamic version of the picture view. For instance, Leibniz writes: '. . . characters must show, when they are used in demonstrations, some kind of connection, grouping and order which is also found in the objects. . . . Some kind of characters is surely always required in thinking.'[21] C. S. Peirce likewise asserted that deduction 'invariably requires something of the nature of a diagram; that is, an "Icon", or Sign that represents its Object in resembling it'.[22] Elsewhere Peirce makes it clear that the resemblance in question need not consist in an unanalysed qualitative similarity but rather consists normally in a structural similarity. According to him, many icons 'resemble their objects not at all in looks; it is only in respect to the relations of their parts that their likeness consists' (vol. 2, sec. 282). In comparison, in the *Tractatus* the picture view is rather static. It is applied primarily to atomic sentences. Its connection with the other main doctrine of the *Tractatus*, i.e., with the truth-function theory, is not very strong.[23] It is not related

---

[21] Leibniz, 'Dialogue on the Connection Between Things and Words', August 1677, printed several times; see, e.g., C. I. Gerhard, ed., *Die Philosophische Schriften von Gottfried Wilhelm Leibniz* (Berlin, 1875–90), VII, 190–4; Philip P. Wiener, ed., *Leibniz Selections* (Charles Scribner's Sons, New York, 1951), pp. 6–11.

[22] For Peirce's theory of icons, see, e.g., *Collected Papers of Charles Sanders Peirce*, ed. by Charles Hartshorne, Paul Weiss, and Arthur Burks (Harvard University Press, Cambridge, Mass., 1931–58), vol. 2, sections 276–82; vol. 3, sections 362–3, 641. Notice especially the ubiquity icons *apud* Peirce: 'The only way of directly communicating an idea is by means of an icon' (vol. 2, sec. 278); 'icons of the algebraic kind, though usually very simple ones, exist in all ordinary grammatical propositions' (ibid., sec. 280).

The passage I quoted is from 'A Neglected Argument for the Reality of God', *Hibbert Journal*, no. 7 (1908), pp. 90–112.

[23] The picture theory of the meaning of (atomic) sentences and the theory of truth-functions have been called 'the two pillars of the *Tractatus*' by G. H. von Wright in *Logik, filosofi och språk* (Helsingfors, 1956).

to quantificational proofs in any interesting way. In extending the picture view to quantification theory we have thus brought it much closer to parts of the earlier tradition than the picture theory of the *Tractatus*. In some ways, our extension may perhaps serve as a connecting link between the two.

The relation of the ideas of the *Tractatus* to this tradition might repay a closer study. The basic idea of Wittgenstein's picture theory is the idea of an isomorphism obtaining between language and reality, an isomorphism in the abstract general sense of an isomorphism which can be established by any correlation on mapping. Now the gradual development of this general idea of an arbitrary mapping, which is essentially the idea of an arbitrary function, has been one of the most significant general features in the history of mathematics. As was pointed out earlier, appreciating the picture view in the form in which I have presented it presupposes appreciating the generality of the notion of mapping on which it is based. In so far as the picture theory is successful as a theory of language, it has related the philosophical study of language to one of the main streams of the conceptual development of mathematics. Hence in so far as I have been able to integrate the logic of quantification with the picture view, to that extent this central part of logic has also been related to the same feature of the development of mathematics.

The way in which we have related the picture view to logical deduction may nevertheless be compared with certain ideas Wittgenstein puts forward in the *Tractatus* concerning logical proof. He says there, that 'it is always possible to construe logic in such a way that every proposition is its own proof' (6.1625). This idea is closely related to the picture theory. Elsewhere Wittgenstein says: 'Propositions show what they say: tautologies and contradictions show that they say nothing' (4.461). These statements may be understood as follows: a sentence must be a picture or a number of alternative pictures. In order to understand it, we must bring out the (alternative) pictures which are implicit in it. If it is a contradiction, then it turns out not to yield any picture of a possible state of affairs at all. Thus the process by means of which we come to understand what a sentence means coincides in the special case of a contradiction with the process of showing that it is contradictory, i.e., with disproving it. Similarly, in the case of a tautology, the process of spelling out its meaning will also bring out the fact that it is a tautology.

On our extended picture view, it is obviously not true any longer that each contradictory sentence can be considered as its own disproof in the sense Wittgenstein intended. But in another, perhaps deeper sense, I find myself agreeing with Wittgenstein. On our extended picture view, it remains in a sense true to say that the process by means of which we come to understand what a sentence means is the same as the process by means of which a contradictory sentence is disproved. For on our picture view the former process is obviously the process of constructing the different model sets into which the sentence in question can be embedded; these model sets are pictures of reality in the sense of the picture theory, and they are what shows what the world is like when the sentence is true. But I have pointed out that unsuccessful picture (model set) constructions of this kind are exactly the disproofs of quantification theory (under our formulation). In a sense, therefore, on our view too it can be said that 'in logic, process and result are equivalent' (6.1261). (There are other senses, however, which necessitate further qualifications here.)

8. *Logical proofs as frustrated picture constructions: comparisons and examples*

My interpretation shows that all quantificational proofs may be taken to be *constructive* in a certain sense of the word. This is not the sense of the word in which constructive methods of proof are contrasted to non-constructive methods. The arguments by means of which we can prove, e.g.,

$$`(Ex)B(x) \supset (Ex)[A(x) \supset (Uy)A(y)]`$$

are not of the kind which an intuitionist would accept as a proof of this proposition. However, from the point of view I have sketched, all quantificational proofs are constructive in a wider sense. They are constructive in that in conducting them we are carrying out acts of construction: we are literally trying to build up certain 'pictures of reality', namely, of reality such as it would be if a certain sentence S were true. For the purpose, we introduce one by one representatives of such individuals as would have to exist if S were true. We are not merely considering predicates which represent properties and relations of individuals but we are also considering particular individuals through their representatives. It is interesting to observe that this is to all intents and purposes what Kant means by the use of constructions in mathematics.[24] 'To *construct* a concept means to exhibit *a priori* the intuition which corresponds to the concept', he says.[25] By an intuition Kant by definition means nothing more and nothing less than a (direct) representation of an individual. Intuitions so defined may have little 'intuitiveness' about them in the present-day sense of the word; but this is how Kant intended his notion to be understood. In his usage, intuitions are contrasted to general concepts (*Begriffe*). An intuition is what represents an individual directly, without going 'by way of' the attributes and relations which the individual may share with other individuals. Thus to introduce an intuition corresponding to a concept for Kant simply means to introduce a singular term referring to an individual to which this concept applies.

An example perhaps makes this clearer. Consider the pair of statements

> (7) There exists everyone's teacher
> There exists nobody's pupil.

Expressing the relation of being a teacher of by 'R' and by realizing that the relation of being a pupil of is the converse of R we can write instead of these

> (8) '$(Ex)(Uy)R(x, y)$'
> (9) '$(Ex)(Uy) \sim R(y, x)$'

This pair of statements is clearly inconsistent. What is the relation of the former individual to the latter? Because he is

---

[24] I have discussed the interpretation of Kant's philosophy of mathematics, and especially the meaning of his notion of intuition, on a number of occasions. See Chapters V, VII, VIII, and X below, the papers referred to in note 38 to Chapter I above, as well as my papers 'Kant's "New Method of Thought" and His Theory of Mathematics', *Ajatus*, vol. 27 (1965), pp. 37–47; 'Are Mathematical Truths Synthetic *A Priori*?', *Journal of Philosophy*, vol. 65 (1968), pp. 640–51.

[25] Kant, *Critique of Pure Reason*, A = 1st ed. (1781), p. 731; B = 2nd ed. (1787), p. 741.

everybody's teacher, the former ought to teach the latter. But he cannot, because the latter is nobody's pupil.

This intuitive argument is neatly recaptured by our model set technique.[26] The informal attempt to describe a world in which (8)–(9) are both true, which the intuitive argument in effect was, is systematized by the following argument:

Suppose that the only members of μ are the following:

(10) '$(Ex)(Uy)R(x, y)$' $\in \mu$
(11) '$(Ex)(Uy) \sim R(y, x)$' $\in \mu$

Then by (A.E) we can enlarge μ so as to have

(12) '$(Uy)R(a, y)$' $\in \mu$
(13) '$(Uy) \sim R(y, b)$' $\in \mu$

for some new free singular terms 'a', 'b'. (This may be thought of as simply giving a name to everybody's teacher and nobody's pupil.)

Because of (12)–(13), we can put (in virtue of (A.U))

(14) '$R(a, b)$' $\in \mu$
(15) '$\sim R(a, b)$' $\in \mu$

This substitution of 'b' for 'y' in (12) and 'a' for 'y' in (13) can be considered simply as an attempt to answer the question: how is a (= everybody's teacher) related to b (= nobody's pupil)? The fact that (14)–(15) (the different answers to these questions) violate (C.$\sim$) shows the desired inconsistency.

What is pictorial or 'constructive' about this argument? I have spoken of the terms 'a' and 'b' as if they stood for or represented certain individuals. The pictorial character of their use can be illustrated by correlating the proof with a schematic diagram.

Thus step (12), i.e., the introduction of '$(Uy)R(a, y)$' by (A.E), may be expressed in words saying 'consider by way of example one individual, let us name it "a", of the kind which is asserted to exist by "$(Ex)(Uy)R(a, y)$".' Likewise, the introduction of '$(Uy) \sim R(y, b)$' by the rule (A.E) means the introduction of a new individual to our considerations, referred

---

[26] The rules for those attempted model set constructions whose failure will show the inconsistency of a set of sentences are given in the Appendix to Chapter I above.

to by '*b*'. The introduction of '*R*(*a*, *b*)' may be illustrated by some such diagram as the following:

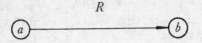

The introduction of '∼*R*(*a*, *b*)' would have to be illustrated by a similar diagram from which the arrow between '*a*' and '*b*' is missing. Such a diagram is of course incompatible with the one just drawn. This incompatibility illustrates the use of the condition (C. ∼). This procedure can obviously be applied quite generally.

As long as (C. ∼) is not violated, I can likewise illustrate each set of atomic sentences and their negations by means of a figure with arrows and other paraphernalia. If the relations in question were geometrical ones, I could draw a diagram to illustrate the set of sentences. The role of the rule (A. E) deserves special attention here. Each time (A. E) is applied the construction proceeds further by one step: a new individual is introduced to the figure or the diagram, an individual related to the old ones in certain specifiable ways. (There may be several alternatives to be considered separately here.) Each application of (A. E) is thus essentially a new act of construction—a fact which graphically brings out the sense in which a quantificational argument is on this view an attempt to *construct* a counter-example.

9. *Sentences as recipes of picture construction*

The constructivity which quantificational proofs and disproofs have on our interpretation serves to distinguish it from certain earlier attempts to extend the picture view beyond atomic sentences. There are obvious similarities between our interpretation and certain earlier suggestions. Stenius has already interpreted the logical rules which govern the use of compound sentences as indicating 'how a compound sentence *P* can be transformed into a system of alternative pictures presenting the different states of affairs the existence of one of which verifies *P*' (*Wittgenstein's Tractatus*, p. 151). However, there are also dissimilarities. In propositional logic, one can hope to get along with a much simpler extension of the picture view. We may try to understand the propositional connectives which occur in a sentence as merely indicating how one should take the various *Urbilder* or 'proto-pictures' which the various atomic sentences give us. As Wittgenstein himself suggested, we might try to view the propositional connectives as 'projecting the picture of the elementary propositions on to reality—which may then accord or not accord with this projection' (*Notebooks 1914– 1916*, p. 29).

The constructive character of quantificational proofs and disproofs shows that this interpretation does *not* work in quantification theory. Here the transition from a sentence to the associated pictures of reality does not merely establish a connection between ready-made proto-pictures and reality, for the simple reason that there normally are no suitable proto-pictures present in a quantificational sentence. The model set constructions are constructions in a rather strict sense of the word. We actually have to build the pictures (model sets) step by step; they only come to existence during the process of construction. For instance, most of the individuals of the pictures are not present in the original sentence (or set of sentences): they are introduced one by one by the rule (A.E). The tempting idea of a proto-picture must therefore be discarded. Sentences do not *contain* pictures somehow hidden inside them. Rather, they are *recipes* for constructing alternative pictures of the world.

10. *Picture view suggests a theory of language use*

Thus far, I have emphasized the gains that can be obtained by extending the picture view to quantification theory. I believe that something like the interpretation I have outlined is the only satisfactory way of reconciling a picture view of language with the presence of quantifiers.

But what about the losses? Have we been able to preserve all the important aspects of the more familiar picture theories? One's answer to this question depends on one's order of priorities, which is likely to be different for different philosophers. In any case, it seems to me that, however natural and even inevitable our extension of the picture view to quantification theory may be, certain desirable features of the earlier picture theories have been irrevocably lost. If so, then a part of the interest of our observations may also lie in the fact that they bring to light certain essential limitations of the picture view.

The desirable features which are likely to be lost have not always been explicitly specified. They seem to have been among the main tacit attractions of the picture theory, however. In order to see one of them, we may ask: what is required, on the picture view, for the purpose of understanding a given atomic sentence? An answer is obvious: one needs little more than knowledge of the key which correlates the elements of the sentence with the elements of the world of which it speaks. This is all the specifically linguistic and conventional knowledge one needs. If one knows the key, one understands what a sentence means by means of its pictorial character. One understands it by understanding the notion of an isomorphism. This is a 'natural' notion, not an 'artificial' one. It does not depend on the particular language in question. Understanding it is the essence of understanding all languages. As soon as we have been given the key to the sentence in question, we can compare its structure with that of reality. We can, so to speak, simply go and see whether the reality corresponds to it or not.[27]

The original picture theory of the *Tractatus* thus contains, or at least suggests, a simple theory (or a model) of how language is understood and how it operates. This explanation of sentence meaning is one of the attractive features of a picture theory. It has to be modified, however, if the picture view is extended in the way we have done. On our extended view, a quantified sentence cannot be compared with the reality directly. It is not an isomorphic representation of reality even if it is true. In order to compare it with reality we have first to build the different model sets in which it can be embedded. Rules are needed for this purpose. They add a further conventional element into the model of the workings of a language which the picture view suggests.

11. *Picture view has to be complemented by a theory of stepwise comparisons between language and reality*

This, by itself, does not amount to a serious objection to the picture view. However, if we consider what is involved in a

---

[27] Cf. the blunt statement in *Tractatus* 4.05: 'Reality is compared with the sentence.'

comparison of language with reality on our picture view, we can see that the model it gives us of the way in which we come to understand a quantified sentence is no longer very realistic, not even if it is restricted so as to apply only to the symbolic languages of a formal logician. In order to understand what a quantificational sentence of ordinary discourse means, we do not have to construct the different model sets in which it can be embedded. This does not even seem to be possible in many cases, for many model sets are infinite and scarcely available for us in the time we in fact need to grasp a quantified sentence. Nor does it seem feasible to compare them with reality in the way in which the picture view envisages. It is plausible to suggest that a comparison of the structure of an atomic sentence with that of the world is an operation anyone can easily perform who is in the possession of the key without having to master any special rules or techniques. (Even this is not completely obvious, for it may depend on the particular predicates with which the atomic sentence in question deals. However, this difficulty is beside my present point.) This is no longer the case when one is comparing a large (possibly infinite) model set with that part of the world of which it speaks. Such a comparison cannot be effected at a glance. It can only be effected by means of step-by-step processes. These processes are on the assumptions of our picture view absolutely crucial for the workings of a language to which this view applies. However, the picture view itself has nothing to say of these processes.

In so far as these step-by-step comparisons are emphasized, the role of the pictures themselves (i.e., the model sets) in understanding a quantificational language becomes less important in comparison.

This impossibility of comparing model sets with reality 'at a glance' is made all the more acute by another discrepancy between the sense in which model sets are pictures of reality and the sense in which Wittgensteinian atomic sentences were supposed to be pictures. In understanding an atomic sentence, we were supposed to know the individual to which each of the free singular terms of the sentence referred. This is not any longer true of model sets needed to interpret logical proofs. The free singular terms which are introduced by (A. E) do not refer to any particular individuals. At least, we do not assign any particular individual to one of them when we introduce it. Such model sets as result from constructions by means of our (A)-rules may be pictures of reality, but they are not unique pictures. They may represent the reality in more than one way. In comparing a model set with reality, there is usually more than one possible correlation to be considered. We have to consider all the different ways in which an individual may be assigned to each of the free singular terms introduced by (A.E) as its reference, and we have to see whether any of these assignments makes the model set in question into an isomorphic representation of the reality or aspect of reality of which its sentences speak. This multiplicity of possible correlations already makes it inadmissible to consider the comparison of the structure of a model set with that of reality as an unproblematic one-shot process. This difficulty is connected with the problem of the status of the 'ambiguous names' introduced by (A.E). I shall try to say something of this problem in Chapter V below.

12. *The failure of Wittgenstein's 'Logik der Abbildung'*

This failure of the picture view cuts deeper to the fundamental aims of Wittgenstein's picture theory than one perhaps first realizes. One of the very first aims of his search for a satisfactory theory of language was to find the 'logical identity' which he felt must obtain between the sign and the thing signified. For if there were no such identity, 'there would have to be something still more fundamental than logic' (*Notebooks*, p. 4; cf. *Tractatus* 6.123). This identity he came to see in the possession of the common logical form, i.e., in the isomorphism which he thought obtains between a sentence and what it represents (cf. *Tractatus* 4.03). What we have found shows that in the case of quantificational sentences there is after all something more fundamental than the logic of isomorphisms on which the picture view is based. (Cf. Wittgenstein's expression 'Logik der Abbildung' in *Tractatus* 4.015.) There is on the one hand the 'logic' of the model set constructions and on the other hand the logic of the step-by-step comparisons of model sets with reality. Thus my extension of the picture view to quantification theory may have the additional merit of suggesting directions in which we should develop the picture view further so as to overcome its imitations. We may ask, for instance, whether the two processes just mentioned are perhaps connected with each other.

It may be mentioned that the view I am putting forward was not perhaps completely foreign to Wittgenstein. At one time, he apparently was willing to consider sentences as starting-points of model construction. In his *Philosophische Bemerkungen*[28] which precede the *Blue Book*, he writes: 'If one thinks of sentences as directions for building models, their pictorial character (*Bildhaftigkeit*) becomes still clearer. For in order for a word to be able to guide my hand, it must have the multiplicity (*Mannigfaltigkeit*) of the desired activity' (§ 10). Wittgenstein goes on to suggest that this idea also serves to explain the nature of negative propositions.

There are also dissimilarities, however, between the quoted passage and my suggestions. Wittgenstein seems to think in this passage that the sentence which serves as the starting-point of a model construction must have the same 'multiplicity' as the construction activity, and therefore presumably also its outcome. In the extension of the picture view which I have outlined this is not the case. Each of the alternative outcomes of model set construction is an isomorphic representation of a part of reality such as it would be if all the members of the model set were true, and hence must have the same multiplicity as this reality. But this does not imply that the original sentence which serves as the starting-point of the construction already had the same multiplicity.

In fact, it may be worth generalizing this observation. Often it is apparently thought that what a sentence expresses is a fairly straightforward function of the concepts its component words express. Our extension of the picture view to quantification theory may perhaps serve as an antidote to this oversimplification. It shows that what most immediately corresponds to the reality of which quantificational sentences speak are the outcomes of model set construction which are often obtained only by a long and complicated process. In the original sentence there is therefore very little which would correspond to the elements of the world as it would be if the sentence were true. The proposition which a quantificational sentence expresses, we

---

[28] Ludwig Wittgenstein, *Philosophische Bemerkungen* (Basil Blackwell, Oxford, 1966).

might thus say, is not a simple combination of the concepts which its component words express. In Chapter VI below I shall try to bring this observation to bear on the concept of analyticity.

13. *Suggestions for quantification theory*

We have seen that there is a much closer connection than most philosophers seem to have realized between the picture view of language and the logic of quantification, including both the semantics (model theory) of first-order logic and suitable deductive rules for actually proving certain first-order sentences. It was also seen, however, that when the Wittgensteinian theory is extended so as to accomplish all this, its insufficiency as an account of how our language (even just first-order discourse) actually operates becomes evident. In order to obtain a satisfactory account, we obviously have to shift our main attention from the 'pictorial' relations of isomorphism based on a given static 'key' to the processes by means of which we compare language and reality step-by-step and in the course of which the 'key' is gradually established. The close relationship between quantification theory and the picture theory suggests that a similar change of emphasis is perhaps in order in the more usual ways of looking upon the logic of quantification.[29]

[29] See next chapter.

III

LANGUAGE-GAMES FOR QUANTIFIERS

1. *Logical expressions*

ONE way of looking at logic is to view it as a study of certain words and phrases which we may label *logical expressions*. Whether or not one can thus obtain a general definition of the province of logic, this point of view is useful for many purposes.[1] For instance, quantification theory may be characterized from this point of view as the study of the phrases 'there is', and 'for every' over and above the study of the words 'not', 'and', and 'or', which are already studied in propositional logic, plus whatever terms are required to express predication. I shall call these phrases and other expressions with similar meanings *quantifying expressions*.[2]

In books and papers on logic, some aspects of the behaviour of these expressions are studied. However, they are usually studied mainly as they appear in more or less strictly regimented systems of formal logic. The meaning they have in unregimented discourse is not often discussed directly, nor is the relevance of these formal studies to the more ordinary uses of the quantifying

[1] On the subject of logical vocabulary, see P. F. Strawson, *Introduction to Logical Theory* (Methuen, London, 1952), pp. 47–9, 57; W. V. Quine, 'Mr. Strawson on Logical Theory', *Mind*, vol. 62 (1953), pp. 433–51, especially p. 437.

[2] In this chapter, only those quantifying expressions are studied which are roughly synonymous with the usual existential and universal quantifiers. Non-standard quantifiers, such as 'at least two', 'at most three', 'many', 'most', etc., are illuminated only in so far as they behave in the same way as standard quantifiers or are definable in terms of these. Furthermore, all differences between the different ordinary-language equivalents to standard quantifiers are disregarded, although some of them are of considerable interest. In particular, I shall disregard the close relation which there is between some of these idioms (e.g., 'some', 'all', etc.) and the 'quantitative' relation of a whole to a part. Interesting as this relationship is in many respects, not just as a reason for some of the differences between different quantifying expressions, it is in my view less important than the problem of interpreting quantifying expressions when they are conceived of in the usual terms of 'ranging over' a domain of discrete individuals. Of the quantifying expressions of ordinary language, 'there is' (or 'exists') and 'for every' perhaps come closest to this type of quantifying expression and are therefore considered here in the first place.

expressions 'there is', and 'for every'. In this chapter I shall deal with these questions, questions on whose importance I scarcely need to enlarge.

2. *Meaning as use*

Plenty of advice is in fact available to tell me how to straighten the defect just mentioned. Much of this advice is summed up in the famous remark of Wittgenstein's: 'The meaning of a word is its use in the language.'[3] This dictum is not unequivocal, however, not even if we recall that it was only supposed by Wittgenstein to cover a large class of words, not the meanings of all possible words that there are. Here I am not interested in bringing out all the different aspects of Wittgenstein's advice. For my present purposes it suffices to confine our attention to one of the most important things Wittgenstein apparently meant by his dictum. This aspect of his remark has not always been brought out as clearly as it ought to have been.

It is perhaps easier to say what in Wittgenstein's dictum I am *not* interested in (for the purposes of this chapter). Often, a distinction is made between the use of words and the use of language.[4] Under the former title philosophers have considered the use of words for the purpose of forming sentences or for referring. Under the latter title, they have usually considered the different language acts or speech acts which one can perform by uttering or by writing a sentence. The uses of language are then those uses which one can make by uttering or writing something.

It seems to me that this distinction is not an exhaustive one, and that the uses of words which I am primarily interested in here are largely forgotten if the situation is described in these terms. It is obvious that Wittgenstein did not have in mind only the uses of words for the purpose of constructing sentences out of them when he coined his slogan. Furthermore, he certainly did not have in mind only the acts one can perform by saying something or in saying something.[5] The study of the different

---

[3] Ludwig Wittgenstein, *Philosophische Untersuchungen—Philosophical Investigations* (Basil Blackwell, Oxford, 1953), Pt. I, sect. 43: 'For a *large* class of cases—though not for all—in which we employ the word "meaning" it can be defined thus: the meaning of a word is its use in the language.'

[4] Cf., e.g., Gilbert Ryle, 'Ordinary Language', *Philosophical Review*, vol. 62 (1953), pp. 167–86.

[5] *Philosophical Investigations*, Pt. I, sects. 6, 9, 10, and 11.

types of speech-acts does not exhaust the import of Wittgenstein's advice. The uses we are invited to consider do not always
take the form of locutionary or illocutionary acts. Wittgenstein
is not only asking what we do or can do by uttering a sentence.
He is also asking what we must be able to do or what people
must generally do in order for us to understand a word.[6] He is
calling our attention to a certain environment of types of action
or activities which a word often has and outside which it loses
its meaning (or its use, if you prefer).

These activities may be activities one performs by uttering a
sentence, but they need not be. The verb 'thank' loses its use (or
meaning) in the absence of the custom of thanking. This custom
happens to be such that one can thank by saying 'thank you'.
However, the fact that one can do this is largely inessential to
the connection which there is between the custom (or institution)
of thanking and the meaning of the verb 'to thank'. For we
could use this verb meaningfully even if it were not our custom
to thank by saying anything but (for instance) merely by means
of certain gestures. As our actual customs go, it is certainly
possible to thank someone without using the verb 'to thank'. In
the case of certain other words, for instance, of the verb 'to
score' (in a game), the activities we must be able to master, if
only from the point of view of a spectator, are such that they are
never performed merely by saying something. Thus, for one who
is primarily interested in the activities which constitute the
natural environment of a word and from which it gets its
meaning, the things one can do by means of words are not
of central importance. What is important is the connection
between a word and the activities which typically surround it.
The aspect of Wittgenstein's advice which I want to take up
here is therefore closely related to his notion of a language-game.
'I shall also call the whole, consisting of language and the
activities into which it is woven, the "language-game"'; 'Here

---

[6] Ryle, op. cit., warns us not to mistake *use* (in speaking of the use of language)
to mean *utilization*. But surely Wittgenstein constantly assimilates these ideas to each
other. His favourite term *Gebrauch* is ambiguous in the same way as the English
word *use*, and could often be taken in the sense of usage; but on other occasions
the presence of the ideas of application and utilization are unmistakable. These
ideas are often still more obvious when Wittgenstein uses words like *Verwendung* or
Anwendung, which he also frequently does. (See *Philosophical Investigations*, Pt. I,
sects. 11, 20, 21, 23, 41, 42, 54, 68, and 84.)

the term language-game is meant to bring into prominence the fact that the speaking of language is part of an activity, or a form of life.'[7] The emphasis is here as much and more on the actions in the framework of which the use of words occurs as on the actions which one can perform by using certain words. The activities which typically surround a word and from which it gets its meaning might be called the language-game in which the word in question is at home.

3. *Relation to operationism*

An extreme, and exaggerated, form of this dependence of certain words on non-linguistic activities for their meaning is claimed to obtain by the group of doctrines known as operationism.[8] In spite of the vagueness and crudity of operationistic doctrines some aspects of these views merit a comparison with those aspects of Wittgenstein's ideas we are interested in here. It is important to realize, however, that the interpretation I am putting on Wittgenstein's words does not commit me to anything like operationism. On a typical operationistic view, to make a statement containing operationally defined words is to make a prediction, as it were, concerning the outcome of the operations which are associated with these words. What is more, it is normally required that these operations can be performed once and for all. It is required, moreover, that they can be performed in only one way. It is also required that to each operationally defined word there is but one defining activity or 'operation' associated with it.

These three requirements (together with other similar requirements which strict operationism imposes on the activities from which our words receive their meaning) seem to be exceedingly narrow-minded. There does not seem to be any reason to deny that a word may be connected with an activity or mode of action which does not necessarily terminate or whose termination point is at least unpredictable. There also seems to be no reason whatsoever to deny that the activities in question can be performed

---

[7] *Philosophical Investigations*, Pt. I, sects. 7 and 23.

[8] For operationism, cf., e.g., the symposium on 'The Present State of Operationalism' in *The Validation of Scientific Theories*, ed. by Philipp G. Frank (Beacon Press, Boston, 1955), and Carl G. Hempel, 'A Logical Appraisal of Operationism', in Carl G. Hempel, *Aspects of Scientific Explanation and Other Essays in the Philosophy of Science* (The Free Press, New York, 1965), pp. 123–33.

in many alternative ways. Furthermore, one has to realize that a word may be connected with reality not through a single operation, but rather through a network of subtle interrelations which involve a good many theoretical assumptions.

In spite of these shortcomings, there are some purposes which an operationistic view of language may serve. It serves to bring out, albeit in a distorted form, one aspect of the notion of 'the use of language' which is sometimes forgotten. If its exaggerations are removed, it offers a simplified model with which we may compare some of the things which actually happen when a language is being used. In any case, this is the assumption I shall be working on in this paper.

4. *Verbs and activities*

It can be given a somewhat more linguistic turn. Actions and activities are in our language typically represented by verbs. As a consequence, an answer to the question: 'What activities constitute the natural environment of a word?' may sometimes be reformulated as an answer to the question: 'What verbs are there to which the word in question has an especially intimate logical relation?'[9] Of course, it cannot be assumed that this reformulation is viable in all cases nor assumed that for every word there is but one verb to which it is related logically. For instance, the word which has probably been studied more than any other philosophically interesting word, the word 'good', has several different verbs associated with it in this manner. They include the verbs 'to evaluate', 'to grade', 'to praise', 'to commend', 'to recommend', and 'to appreciate'.[10] On a given occasion, a statement which contains the word 'good' can perhaps be paraphrased in terms of one of these verbs, but no single one of them enables us to reformulate (in context) all the sentences containing the word 'good'. It is also obvious that if the activities which are expressed by the verbs just listed would cease, the

[9] The multiplicity and variety of the different language-games which are involved in the use of language partly explains the Protean character of the grammatical category of verbs. The variety in the logical functions of different verbs is in fact much greater than one would gather from most logical and philosophical discussions of the different grammatical categories.

[10] Cf. R. M. Hare, *The Language of Morals* (Clarendon Press, Oxford, 1952), and Paul Ziff, *Semantic Analysis* (Cornell University Press, Ithaca, N.Y., 1960), last chapter.

word 'good' would lose much of its use and in a sense therefore much of its meaning. There is thus a logical connection between the word 'good' and the verbs listed, a connection which is the more interesting the more clearly the paraphrases we can obtain in terms of these verbs bring out the logical conditions of the use of the word 'good'.

5. *Verbs for quantifiers*

It seems to me that there is an even more interesting instance of this in the philosophy of logic. There are verbs which are not merely logical relatives of the quantifiers 'there is', and 'for all', but which are veritable next of kin of theirs. These verbs are not to be found among the verbs a philosopher is apt to think of in connection with logic, for instance, not among the verbs 'to infer', 'to follow', 'to deduce', 'to contradict', and 'to refute'.[11] In no important case can a quantifier be paraphrased in terms of them, although interesting attempts have been made to connect the most important rules for operating with quantifiers with the notions of inference and deduction.[12]

There are much better candidates for the role, namely, such verbs as 'to search', 'to look for', 'to seek', and 'to find'. In more than one natural language, existence is in fact expressed by speaking of what 'can be found' (cf., e.g., the Swedish phrase 'det finns' which literally taken means just this). E. Gilson writes that according to Averroës, 'the Arabic word meaning "to exist" came from a root originally meaning "found", because it seems to have been a common notion that, for any given thing, to exist meant approximately "to be found there"'.[13] In the everyday parlance of mathematicians, existence is typically expressed in this way. It is also obvious enough that instead of 'there are

---

[11] Cf. P. F. Strawson, op. cit., pp. 1–4, 15–25.

[12] Notice that one cannot teach the meanings of quantifiers as a radically new idea by listing, e.g., semantical truth conditions. The learner must know the meta-language in which these truth-conditions are formulated. These formulations will themselves turn on the use of the quantifiers of the meta-language. Hence the most that one can accomplish in this way is to teach the meaning of quantifiers in one language in terms of the quantifiers of another language. From our point of view, to convey the meaning of quantifiers to someone as a radically new idea is to teach him to play the language-games that go together with quantifiers, and to teach him the relation of the different quantifying expressions to these games.

[13] Etienne Gilson, *The Christian Philosophy of St. Thomas Aquinas* (Victor Gollancz, London, 1957), p. 39.

black swans' we can in many contexts say 'one can find black swans', and, instead of 'all swans are white', one can sometimes say 'no swans can be found which are not white'. One 'language-game' in which quantifiers can naturally occur is what I shall call the language-game of seeking and finding; and it seems to me that this is by far the most important kind of language-game in which they can occur. In this respect, the case of quantifiers is different from that of the word 'good' which can occur in the context of many different types of activity none of which seems much more interesting logically than the others.

6. *Caveats*

There are, of course, circumstances in which quantified sentences cannot naturally be rewritten in terms of seeking and finding. 'There are mountains on the Moon' is more naturally paraphrased as 'One can see mountains on the Moon' than as 'One can find mountains on the Moon'. In this case, coming to know the existence of the objects in question is a matter of direct observation and therefore ill suited to the verbs 'to seek' or 'to search' which normally suggest that some amount of effort and of shifting one's point of view is needed. It is important to realize, however, that ascertaining the existence of individual objects by direct observation is a very special case of coming to know the existence of individuals. What is apt to mislead one is that in the most typical cases a search terminates in a situation in which one is confronted by a directly observable object. However, this does not make it true to say that the existence of the object in question was discovered by direct observation, for that would entirely overlook what seems to be the most important element in the situation, viz. the activities of seeking or trying to find.[14] Saying that we always come to know the existence of individual objects through sense-perception is like saying that one comes to London from New York by bus when what one

---

[14] For the conceptual situation, the crucial question is perhaps not whether one's mind is a 'ghost in a machine' which can only receive messages from the external world through the receptive mechanisms of the 'machine', but whether the mind can actually move the machine around so as to have a choice of what it can or cannot perceive. The possibility of active operations on one's environment at will seems to be deeply embedded in our conceptual structure, although in some curious way it gets eliminated in our conscious experience. On this point, cf. Eino Kaila, 'Die konzeptuellen und perzeptuellen Komponenten der Alltagserfahrung', *Acta Philosophica Fennica*, vol. 13 (1962), especially pp. 71–3.

means is that one flies over and then takes a bus to London from the airport.

It can also be pointed out that when the situations are described more closely in which we allegedly become aware of the existence of certain objects merely by witnessing them, we very often find ourselves using words that are closely similar logically to words for searching and seeking. In order to see an object which is at hand, it does not always suffice to open one's eyes; we very often have to scan our visual field even though we do not have to move ourselves from place to place bodily. Words like 'scan' are obviously related to words for seeking and searching. (Scanning as *visual* searching.)[15]

There is also an opposite type of case in which a paraphrase of a quantified sentence in terms of searching and finding does not sit quite happily. It may be illustrated by the sentence 'there are transuranium elements' which it would be a little awkward to paraphrase as 'one can find transuranium elements'. What misfires here is the fact that to speak simply of seeking and finding often suggests that no highly technical methods are required to get at the entities in question. It is more natural to say, e.g., that one can produce transuranium elements. It is of some interest to note that paraphrases in terms of seeking and finding become perceptibly less awkward if the methods used are specified, thus eliminating the source of awkwardness. It is perfectly natural to say, for instance, that transuranium elements were found by such-and-such methods.

In general, the words 'to seek' and 'to find' apply most aptly to the middle range of cases in which an effort has to be made to become aware of the existence (or non-existence) in question but in which no greatly sophisticated procedures are needed. We may of course imagine circumstances in which this middle range of cases becomes increasingly less important. Then verbs other than 'to seek' and 'to find' might become more important for the meaning of the quantifying expressions of the language in question.

These qualifications nevertheless do not seriously reflect on the importance of the two verbs for appreciating the logic of

---

15 I find that Kurt Baier makes use of this very word in his discussion of the concept of existence. See 'Existence', *Proceedings of the Aristotelian Society*, vol. 61 (1960–1), pp. 19–40, especially p. 24.

quantifying expressions. It may be that quantifiers are sometimes better served by the verb 'to produce' than by 'to find',
but many of the relevant logical features of these two verbs are
closely similar. Nor do our qualifications sever the discussion
from what we find in ordinary discourse. In natural language
existence and universality are often expressed by speaking of the
outcomes of different courses of action. A case in point is the
German idiom 'es gibt' whose origin is betrayed by such sentences as 'Wenn du hingehst, so gibt es Unglück' (meaning
literally: 'if you go there, "it gives" misfortune'—an example
listed in Hermann Paul's *Wörterbuch*). In the informal jargon of
mathematicians, universality is often expressed by such phrases
as 'no matter which number you take . . .'. The exceptional
cases in which 'to seek' and 'to find' do not give us very natural
paraphrases of the quantifiers may even be considered, for our
limited purposes, as special cases of seeking and finding in an
extended sense. Direct observation is a 'trivial case' of finding,
and the discovery of an object by a complicated technical procedure may perhaps be considered as the issue of a search conducted by very special means. In this extended sense, it may
thus be said that all our knowledge of the existence of external
objects is obtained by means of the activities of seeking and
finding.

7. *Quantifiers not operationistically interpretable*

In a sense, the meaning of quantifiers is thus their role ('use')
in the language-games of seeking and finding, with all the qualifications which I have indicated. On this view, a statement
containing quantifiers is comparable with a prediction concerning the outcome of certain processes of searching. These processes are the processes of seeking which we should have to carry
out in order to verify the sentence in question. Of course, nothing
is said of how these procedures should be conducted. One is also
abstracting from all the contingent limitations of our actual
capacity of search. Thus the processes of seeking and finding are
not 'operations' of the kind an operationistic theory of meaning
envisages. One can almost say that, on the contrary, the notions
of existence and universality receive their importance from the
fact that all the individuals that are known to exist cannot be
produced by 'operations' whose course is determined in advance.

In so far as there is an effective method of verifying or falsifying existential sentences, there is little point in using these sentences. If there were such a method, existential sentences could be replaced by sentences which speak of those particular instances of the claimed existence that would then be obtainable *per hypothesin*.

How deeply this uncertainty about the outcome of seeking and finding really cuts is indicated by the undecidability of quantification theory. What this undecidability means may be roughly explained by saying that one cannot always predict how far one would have to go in an attempted model set construction in order to bring out the possible inconsistency which may lurk in the set which we are trying to embed in a model set. In Chapter V below I shall argue that there is a certain analogy between the processes of model set construction and the activities of seeking and finding which one has to perform in verifying or falsifying sentences.[16] In view of this analogy, we may perhaps say that the processes of seeking and finding are as unpredictable as model set constructions.

Furthermore, there usually are many alternative ways of trying to construct a model set for a given set of sentences. Correspondingly, there usually are many alternative ways of trying to verify a sentence by looking for suitable individuals. It is impossible to give general rules as to which alternative will yield a model set, if such there be. Likewise, there does not seem to be much hope of telling which one of many alternative ways of looking for individuals, which would verify a given sentence, is the likeliest one to produce results. In some sense, the activities of seeking and finding therefore present irreducible alternatives. All this shows how far a cry the activities of seeking and

---

[16] For the concept of a model set, see the first chapter of the present book and the literature referred to there. Model sets may be thought of as partial descriptions of possible states of affairs; they are consistent, and any consistent set of first-order sentences can be embedded in at least one of them. A suitable complete proof procedure for first-order logic can be thought of as a method of trying to construct such a description for $\sim F$. If this attempt comes to a dead end, we have proved F. To decide whether F is provable, we thus have to know how far an attempted counter-example construction has to proceed in order to bring out whatever inconsistency there may lurk in $\sim F$. Because a decision procedure is impossible, we know that this cannot be recursively predicted. This unpredictability of model set constructions illustrates vividly the tremendous difference between them and the predictable operations of the operationists.

looking for are from the operations which an operationist is willing to countenance.

8. *Language-games as games proper*

One way of explaining my theory of what it means to understand quantifiers is to say that according to it one can understand quantifiers if one knows how to play certain kinds of *games*. Whatever there is to be said of the use of the Wittgensteinian term 'language-game' in general, here the word 'game' at any rate sits especially happily. This happiness is not due only to whatever informal similarities there are between games proper and those activities which Gilbert Ryle has called 'the game of exploring the world'.[17] It is primarily due to the fact that in the case of quantifiers, the relevant 'language-games' can also be formulated as games in the precise game-theoretical sense of the word.

In these games, one's opponent can be thought of in different ways: he may be simply nature, but he may also be some recalcitrant *malin génie* making the most of his chances of frustrating us. The game is most easily explained in the case of sentences in the prenex normal form (initial string of quantifiers followed by a 'matrix' which does not contain any quantifiers). Since all quantificational sentences (classically interpreted) can be converted into this form, the explanation of the 'game' that goes together with such a sentence will be in effect rather general.

My end in the game is to make a substitution-instance of the matrix true. My opponent's ('nature's') aim is to make the outcome of the game to be a false substitution-instance of the matrix. Each existential quantifier marks my move: I choose (produce, find) an individual whose name is to be substituted for the corresponding bound variable.[18] Each universal quantifier marks a move by my opponent: he is free to produce an individual whose name is to be substituted for the variables bound to the universal quantifier. The order of the moves corresponds to the order of the quantifiers.

It is readily seen that quite a few things which are ordinarily expressed by speaking of quantified sentences can be expressed

---

[17] Gilbert Ryle, 'Sensations' in *Contemporary British Philosophy*, Third Series, ed. by H. D. Lewis (Allen & Unwin, London, 1956), p. 442.

[18] Notice that this individual need not have a name prior to a move of this kind.

by speaking of the correlated games. For instance, for a sentence to be true it is necessary and sufficient that I have (as a matter of fact) a winning strategy in the correlated game, in the sense of game theory.[19]

On the other hand, it is quite clear that the games which this interpretation associates with quantificational sentences are to all intents and purposes tantamount to the games ('language-games') of looking for and finding. The imaginary opponent merely serves to highlight our own attempts to make sure that certain kinds of counter-examples cannot be found (that the opponent 'cannot defeat us'). Hence our interpretation does in a sense bring out all there is to be brought out in the logic of quantification.

The naturalness of the game-theoretic point of view is illustrated by the fact that this interpretation is sometimes resorted to spontaneously by writers who are explaining the meaning of quantifiers in non-systematic contexts. Developed more systematically, it has been employed by Leon Henkin, not only to explain the meaning of the usual kind of quantification, but to extend it further in one direction.[20]

Notice that the question as to what the individual moves are to be *called* is left open by the game-theoretic interpretation which I have sketched. The applicability of whatever term we want to use will depend on the details of the situation. In one of them, seeking and finding may be the most apt words; in another, producing might be a better one. In this respect, the game-theoretic interpretation is neutral with respect to the choice between these different descriptive expressions. It also brings out the fact that this choice is largely immaterial for my purposes, for clearly the games in question have the same charac-

---

[19] See R. Duncan Luce and Howard Raiffa, *Games and Decisions* (John Wiley, New York, 1957), Anatol Rapoport, *Two-Person Game Theory: The Essential Ideas* (University of Michigan Press, Ann Arbor, 1966), or Morton D. Davis, *Game Theory: A Nontechnical Introduction* (Basic Books, New York and London, 1970).

[20] See Leon Henkin, 'Some Remarks on Infinitely Long Formulas', in *Infinitistic Methods: Proceedings of a Symposium on Foundations of Mathematics* (Pergamon Press, London, and Państwowe Wydawnictwo Naukowe, Warsaw, 1961), pp. 176–83. For a further development of Henkin's observations, see J. H. Keisler, 'Finite Approximations of Infinitely Long Formulas', in *The Theory of Models: Proceedings of the 1963 International Symposium at Berkeley*, ed. by J. W. Addison, Leon Henkin, and Alfred Tarski (North-Holland Publishing Company, Amsterdam, 1965), pp. 158–69, especially pp. 160–1. Cf. also the Appendix to this chapter, below, pp. 77–82.

ter (same structure) no matter what the procedures are *called*
that lead me to choose one individual rather than another.
Hence many of the language-games which I have called games
of seeking and finding might be as well (and better) called
something else. All this is closely related to what I said earlier
of the applicability of the various words of the natural language
to the language-games in question.

The games just described are in many ways closely related to
the systematic theory of quantification, and might even open
possibilities of generalizing it. Some possibilities and some results
that have already been reached in this direction are indicated
in the appendix. Here I shall only explain how the game-
theoretic interpretation can be extended to sentences which are
not in the prenex form. Again the game proceeds from the whole
sentence to substitution-instances of its subsentences. My aim is
to end up with a true atomic sentence. The rules for quantifiers
remain the same. Disjunction now marks my move: I have to
choose a disjunct with reference to which the game is continued.
Conjunction marks a move by my opponent: he chooses a conjunct with reference to which the game is continued. Negation
$\sim F$ has the effect of changing the roles of the players, after
which the game continues by reference to F. This serves to define
the game correlated with any quantificational sentence, assuming that a domain of individuals is given with the appropriate
predicates defined on this domain.

The games which are thus correlated with quantificational
sentences are closely connected with the activities by means of
which one can try to verify these sentences. As far as my own
moves are concerned, precisely the same things are involved in
the verification of quantificational sentences and in the games
we have correlated with them. In the case of my opponent's
moves, I have to make sure that I cannot be defeated by any
of his strategies. This can be thought of as involving a temporary
switch of roles: I have to play the role of the devil's (rather
nature's) advocate—that is, the role of my opponent—for a
while in order to see what possibilities he has of defeating me.
This is neatly reflected by the possibility of replacing the universal quantifier '(Ux)' by '$\sim(Ex)\sim$', which eliminates my opponent's move but involves a temporary exchange of roles.

With this proviso, the games I have described are in effect the activities by means of which one can try to verify quantificational sentences. By describing these games in some detail one can thus see what the activities are of whose outcomes we are making, as it were, a prediction when we assert a quantificational sentence. All this illustrates the close logical connection which (I am arguing) there is between quantifiers and the 'games' of looking for and finding.

9. *Presuppositions of the language-games of seeking and finding*

The justification for this connection must lie to a considerable extent in the light which this connection throws on the logical behaviour of the quantifying expressions of ordinary language and of formal logic. Does it throw any such light?

If quantifiers go together with the verbs 'to seek', 'to look for', and 'to find', the conditions for the significant (or, as some students of language would like us to say, non-deviant) use of quantifiers must be approximately the same as the conditions for the use of these verbs. Now what is required for the notions of seeking and looking for to make sense? Two main requirements obviously have to be met. First, the field of search must somehow be defined, however partially. Second, there must be ways of ascertaining when one has found the individual or the kind of individual one has been looking for. These are obviously also requirements that have to be satisfied in order for the games properly described above to be playable.

I shall call these requirements the first and second requirement. Both of them are relevant to the logical behaviour of quantifying expressions in ordinary language and in the formal systems of logic. We shall examine them in the order in which they were mentioned.

The first requirement helps us to understand, *inter alia*, why unqualified statements of existence are apt to strike one as odd (deviant). We are likely to find any number of perfectly natural utterances of the form 'there are chairs upstairs', or 'there is an infinity of prime numbers', but it is doubtful whether we can find many non-deviant utterances of the form 'there are numbers' or 'there are chairs' outside philosophers' discussions.

It is now easy to see what is wrong with these unqualified statements. Part of the function of the missing qualification is to indicate what this field of search is: hence the meaning of these statements is incomplete, and can only be gathered from the context at best.

It is interesting to note that a very small change alters the situation radically. The statement 'there are black swans' is perfectly in order, as might indeed be expected from our point of view. In this statement the class of swans constitutes the relevant field of search, or part of it, which is taken to be given clearly enough for the operations of seeking and finding to make sense. Attention is concentrated, so to speak, on the additional question whether within this well-defined universe of discourse one can find swans of a particular colour.

There is an interesting asymmetry here between positive and negative statements. Although sentences like 'there are swans' are very often awkward to utter, similar negative statements like 'there are no dodos' are perfectly in order. Again an explanation is forthcoming. In an unqualified negative statement the field of search does not matter (if it does, the statement is dangerously vague), and hence the need for specifying it is much smaller than is the corresponding positive statement. These, in turn, can lose their awkwardness when contrasted to a real or imagined effort to deny the existence of the individuals in question. As Peter Geach has urged on me,[21] there is nothing wrong with a sentence like 'Yes, Virginia, there *are* swans, and they really are ugly in their first year, just as Hans Andersen says.'

The same point emerges also from the observation of other quantifying expressions of ordinary language. Such words as 'some', 'any', and 'all' are, in Austin's phrase, substantive-hungry. No matter whether the statement 'there are swans' makes sense or not, it cannot be paraphrased in terms of 'some' without bringing in new words which serve to indicate the relevant field of search, for instance, 'Some extant birds are swans'. The words 'some' and 'any' occur in such constructions as 'some X' or 'some Xs' and 'any X', where X is a general noun. Part of the function of this general noun, and a reason why it is needed, is to indicate the field of search which is being presupposed. Where such a field of search or part of it is available, these words can be used. Thus 'There are black swans', becomes 'Some swans are black'. A statement like 'All ravens are black' is therefore not quite accurately translated into the language of

[21] Private communication.

formal logic by '$(Ux)(x$ is a raven $\supset x$ is black)', for in this translation some definitely given large universe of discourse is being
presupposed while in the original the extent of the underlying
field of search was left largely unspecified, the only relevant
assumption being that it must include all ravens.[22]

Often the exact boundaries of the field of search are not
clearly defined; there is a similar vagueness in the meaning of
the corresponding quantified sentences. Austin once posed the
question (it was one of the problems which have been published
in *Analysis*) whether the statement 'All swans are white' refers
to whatever swans there may be on the canals of Mars.[23] As
emerged from the answers, there is a complication here in that
the inductive evidence on which we may think of the statement
to be based may tacitly restrict its scope to terrestrial swans.
Apart from this complication, however, the statement serves to
illustrate the vagueness I have in mind.

Formal logicians usually assume that all the different fields of
search can be happily pooled together into one big 'universe
of discourse'. There may be reasons for this complacency, but
the situation would merit a closer look. The difficulty of pooling
different fields of search together does not lie primarily in the
dissimilarity of the entities which thus have to be treated as
equal. A more important problem is due to the fact that there
may be interdependencies between individuals in the different
fields of search. One may look for rivers of different kinds, and
one may look for waters of different kinds. However, there
cannot exist rivers without there also existing waters.[24]

In the applications of logic the frequent indeterminacy of the
pertinent field of search is shown especially clearly by the odd
results of the process of contraposition. It seems rather odd to
paraphrase 'every man is selfish' by 'no unselfish thing is a man'.
These two sentences will be logically equivalent as soon as the
relevant field of search has been fixed. But the sentences them-

---

[22] For a detailed discussion of a number of problems in this area (from a some-
what different point of view), see Ernest W. Adams, 'Probability and the Logic of
Conditionals', in *Aspects of Inductive Logic*, ed. by Jaakko Hintikka and Patrick
Suppes (North-Holland Publishing Company, Amsterdam, 1966), pp. 265–316.

[23] See J. L. Austin, 'Report of Analysis "Problem" No. 12', *Analysis*, vol. 18
(1957–8), pp. 97–101 (with two 'solutions' to the problem).

[24] Cf. Peter Geach, *Reference and Generality* (Cornell University Press, Ithaca,
N.Y., 1962), and W. V. Quine, 'Unification of Universes in Set Theory', *The
Journal of Symbolic Logic*, vol. 21 (1956), pp. 267–79.

selves do not specify this field, and they presuppose different things concerning it. 'Every man is selfish' presupposes that the class of all men is part of the field of search. 'No unselfish thing is a man' presupposes that the totality of unselfish things has been defined clearly enough to be amenable to our activities of seeking and finding. Hence these two sentences do not have the same logical powers in ordinary discourse.

These odd results of contraposition cannot be explained away in the way in which some philosophers have sought to explain away some of the paradoxes of confirmation, that is to say, by reference to the relative sizes of the classes involved. In the case at hand such an attempt would presumably consist in pointing out that there are many more things (and things of many different sorts) which cannot be said to be selfish than there are human beings, and of arguing that this makes it more natural to use the former class as an antecedent of a general implication than the latter. However, this manœuvre does not help at all. 'No indivisible entity is a material body' is markedly more deviant than 'every material body is divisible', all the more so in the mouth of a materialist.

In the same way, the statements 'some swans are black' and 'some black objects are swans' are not equivalent in ordinary discourse. The former presupposes that the relevant field of search includes all swans, the latter that it includes all black objects.

In relation to the requirement that the field of search is to be delineated, the verb 'to produce' behaves somewhat differently from the verb 'to look for'. The methods of producing an object of a certain kind both with respect to their scope and with respect to the nature of the procedures involved are restricted somewhat less narrowly than the methods of finding one. In this sense, the 'field of search' connected with production is wider and more flexible than those connected with searching and finding. This may be part of the reason why it is more natural to say, for instance, 'we can produce transuranium elements' or 'we can produce neutrinos' than to say, 'we can find transuranium elements' or 'we can find neutrinos'. Sometimes this difference is connected with doubts about whether the objects produced exist objectively apart from our methods of production. However, even where this is not at issue, the difference between the verbs 'to produce' and 'to find' is marked enough, as it seems to be in the examples I just gave. All this tends to make the verb 'to produce' somewhat more amenable to the purposes of a formal logician, who needs a large, all-comprehensive field of search for his 'universe of discourse', than the verb 'to find'.

10. *End-points of search*

The second requirement is likewise of considerable interest. In order for the notions of seeking and finding to make sense, and hence for the quantifiers to make sense, we must have some idea of the circumstances in which we can stop and claim to have found what we have been looking for. In brief, the conditions of having found the thing we are looking for must be determined. These may often be defined with reference to the results of further search; i.e., quantifiers may occur within the scope of other quantifiers; but ultimately our conditions will normally specify absolute stopping-points for our search. Of course, the conditions of 'really having found' something are not always without a certain vagueness. The paradigmatic case is that of being able to point to a physical object or to a man and to say: 'There is one!' But how the other cases shade into this one is not always very clear. However, this vagueness does not sever the logic of seeking and finding from that of existence. The difficulties which there often are in deciding whether entities which we cannot immediately confront (such as a neutrino, a field, or a gene) 'really exist' or not are largely difficulties in deciding what is to count as finding or producing one of these entities.[25] As Stephen Toulmin puts it, certain things are generally taken to be sufficient for the purpose of showing the 'real existence' of physical entities, 'for instance, cloud-chamber pictures of α-rays, electron microscope photographs, or, as a second best, audible clicks from a Geiger counter'.[26] The reason why these count as demonstrations of actual existence is that they are, again in Toulmin's words, 'sufficiently like being shown a

---

[25] According to some reports, Ernst Mach's standard reply to those who claimed that atoms exist was 'Have you seen one?' For these reports, and the qualifications they need, see Stephen Brush, 'Mach and Atomism', *Synthese*, vol. 18 (1968), pp. 192–215, especially p. 208.

[26] Stephen Toulmin, *Philosophy of Science* (Hutchinson, London, 1953), pp. 135–7.

living dodo on the lawn' or, in my terms, sufficiently like the paradigmatic cases of finding an object by directly confronting it. Thus for a working physicist 'the question, "Do neutrinos exist?" acts as an invitation to "produce a neutrino", preferably by making it visible'—or, as we may equally well say, to find a neutrino for us to witness.

The second requirement also seems to me to be relevant to the evaluation of a famous 'argument' of G. E. Moore. Norman Malcolm has suggested that what look like arguments in Moore should often be construed as reminders that certain concepts have a logically correct use in our language.[27] On this view, Moore did not have to produce *true* or *indubitable* examples of the use of these concepts in order to accomplish his end, although he certainly did try to do so himself. What happens now to this view if it is applied to Moore's famous 'proof of the external world'?[28] The crucial concept here is that of existence. What do we have to be reminded of in order to bring it home to us that we can use it impeccably as applied to what Moore calls 'external objects' or 'objects which are to be met with in space'? It follows from what I have said that there are two main things one has to ascertain in order to make sure that a concept of existence applies to objects of a certain sort; they are incorporated in my first and second requirement. The first is not crucial here, partly because we are dealing with the question whether there are any 'external objects' at all. This being so, we are in effect facing a potential denial of the existence of any 'external objects' at all, which makes the precise specification of the field of search less crucial in the same way it did in our dodo example earlier.

Hence the main burden falls on the requirement that we must have criteria for having found whatever we are looking for. This requirement in effect says that it must make sense to say, 'Now I have found an *X*' in order for the concept of existence to be applicable to *X*s. How could one hope to bring home to an audience that we do in fact have such criteria for deciding when we have found 'an external object' or have met 'an object to be met with in space'? Clearly by staging as paradigmatic an

[27] Norman Malcolm, 'George Edward Moore' in his *Knowledge and Certainty: Essays and Lectures* (Prentice-Hall, Englewood Cliffs, New Jersey, 1963), pp. 163–83.
[28] G. E. Moore, 'Proof of an External World', *Proceedings of the British Academy*, vol. 25 (1939); reprinted in G. E. Moore, *Philosophical Papers* (Macmillan, London, 1959), Ch. 7.

instance of a confrontation with an 'external object' as one could imagine. One displays an 'external object' and says, 'Here is one'; one displays another and says, 'Here is another.' And this is precisely what Moore does in his 'proof of the external world': he waves a hand and says, 'Here is a hand.'

What Moore does thus receives a perfectly reasonable and indeed predictable sense when seen in the light in which Malcolm wants to view Moore's philosophical activity in general. By enacting his little scene, Moore reminds us that we know perfectly well what it means to be confronted with an 'external object' so as to be able to say, 'Here is one!' and that one of the main presuppositions of our use of the concept of existence is therefore satisfied. In Moore there is, of course, also the implication that in the ensuing sense of existence, it is indeed obvious that there are 'external objects'. I would agree with Malcolm, however, that for this purpose Moore's skit is both unnecessary and perhaps even insufficient. It matters little whether on the actual occasion before the British Academy Moore actually succeeded in pointing to his hand or to any other external object.[29] What matters is only the fact that we can in principle do this and that we also often succeed in doing so. Moore is not as much proving the existence of the external world as pointing out that we have in fact an impeccable concept of existence as applied to hands, chairs, houses, and other commonplace 'external objects'.

I am not quite sure whether our concept of existence as applied to commonplace external objects is quite as unproblematic as Moore's argument presupposes (on the construction I have put on it). However, even if it is not, there is a point Moore's argument makes: in so far as we do have a satisfactory idea of what it means for external objects to exist, it must make sense to speak of finding them and confronting them. If we want to criticize the former idea, we have to examine the latter idea more closely.

It may be argued that the interest of Moore's 'proof' is difficult to bring out in other ways. For instance, it does not help to ask what Moore was doing when he said, 'Here is one hand, and

---

[29] If you have inverting goggles on (of the kind now used in some psychological experiments), then it may actually be difficult for you to point to your hand. Does this make it more difficult for you to 'prove the existence of an external world' in Moore's sense?

here is another.' He certainly was not informing his audience of something they did not know before. Nor is there any other natural purpose in view which his statement could serve. The whole question of the *use* of his statement seems oddly out of place.

Moore's argument cannot be construed as a formal inference, either. We may admit that hands are external objects, but this does not carry us very far. The crucial statement 'this is a hand' or 'here is a hand' should presumably be taken as a subject-predicate of the form $P(a)$. I have pointed out elsewhere that from this we can only infer '$(Ex)P(x)$' (i.e., 'hands exist') if we have an additional premiss of the form '$(Ex)(x = a)$' which ensures that the object referred to by the term 'a' ('this object') exists.[30] However, this is just what we cannot assume here. To assume that the hand Moore is waving really exists is to beg the very question he is asking. Hence his argument does not have any validity as a formal proof. We can draw existential conclusions without explicit or hidden existential premisses as little as we can derive an 'ought' from an 'is'. Whatever persuasiveness Moore's famous 'proof' has derives from its being the kind of paradigmatic confrontation with an external object which we must have in order for the notion of existence to be applicable.

11. *Marking the different moves*

In order to bring out more fully the connection between quantifying expressions and the activities of seeking and finding and to perceive some of the consequences of this connection it is advisable to consider somewhat more complicated cases. Consider as an example the sentence 'Some Englishman has seen all the countries of the world.' In order to verify this sentence, we therefore have to fix upon one individual at a time and investigate whether he perhaps satisfies this double requirement. This means that we have to distinguish him, for the time being at least, from the other individuals whom we also have to keep an eye on. If we know his name, we may use it. If not, we may assign some conventional designation to him, like the John Does

[30] See Jaakko Hintikka, 'On the Logic of Existence and Necessity', *The Monist*, vol. 50 (1966), pp. 55–76, reprinted (with changes) under the title 'Existential Presuppositions and Their Elimination' in Jaakko Hintikka, *Models for Modalities: Selected Essays* (D. Reidel Publishing Company, Dordrecht, 1969), pp. 23–44.

and Richard Roes of legal parlance. If the context allows, we may also speak simply of *this* man or *that* man. The necessity of distinguishing him from others in some way or another is closely related to our second requirement for the meaningfulness of quantifying expressions. We must have ways of marking the different moves in our game; we must be able to distinguish not only the end-points but also the branching-points of the different possible courses which our interconnected processes of seeking and finding may take. Even if we have already come across an Englishman such as we are looking for, we still have to distinguish him from others while we make sure that he is related to each of the countries of the world in the required way.

This new requirement is closely related to recent disputes concerning the dispensability of free singular terms in favour of mere variables of quantification. (Certain aspects of the controversy cannot be touched here; for instance, the question whether it is possible to teach and to learn a language without free singular terms—a subject of which we all seem to know very little.) The requirement just mentioned is probably part of the truth which there seems to be in the contention of those who think of singular terms as being indispensable. It is, e.g., closely related to the point which P. F. Strawson has expressed by saying 'there could not be a form of words having the meaning "There is something or other which has attribute *A*" unless there were also a form of words having the meaning "*This* thing has attribute *A*".'[31] We must have, it seems, some ways of referring to one particular individual rather than to others for a while at least, in order for the language-games of seeking and finding to be practicable and hence for quantifying expressions to make sense.

This much is certainly true. However, certain other contentions of the defenders of free singular terms do not follow from it. For instance, it does not follow that there is something in the actual body of our knowledge which we cannot express in terms

---

[31] Cf. W. V. Quine, *Methods of Logic* (Henry Holt, New York, 1950), pp. 220–4; id., *From a Logical Point of View* (Harvard University Press, Cambridge, Mass., 1953), pp. 7–8, 13, 146, and 166–7; id., *Word and Object* (Harvard University Press, Cambridge, Mass., 1960), pp. 179–86; P. F. Strawson, 'Singular Terms and Predication', *Journal of Philosophy*, vol. 58 (1961), pp. 393–412; id., *Individuals* (Methuen, London, 1959), pp. 199–203; id., 'Singular Terms, Ontology, and Identity', *Mind*, vol. 65 (1956), pp. 433–54.

of quantifiers and bound variables although we can express it by means of free singular terms.

It does not follow, either, that there must be a category of proper names or other free singular terms in one's language. We must require that there are ways of marking the end-points and other crucial junctures of our interlocking processes of search, processes which are (*inter alia*) required for the verification of sentences with more than one layer of quantifiers. Consider the simplest case as an example. This is what was called the second requirement. It says that the end-points of search must be somehow recognizable. This recognition must of course be marked in the language-game in question. It may be the case that we can simply say: '*This* is the kind of object we have been looking for' (say one with the attribute *A*). It does not follow, however, that we must be able to mark the end-points by *saying* of the particular object we have reached that it has the attribute *A*. Instead of saying anything about this particular individual we might say in general terms, 'Now we know that there is an object with the attribute *A*.' Of course, in order for such utterances to serve to mark the end-points of search we must have some non-verbal means of making it known that we assert the existence of at least one individual of the appropriate kind on the basis of witnessing that particular individual we actually witnessed. From the necessity of employing such non-verbal devices of communication it does not follow, however, that there must be an expression in the language which can serve this purpose. Turning Strawson's formulation around, we might say that there need not be any *form of words* having the meaning 'This thing has attribute *A*' in a language although the language in question contains a form of words having the meaning 'there is something with the attribute *A*'. However, there must be some alternative way of indicating the same thing, that is to say, of bringing out what the former expresses over and above the latter. There must be non-verbal means to call one's attention to particular individuals even though there need not be verbal means for doing so.[32] Some sort of demonstrative device is thus needed in any case for the language-games of seeking and finding and hence for

---

[32] It may also be admitted that it is in many cases *practically* impossible to get along with non-verbal means only. I do not see, however, any general logical argument for not being able to do so in some cases.

first-order languages in general. However, the use of proper names (or of other singular terms different from demonstratives and from the variables of quantification) can be viewed as a mere mnemonic device.

12. *General morals*

There is also a general moral or two to be drawn from our observations. If there really obtains the close relationship between quantifiers and the activities of searching and trying to find, we have a stronger reason than ever to be suspicious of the Carnapian methods which are criticized elsewhere in this volume.[33] The use of these methods sometimes presupposes, it will be argued, that all the individuals in the universe of discourse are known. In any case, not very much attention is paid in these methods to the discovery and introduction of new individuals. If the use of quantifiers is essentially connected with the activities of seeking and finding new individuals, we cannot hope that any methods which make no provision for such activities will throw much light on the logic of quantification. It seems to me significant that some of the main theoretical difficulties to which the application of Carnapian methods lead arise in connection with quantified sentences.

To conclude with another general point: we can perhaps now see one partial reason for the interest of the formal logic of quantification. If it is true that the processes of seeking and finding are the most important processes by means of which we become aware of the existence of individuals, and if it is also true that the language-games of seeking and finding are the natural context of quantifiers, then the study of the logical behaviour of quantifiers is largely a study of the structure of some of the most important processes by means of which we obtain our knowledge. It is perhaps worth noting that the formal logic of quantification can have this interest independently of how closely it reproduces the ways in which we in the natural language refer to the activities of seeking and finding. As a brief dictum we might perhaps say this: quantification theory is a regimented way of speaking of the activities of seeking and finding. It is not a regimentation of the ways in which we speak

---

[33] See above, pp. 8–9 and below, Ch. VII.

of these activities in *ordinary language*. If quantification theory helps us to carry out the processes of seeking and finding or at the very least helps us to clear up our ideas concerning them, it has an interesting application even if it should turn out not to apply very well to a direct study and regimentation of ordinary language. In a later chapter (see below, pp. 106–14) I shall try to bring out at least one way in which the formal logic of quantification helps us with our language-games of seeking and finding.

APPENDIX

Language-Games and Systematic Logical Theory

Although the game-theoretic point of view on first-order logic which was sketched in the body of this paper apparently has never been discussed in its full generality before, it is obviously closely related to a number of issues and approaches in systematic logical theory. Here only a few relatively informal remarks will be made to illustrate the naturalness and importance of the connection between the logic of quantification and the games of searching and looking for.

The game-theoretic approach is closely related to the idea of eliminating quantifiers in favour of functions and functionals, and to the basic idea of the so-called 'no counter-example interpretation'.[34] For instance, there is obviously a very close connection between the truth of a statement of the form

(I) $$(Ex)(Uy)(Ez)F(x, y, z)$$

where the variables are assumed to range over natural numbers, and the statement

(II) $$(Ex)(Ef)(Uy)F(x, y, f(y))$$

with a function variable 'f'. This function and a number x are precisely what determines 'my' strategy in the game correlated with (I). Hence the force of (II) is in effect to say that there is a winning strategy in the game correlated with (I). If a suitable x and f can in fact be given, the existential quantifiers in (II) can be dropped, leaving us with a quantifier-free statement.[35]

[34] See, e.g., Georg Kreisel, 'A Variant to Hilbert's Theory of the Foundations of Arithmetic', *British Journal of the Philosophy of Science*, vol. 4 (1953–4), pp. 107–29 (cf. p. 357), and William Tait, 'The Substitution Method', *Journal of Symbolic Logic*, vol. 30 (1965), pp. 175–92.

[35] For a brief survey of a number of developments in this direction, see Andrzej Mostowski, *Thirty Years of Foundational Studies* (Acta Philosophica Fennica vol. 17, Basil Blackwell, Oxford, 1966), lecture IV.

I shall not discuss how simple observations of this sort are utilized in the 'no counter-example interpretation' or in other developments in logical theory. I have merely tried to illustrate the main idea, which seems clear enough: we take a sentence or formula (e.g., a number-theoretic one), correlate with it a game along the lines indicated, and then express by an explicit statement the fact that there is a winning strategy in this game. This new statement will then serve as an interpretation of the original sentence or formula.

This general technique admits of many variations. One may try to consider, not the game correlated with a statement, but rather the game correlated with its negation. If games of infinite length are used, we may require that they have to be won in a finite number of moves, and so on. Perhaps the most important variation is the possibility of choosing the strategy set in different ways.

If f is allowed to range over *arbitrary* (number-theoretical) functions in our example, (II) is true if and only if (I) is true in the classical arithmetic. It lies very close at hand, however, to suggest that the class of pure strategies we 'really' have available is narrower than that. This means restricting the range of the function quantifier in (II). For instance, it might appear natural to let f range over recursive functions only. (How could anyone actually use a strategy given by a non-recursive function?) This will correspond to some non-classical sense of truth and falsity for (I).[36] In this way, we can perhaps see with some clarity what it could mean actually to employ a non-classical logic in one's 'games of exploring the world': it could mean to use a restricted pure strategy set in the game correlated with (I). Alternatively, or in addition to this, the use of a non-classical conception of logic could also mean defining the moves of the game which are connected with the different connectives and quantifiers in a way different from the characterizations of these moves given earlier.

It seems to me that a number of approaches and arguments in the foundational studies might become more accessible to a philosophical scrutiny when looked upon from this game-theoretic point of view, although their precise connections with the game-theoretical concepts and ideas often remain to be worked out.

The following observation has struck me as being especially suggestive: there is a very close connection between the concept of a truth-value of a sentence and the game-theoretical concept of the value of the correlated game. If I have a winning strategy, the value of the game is the pay-off of winning, i.e., the 'value' of winning the game. This is also precisely the case in which the sentence is true.

[36] Of course, the interpretation of sentential connectives is also important here.

Hence the pay-off of winning as a value of the game can be identified with the truth-value 'true' of the sentence, and correspondingly for falsity.

It follows that the fact that classical logic is two-valued is virtually tantamount to the fact that the games correlated with classically interpreted statements like (I) admit of pure optimal strategies. That this should be the case is not quite immediate, for in the case of an infinite domain the games have infinite (pure) strategy sets. The existence of pure optimal strategies nevertheless follows from well-known general results which rely essentially on the fact that we are dealing with games with perfect information.

However, if suitable changes are made in our assumptions, optimal strategies (if any) might turn out to be mixed. The weights of the different pure strategies involved in this mixture could then perhaps serve as models of non-classical truth-values.

This idea remains to be explored, as far as I know. However, it is obvious that there are extant theories which could be, and perhaps have been, conceived of in a game-theoretic spirit. One example among many is Gödel's suggested extension of the finitistic point of view.[37] Here each arithmetical statement is interpreted in terms of another one which can be taken to be essentially a statement to the effect that a certain game correlated with the first statement has a winning strategy. The pure strategy sets are assumed to be restricted to those that can be defined by means of recursive functions and functionals.

Furthermore, a not insubstantial amount of important systematic work in the model theory of first-order logic either has been or can readily be described in game-theoretic terms. Here I shall give only a few indications of some of the results that have been reached. In the application of game-theoretic ideas just outlined, a game is connected with each statement, interpreted so as to speak of a certain piece of world or of a 'model'. Two such models are said to be elementarily equivalent if and only if they are equivalent with respect to all the different games we have described. Now Ehrenfeucht and Fraïssé have in effect shown how for the purpose of describing elementary equivalence this variety of games can be replaced by a single game of comparing the two models.[38] In this game, a move by my opponent (who has the first move) consists in picking out an individual a from one of the two models, say M (of his own choosing). My next move

[37] Kurt Gödel, 'Über eine bisher noch nicht benützte Erweiterung des finiten Standpunktes', *Dialectica*, vol. 12 (1958), pp. 76–83.

[38] A. Ehrenfeucht, 'An Application of Games to the Completeness Problem for Formalized Theories', *Fundamenta Mathematicae*, vol. 49 (1960–1), pp. 129–41; R. Fraïssé, 'Sur quelques classifications des relations basées sur des isomorphismes

consists in trying to choose from the other model M' an individual a' whose relations to those members of M' which have been picked out earlier match the relations of a to the corresponding members of M and whose attributes match the attributes of a. If I cannot do this, I lose; if I do not lose after any finite number of moves, I win. Then M and M' are elementarily equivalent if and only if I have a winning strategy in the game so defined.

It turns out that this game, and all the truncated versions one obtains by restricting both players to a finite number of moves, are connected very closely with what I have called distributive normal forms and discussed elsewhere in some detail.[39] For instance, I have a winning strategy in the truncated game with precisely d moves for each player if and only if the same constituent with depth d is true both in M and in M'. Then (and only then) the two models M and M' are also equivalent for the purposes of all games correlated with statements of depth d or less. (Depth is roughly speaking characterized as the number of layers of quantifiers in a sentence.) In certain other respects, too, a consideration of constituents helps us to appreciate the close connection which there obtains between the games of comparing two different models and the games correlated with statements.

These examples perhaps suffice to illustrate my suggestion that the logic of quantification is essentially the logic of certain kinds of games of seeking and finding (or whatever you want to call them).

The most systematic earlier use of game-theoretical ideas in quantification theory is due to Paul Lorenzen and developed further by Wolfgang Stegmüller and K. Lorenz (among others).[40] Some connections between their approach and the above remarks are obvious.

restraintes', *Publications Scientifiques de l'Université d'Alger*, Série A, vol. 2 (1955), pp. 15–60 and pp. 273–95.

[39] Jaakko Hintikka, 'Distributive Normal Forms in First-Order Logic' in *Formal Systems and Recursive Functions*, ed. by J. N. Crossley and M. A. E. Dummett (North-Holland Publishing Company, Amsterdam, 1965), pp. 47–90; Jaakko Hintikka, 'Distributive Normal Forms and Deductive Interpolation', *Zeitschrift für mathematische Logik und Grundlagen der Mathematik*, vol. 10 (1964), pp. 185–91. The truncated versions of the comparison-game are also very closely related to the games which were correlated with distributive normal forms in the first place.

[40] See Paul Lorenzen, 'Ein dialogisches Konstruktivitätskriterium' in *Infinitistic Methods*, Proceedings of a Symposium on Foundations of Mathematics, Warsaw (Pergamon Press, London, and Państwowe Wydawnictwo Naukowe, Warszawa, 1961); Paul Lorenzen, *Metamathematik* (Bibliographisches Institut, Mannheim, 1962); K. Lorenz, 'Arithmetik und Logik als Spiele' (Doctoral Dissertation, Kiel, 1961); K. Lorenz, 'Dialogspiele als semantische Grundlage von Logikkalkülen', *Archiv für mathematische Logik und Grundlagenforschung*, vol. 11 (1968), pp. 32–55 and 73–100; Wolfgang Stegmüller, 'Remarks on the Completeness of Logical Systems Relative to the Validity-Concepts of P. Lorenzen and K. Lorenz', *Notre Dame Journal of Formal Logic*, vol. 5 (1964), pp. 81–112.

However, there is also a difference which from a philosophical point of view is very important. The games I have described are related to the uses of logical symbols in finding out something about the world. They are not 'indoor games'; they are 'played' in the wide world among whatever objects our statements speak about. An essential part of all these games consists in trying to find individuals which satisfy certain requirements.

In contrast to our games of seeking and finding, the games of Lorenzen and Stegmüller are 'dialogical games' which are played 'indoors' by means of verbal 'challenges' and 'responses'. These may be made, e.g., by writing down suitable sequences of symbols.

As was already pointed out, there are of course certain connections between the formal games of Lorenzen and Stegmüller and the games which I have described and which have been called language-games. If one is merely interested in suitable technical problems in logic, there may not be much to choose between the two types of games. However, from a philosophical point of view, the difference seems to be absolutely crucial. Only considerations which pertain to 'games of exploring the world' can be hoped to throw any light on the role of our logical concepts in the meaningful use of language.

In fact, it seems to me that a sharp distinction has to be made between such 'outdoor' games of exploring the world in order to verify or falsify certain (interpreted) statements by producing suitable individuals and such 'indoor' games as, e.g., proving that certain uninterpeted formulae are logical truths by manipulating sequences of symbols in a suitable way. Unless this distinction is made, the relevance of games of the latter type cannot be satisfactorily described. In Chapter V below, I shall try to show in what way the formal language-game of proving or disproving quantificational formulae can help us in the 'field games' of trying to verify or falsify quantificational statements.

If there is anything to be learned from the possibility of applying game-theoretic concepts to the systematic theory of first-order logic, it is that the study of the *use* of a language (or a part of a language) can be as purely logical and philosophical an enterprise as the study of logical syntax or the study of the referential relations between language and the world. It seems to me that the familiar Carnapian trichotomy syntax–semantics–pragmatics is often misunderstood to imply that all the study of language in use (as distinguished from its formal aspects and from its referential relations to the world) belongs to the psychology and sociology of language or to some such non-philosophical and non-logical discipline.[41] Without wanting to detract

---

[41] Clear exam ples of this line of thought are found in Colin Cherry, *On Human*

from the interest and importance of these studies, it ought to be clear
that the use of language can be studied in abstraction from the
psychological and sociological conditions of the people using it quite
as well as syntax can be studied in abstraction from the psychological
make-up and social context of the people who write or utter the
sentences whose syntax we are studying. (Of course, this is not to say
that important factual connections might be found in both cases.)
The study of the games correlated with quantificational sentences
perhaps serves to illustrate the possibility and interest of such purely
logical pragmatics.

Communication (M.I.T. Press, Cambridge, Mass., 1957; second edition, 1966), p. 223;
and in A. Pap, *Semantics and Necessary Truth* (Yale University Press, New Haven,
Conn., 1958), p. 434. See also Charles Morris, 'Pragmatism and Logical Empiri-
cism', in *The Philosophy of Rudolf Carnap*, ed. by P. A. Schilpp (The Library of Living
Philosophers, Open Court Publishing Company, La Salle, Illinois, 1963), pp. 87–98,
especially pp. 88–9. Carnap's reply in the same volume (p. 861) shows that the
confusion I am criticizing cannot be attributed to his mature position in the sixties,
whatever effects his earlier statements on the subject may have had.

IV

BEHAVIOURAL CRITERIA OF RADICAL TRANSLATION: A COMMENT ON W. V. QUINE'S *WORD AND OBJECT*

1. *Canonical idiom*

THE observations made in Chapter III can be used to evaluate one of the most frequently discussed philosophical works of the last couple of decades.

For all its impressive merits, Quine's *Word and Object*[1] seems to me a book whose two ends do not quite meet. The difference in approach between the early and the late parts of *Word and Object* is in fact quite striking. With some oversimplification, it can be said that the last few chapters of the book are dominated by the idea of *canonical idiom* of a well-known quantificational variety. Problems of vagueness, ambiguity, opacity, tense, modality, and ontic commitment are studied partly or wholly by showing how the problematic sentences can be paraphrased in the applied first-order language which serves as Quine's canonical notation or how this language can in other ways serve the same purposes as the 'limpid vernacular' of everyday life as well as of science. This vernacular is our familiar English. As Quine writes, in most of the later parts of *Word and Object* 'the language concerned . . . is specifically English' (op. cit., p. 8ð).

To what extent can the results of these discussions be extended to a foreign tongue? They can be extended completely if this foreign language can be translated into English. They can be extended partly to another language if we can recognize quantificational concepts in it, i.e., if we can translate the canonical quantificational notation into it. For instance, such a translation would enable us to discuss the ontic commitments[2] of the speakers of that foreign tongue along the lines of Quine's own discussion of such commitments.

---

[1] W. V. Quine, *Word and Object* (M.I.T. Press, Cambridge, Mass., 1960).
[2] That is, presuppositions concerning the existence of certain classes of entities implicit in a language.

2. *Radical translation*

These questions lead us to the preoccupations of the early parts of *Word and Object*, among which the problem of *radical translation* looms especially large. The success of such translation is what would enable us to relate the apparently language-bound considerations of the late sections to the general discussion about the ways of learning words, stimulus meaning, and stimulus analyticity in the early chapters.

However, the possibility of radical translation is left by Quine unsystematized and dependent essentially on a more or less bilingual translator's analytical hypotheses which in principle can never eliminate completely the indeterminacy of the enterprise. (In particular, this indeterminacy affects the question of ontic commitment: cf. pp. 242–3.) Quine asks 'how much language can be made sense of in terms of its stimulus conditions' but finds that they leave a great deal of scope for 'empirically unconditioned variation in one's conceptual scheme'. For related reasons, the insights which one can gain by comparing English with a canonical first-order language cannot be extended to other languages automatically but only by means of analytical hypotheses which in principle can always leave room for doubt. This indeterminacy of the radical translation of the quantificational idiom is that I had in mind when I said above that the two ends of *Word and Object* do not quite meet.

3. *Canonical idiom* vis-à-vis *radical translation*

Some simple parts of the canonical idiom admit of a behaviourally determinable radical translation. The precise line between cases that can and those that cannot be handled in terms of stimulus meaning is drawn by Quine at a place which might at first seem somewhat surprising. Sentential connectives admit (*apud* Quine) radical translation 'directly'. However, quantifiers do not. What causes this subtle difference?

The difference can be understood if we recall Quine's basic apparatus. It is helpful to think of it in terms of a jungle linguist who is beginning to comprehend a completely foreign tongue. In order to get anywhere, even to reach the concept of stimulus meaning, the linguist must be able to recognize certain modes of behaviour among the natives and in fact secure their co-operation to some extent. What is needed is the recognition and use of the modes of behaviour which we call assent and dissent. Quine admits that there may be difficulties in this enterprise, difficulties both in theory and in practice (pp. 25–30), but he nevertheless grants his jungle linguist this 'working hypothesis'. The notion of assent is subsequently used in Quine's definition of stimulus meaning (pp. 32–3). The affirmative stimulus meaning of a sentence is the class of all stimulations that would prompt one's assent, and its negative stimulus meaning the class of all those stimulations which would evoke one's dissent. Together, they constitute the stimulus meaning of the sentence. Thus the notions of assent and dissent enter into the very heart of the conceptual apparatus of the early parts of *Word and Object*.

That sentential connectives admit of radical translation is now a simple consequence of the fact that they can be characterized in terms of the concepts of assent and dissent. In § 14 of *Word and Object* Quine spells this out in some detail. The main lines of his treatment contain few surprises to anyone who remembers the usual truth-functional definitions of the different sentential connectives.[3]

In contrast, quantifiers do not admit of such a characterization, and hence are not in the same way amenable to radical translation.

4. *Widening the scope of radical translation*

My main suggestion in this chapter is that it is highly arbitrary to select one particular mode of linguistic behaviour for a special role in the way Quine does. If we assume that a jungle linguist can come to recognize assentive behaviour, I do not see any reason to suggest that he could not in principle learn to recognize other modes of activity which are closely related to our use of language. The difficulties in connection with the recognition of assent and dissent are not unique, and in a footnote Quine in fact invites comparison with 'the analogous matter of identifying a gesture of greeting' (p. 30). If this analogy really obtains, and if our identification were successful, we could presumably translate (radically) words for greeting, completely

---

[3] Subsequently, Quine has come to realize that there are more difficulties in principle already in this part of a linguist's enterprise than he envisaged in *Word and Object*.

independently of their relation to stimulus meaning, on the basis of their relation to the gesture.

Furthermore, there are indications in Quine's other writings that he might perhaps have himself occasionally entertained the idea of relying on behaviouristic criteria other than assent, dissent, and stimulus meaning. In any case this seems to be the flavour of his remarks on the possible 'behavioral or cultural factors' which could, if they were forthcoming and were sketched, enable him to understand the notion of analyticity.[4] They can scarcely be expected to reduce to those behavioural factors Quine uses to characterize stimulus meaning.

In fact, if I have understood his responses correctly, Quine does not seem averse in principle to going further in this direction and to examining some other behavioural criteria of the radical translation of certain particular words or expressions. From the fact that he has not done so himself to any marked extent one may perhaps infer that Quine does not think major insights will be forthcoming from such a study, however.

As was already indicated, an important test case here is the problem of the radical translatability of quantifiers. This is important because so many of Quine's observations and results are connected with the canonical notation of quantification theory.

5. *Language-games for the whole canonical idiom*

Can we give behavioural criteria for the radical translation of quantifiers? In the preceding chapter I put forward a thesis which implies such a possibility (in principle). There it was argued that to understand quantifiers in their primary normal use is to know their role in certain activities which may perhaps be called *à la* Wittgenstein *language-games*. These activities are certain 'games' of searching and finding. The Wittgensteinian expression applies to them a shade or two more happily than to many of the other so-called language-games, for they can be thought of as games in the precise game-theoretical sense of the word.

For details, I must refer the reader to the preceding chapter. Suffice it here to recall the basic idea as applied to prenex

---

⁴ W. V. Quine, *From a Logical Point of View: Nine Logico-Philosophical Essays* (Harvard University Press, Cambridge, Mass., 1953), p. 36.

sentences (i.e., sentences which consist of a string of quantifiers followed by a quantifier-free 'matrix'). To each such sentence I associated a two-person game. The players are myself and an opponent who may be thought of as 'Nature' or perhaps as a malicious Cartesian demon. My purpose in the game is to end up with a true substitution-instance of the matrix. If the game ends this way, I win and my opponent loses (whatever the stake is), otherwise I lose and my opponent wins. The game presupposes that we are given a set of individuals (our universe of discourse) on which the appropriate predicates are defined. An existential quantifier marks my move; a universal quantifier marks my opponent's move. A move consists in the selection (production, successful search, or whatever term you prefer) of an individual from our universe of discourse. Its name is substituted for the variable bound to the quantifier in question, whereupon the quantifier is omitted. It was also indicated briefly above how the need to personify my opponent can be completely eliminated.

It is clear that the process of 'selection' or 'production' which I just mentioned normally amounts (in my own case) to a terminating search for an individual among all the members of our universe of discourse. This is why I have called the games in question language-games of *searching* and *looking for*.

6. *Radical translatability of quantifiers*

If the forms of human activity which I have called the language-games of searching and finding are what gives quantifiers their use and thus their meaning, we can recognize certain words in any languages as expressing quantifiers provided that we can recognize the language-games of searching and finding which the speakers of the language engage in (by observing the natives' behaviour) and provided that we can recognize the role the quantifying expressions play in these games. Whatever practical difficulties there might occasionally be in this enterprise, there do not seem to be any major problems in principle here which would not already be present in the case of assent and dissent. Surely it is no more difficult in principle (*or* in practice, for that matter) to ascertain that the game a group of children are playing is hide-and-seek than to find out what the appropriate expressions for assent and dissent are in some heathen jargon. And surely it is most unlikely that any tribe should not engage in the practices of seeking and looking for conspicuously enough for these activities to be recognizable even by a behaviouristically minded 'jungle linguist'. In fact, this appears to me more unlikely than to find a tribe which did not have any standard expressions for assent and dissent.

Presupposing that the thesis of the preceding chapter is acceptable, we thus seem to be led to a genuine possibility of deciding what the radical translations of quantifiers into some completely new language are. However incompletely delineated and however unsystematic this method is, it does not rely on the language-users' co-operation any more than the procedure, as envisaged by Quine, by means of which the expressions of assent and dissent are recognized. In fact, the amount of co-operation with the natives that is presupposed here is less than in the Quinean case of assent and dissent. (Surely we do not have to engage ourselves in the children's play of hide-and-seek in order to understand what they are doing.)

What is even more important, we can speak of searching and finding purely behaviouristically, without any reference to mentalistic notions. If an entomologist should describe a bee as searching for a certain kind of honey, he would scarcely be imputing to the poor insect plans, intentions, or other mental entities. He would not be speaking of the mental life of the bee, but of its behaviour. By the same token, we can obviously speak of seeking and finding in the case of us humans, too, in a purely behaviouristic sense, without overt or covert recourse to intentional or mentalistic concepts. (If we are to believe Gilbert Ryle, this is all that is involved in our ordinary notions of seeking and finding anyway. However, I am not claiming as much as that here.)

Assuming that these characteristic forms of behaviour on the part of a native can be recognized, I can in principle translate between his quantifiers and mine: quantifiers in a foreigner's jargon are those expressions of his which are related to his language-games of seeking and finding in the same way as my quantifiers are related to my seekings and findings. There is nothing in this enterprise that is more problematic in principle than the recognition of the characteristic gestures or expressions for assent and dissent.

7. *Further explanations*

Several different kinds of doubt may nevertheless arise here. The language-games that I have associated with quantificational sentences may seem to involve rather special kinds of seeking and finding. Thus they might seem unlikely to be present in most language-users' conceptual repertoire. This impression is nevertheless an illusion. Whenever we verify or falsify a quantificational sentence by means of our own activities we can be said to 'play' that language-game of seeking and finding which I have associated with this sentence. (And how else can we learn the use of quantifiers except by observing such 'games' and by learning to participate in them?) Furthermore, almost any activity of searching could serve the purpose of attempted verification of a quantificational sentence. If one looks for an individual which satisfies the condition '$A(x)$', one might as well be attempting to verify the sentence '$(Ex)A(x)$'. If one is looking for a particular individual, say a, one might as well be trying to verify the sentence '$(Ex)(x = a)$'. Thus almost any activity of searching and looking for can be thought of as a part of one of my language-games, and the task of recognizing the elements of these games in the natives' behaviour is essentially the task of recognizing the characteristic behaviour that goes together with searching and finding.

The connection between the meaning of quantifiers and the 'games' of searching and finding may perhaps seem so vague as to be uninformative. To what extent it is informative or not can only be determined by examining the different implications of this suggested conceptual connection. It is important to realize, however, that the connection is clear enough to be very intimately related to the truth-conditions (and therefore to the whole logic) of quantificational statements. In fact, a characterization of the truth-conditions of quantificational statements can be given by considering my 'games' of searching and finding in a precise game-theoretical formulation. I have even ventured to suggest that some new light might be thrown in this way on certain systematic problems in the meta-theory of quantificational logic, for instance by providing interesting non-standard interpretations of logic and arithmetic.

In order to appreciate the suggestion I am making here, it is also important to realize that one can recognize searching behaviour without being able to determine for certain what the person in question is looking for. Hence the remarks I have made on the radical translatability of quantifiers are not calculated to insinuate that there is no indeterminacy in radical translation or even in one's own ontology. To adapt Quine's example to my purposes, we can observe a native wandering around in a forest, scanning his environment, examining carefully various medium-sized furry animals he comes across, etc. Finally he comes upon a rabbit and happily goes home to report to his peers. We may have present here all the indeterminacy Quine advertises as to what it was that the native sought and found in the last analysis: rabbit, undetached rabbit part, a portion of a Goodmanesque rabbit-fusion, etc.[5] Nevertheless this indeterminacy would not in the least affect my claim that he was seeking for something and that his finding it made him to believe in the existence of whatever he had been looking for. The radical translation of quantifiers is one thing; the translation of terms and ontologies is another. Here I am not making a point about the latter, although it seems to me that Quine is unduly pessimistic in this department, too.

Formally, we might make the point by saying that we can translate radically the 'E' and the 'U' of the quantifiers '(Ex)' and '(Ux)' without being able to decide what the appropriate style of the variable 'x' is to be or what it is supposed to range over. One should not confuse the translation of quantifiers with the translation of the variables associated with them.

Thus the connection between quantifiers and the 'behavioural' concepts of seeking and finding is in any case clear and sharp enough to be of the greatest interest to anyone who is interested in the precise meaning and potentialities of Quine's 'canonical idiom', which is precisely quantificational.

8. *Linguistic evidence: existentials as locatives*

Unexpected indirect support has been lent to my interpretation of quantifiers by linguistic considerations. Of the two quantifiers, the more controversial is apt to be the existential one, for any theory concerning its meaning amounts to a theory

[5] For the behaviouristic indistinguishability of these, see *Word and Object*, pp. 51–4.

of at least one sense of 'existence'. By way of a slogan it may seem that I am trying to replace Quine's dictum 'to be is to be a value of a bound variable' by 'to be is to be (capable of being) an object of search' or perhaps by 'to be is to be a potential object of finding'. Now by far the most common types of language-games of seeking and finding are obviously the ordinary activities of moving around in space in order to find an object whose spatial location is unknown, although conceptually there could be other types of these games as well. On my view, it is therefore to be expected that the concept of existence should be expressed in natural languages often or perhaps even as a rule in spatial (locative) terms: to be is normally to be an object of search *in space*, to be is to be *somewhere*. Now precisely this consequence of my theory is argued for repeatedly by John Lyons on linguistic grounds.[6] He has presented a case for a derivation—both genetic and systematic, if I have understood him correctly—of existentials from locatives. I cannot recapitulate his evidence here. Suffice it to observe that Lyons's thesis, should he succeed in establishing it, will strongly support my position *vis-à-vis* quantifiers. Our principle 'to be is to be an object of search' would then provide, as it were, a missing genetic and psychological link between the linguistic facts summed up by the dictum 'to be is to be somewhere' and Quine's principle 'to be is to be a value of a variable of quantification'.

9. *Implications for Quine's programme: further behavioural criteria of radical translation are needed*

Here we are primarily interested in the general methodological relevance of our observations to Quine's procedure in *Word and Object*. If I am right, what we are given by the language-games connected with quantifiers is an example which shows the possibility, and the importance, of loosening up the

---

[6] See John Lyons, *Introduction to Theoretical Linguistics* (Cambridge University Press, Cambridge, 1968), pp. 388–90; 'Towards a "Notional" Theory of the "Parts of Speech" ', *Journal of Linguistics*, vol. 2 (1966), pp. 209–36; 'Existence, Possession and Transitivity', in B. van Rootselaar and J. F. Staal, eds., *Logic, Methodology and Philosophy of Science III*, Proceedings of the Third International Congress, Amsterdam, 1967 (North-Holland Publishing Company, Amsterdam, 1968), pp. 495–505; 'A Note on Possessive, Existential and Locative Sentences', *Foundations of Language*, vol. 3 (1967), pp. 390–3. Cf. also Keith Allan, 'A Note on the Source of *There* in Existential Sentences', *Foundations of Language*, vol. 7 (1971), pp. 1–18.

dichotomy between what we can make sense of in terms of stimulus conditions on the one hand and what turns on analytical hypotheses on the other. This broadening of the conceptual basis of *Word and Object* will, one hopes, remove some of its arbitrariness. What we have in the case of the 'language-games' of seeking and finding are behavioural counterparts to certain crucial concepts which we should like to be able to locate (in principle) in any language. However, these behavioural counterparts do not admit of a characterization in the sole terms of assent and dissent or in any other form of purely reactive behaviour, it seems to me. They turn on more complicated regularities in language-users' behaviour. But this does not make them any less behavioural than (say) the notions of assent and dissent. If they can be recognized at all, they can be recognized by observing people's overt movements, initiatives, and reactions. If there are methodological problems connected with these more complicated behavioural regularities (e.g., the question whether a reference to non-public intentions is needed in characterizing them), the same problems often seem to arise already in connection with the notions of assent and dissent. Our 'language-games' of seeking and finding thus seem to show in a striking fashion that there is an important gap between what is (to use Quine's own phrase) 'empirically unconditioned' in one's radical translations and what is in such translations determined by the speaker's stimulus meanings. This gap is to be filled by more flexible *behavioural* criteria of radical translation, of which this chapter strives to give an example or two.

If there is a difference between the radical translation of connectives Quine envisages and the kind of radical translation of quantifiers I am proposing, it does not lie in the fact that one is based on observable linguistic behaviour whereas the other is not. If there is a difference, it lies in the fact that Quine's proposed behavioural analysis of connectives is in terms of a particularly restrictive kind of behavioural framework, viz. in terms of a stimulus–response jargon. Thus in the case of connectives what a jungle linguist has to learn to recognize are affirmative and negative *responses* to a question. It is clear, however, that the kind of behaviour we call searching and looking for cannot be analysed in terms of the stimulus–response framework. It can only be recognized by witnessing longer segments of a native's behaviour. However, this does not mark any shortcoming in my account, for it seems to me unlikely that the stimulus–response framework should be adequate for the description of linguistic behaviour in any case—a point which has been argued at length by Chomsky.[7] If a predilection for it is what has induced Quine to draw the boundary between what admits of radical translation 'directly' and what can only be translated with the aid of 'analytical hypotheses', then this boundary seems to me most unfortunate. Of course the recognition of the behaviour of searching and finding requires hypotheses (assumptions), but they are not analytical hypotheses in Quine's sense. What we need are not tentative equations between a native's words and expressions and some English idioms; what we need are not *linguistic* hypotheses but hypotheses concerning the native's behaviour.

In particular, Chomsky has made essentially the same point as I have been trying to emphasize here, viz. that there is no reason to think that notions based on assent and dissent come close to exhausting what is empirically determinable in language and that Quine's selection of these two for special attention is highly arbitrary. In a reply to Chomsky, Quine has said that he is 'free to pick, from that totality [of speech dispositions], whatever dispositions are most favourable to my purpose of distinguishing ostensive meanings'. This is inconclusive, however, for the moot point is precisely whether dispositions to assent and dissent are in fact particularly well suited for the purpose of distinguishing what is behaviourally determinable in the semantics of a language. For another thing, Quine's notion of 'ostensive meaning' is nowhere clearly defined, and seems to hover uncomfortably somewhere between stimulus meaning (which is by definition exhausted by what we can establish by means of assent and dissent) and the much wider notion of what is behaviouristically determinable in meaning. A reader of *Word and Object* finds it difficult to escape the impression (which admittedly is nowhere expressed in quite so many words by Quine) that Quine there thinks that stimulus meaning pretty much exhausts what we

---

[7] See Noam Chomsky, 'Review of Skinner, *Verbal Behavior*', *Language*, vol. 35 (1959), pp. 26–58, and cf. Noam Chomsky, 'Quine's Empirical Assumptions', in *Words and Objections: Essays on the Work of W. V. Quine*, ed. by Donald Davidson and Jaakko Hintikka (D. Reidel Publishing Company, Dordrecht, 1969), pp. 53–68.

can establish empirically in linguistics. (On p. 26 of *Word and Object* we find an explicit contrast between 'how much of language can be made sense of in terms of stimulus conditions' and what is 'empirically unconditioned . . . in one's conceptual scheme'.) The introduction of a new category of 'ostensive meaning' thus seems to indicate a major shift of emphasis on Quine's part.

10. *New criteria are already needed for the radical translation of connectives*

By widening slightly the definition of my language-games of searching and finding one can also put Quine's behaviouristic characterization of the meaning of propositional connectives into a new perspective and perhaps also argue that this characterization is inadequate in certain respects. This widened definition can be formulated by extending the language-games which were defined above from prenex sentences to arbitrary first-order sentences. A game will now end with a substitution-instance of an atomic sentence. I win if this substitution instance is true, lose otherwise. A disjunction $(F \vee G)$ marks 'my' move: I select a disjunct with respect to which the game is continued. A conjunction $(F \& G)$ marks my opponent's move: he chooses the conjunct to be used in the rest of the game. A negation $\sim F$ means switching the roles of the two players and thereupon continuing the games with respect to F.

This broadening of the original definition of the language-games of searching and finding assigns propositional connectives a role in these games. By observing how people play these games, we can in principle find out whether a word (say) in the language of a Wittgensteinian tribe appears in this role and whether it is therefore to be translated into our canonical notation by means of connectives, or perhaps by a specific connective. This we can in principle recognize even if the tribe have no notions of assent and dissent in their language. Thus the use of these notions, and of the derived notion of stimulus meaning, does not appear indispensable for the purpose of characterizing the meaning of propositional connectives even when we aim at radical translation. Quine's procedure in *Word and Object* thus seems to be at best one possible way among many of characterizing the meanings of propositional connectives.

It may even be a somewhat inadequate way of discussing the meaning of connectives. Although the question needs further study, this inadequacy is in any case suggested by the obvious possibility of modifying slightly the rules of our language games. One type of modification is seen by considering games played on a denumerably infinite (and in fact enumerated) domain, e.g., on the domain of natural numbers. There it is extremely natural to modify my language-games by requiring that their strategy-set be restricted to recursive (computable) strategies in some reasonable sense. (Unfortunately, there appears to be no unique sense of this kind, as demonstrated *inter alia* by Gödel's fascinating extension of the finitistic point of view.[8]) This means, e.g., that my choice of a disjunct in dealing with $(F \vee G)$ will have to be decided effectively by the earlier moves in the game. This means changing the meaning of connectives and quantifiers somewhat, for it means changing the truth-conditions (as formulated in terms of the existence of winning strategies) of first-order sentences. These modified meanings can scarcely be explained in the sole terms of assent, dissent, and stimulus meaning. Yet, these subtle discrepancies notwithstanding, we are unmistakably still dealing with the same old connectives and quantifiers. If a linguistic community consisted (say) of hard-boiled constructivists who insisted on playing the language-games of searching and finding in terms of some suitable set of modified rules, we could nevertheless approximately equate some of their words and expressions with our connectives and quantifiers, in terms of which these words have to be translated. This suggests that the meaning of what we are willing to call a conjunction, a disjunction, etc., cannot be specified by any hard-and-fast relation of theirs to the concept of assent and dissent, but that this meaning admits of certain types of variation which can be partly characterized in terms of stimulus meaning. More complicated behavioural criteria are thus needed, it seems to me, already for some of the purposes which Quine tries to handle by means of the concept of stimulus meaning, including the radical translation of sentential connectives.

[8] Kurt Gödel, 'Über eine bisher noch nicht benützte Erweiterung des finiten Standpunktes', in *Logica: Studia Paul Bernays Dedicata*, ed. by F. Gonseth (Editions Griffon, Neuchatel, 1959), pp. 76–83. Gödel's treatment of connectives gives specific examples of how the rules governing them might be changed.

In fact, the problem of translating sentential connectives now appears as a good example of the kind of situation which has led Quine to emphasize the indeterminacy of radical translation in general: the rules for these connectives can be changed subtly and in many different ways, without there being any hard-and-fast point after which it ceases to be 'the same' connective, i.e., translatable in the same way. This does not imply, however, that there are no behavioural criteria in terms of which the radical translation and the meaning of sentential connectives can be discussed. It nevertheless gives us one more reason to think of Quine's distinction between the behaviour of connectives and the behaviour of quantifiers *vis-à-vis* radical translation as an essentially arbitrary one.

11. *Implications for the concept of ontic commitment*

One interesting possibility opened by our observations (assuming they are essentially correct) is the possibility of discussing ontic commitments without any restriction to one particular language. This enhances greatly the interest of Quine's proposed criterion of ontic commitment ('to be is to be a value of a bound variable').

In fact, the connection between quantification and the notions of searching and looking for helps to clear up a problem which apparently has puzzled several commentators. How can a sentence (of an interpreted language) be committed (or commit its user) to the existence of any entities which it does not assert to exist? Some logicians might be tempted to follow Church[9] who has in effect modified Quine's dictum so as to speak of asserted existence only. This seems alien to the spirit of Quine's own explanations, however. What he appears to mean is that a sentence is committed to the existence of all the values of the bound variables it contains, not just to the existence of those specific values (if any) which are needed to make the sentence true. In short, '$(Ex)A(x)$' and '$(Ux) \sim A(x)$' carry the same ontic commitments.

How is this to be understood? Why should *any* use of bound variables carry a commitment to *all* their values? An answer is suggested by the conceptual connection between quantifiers and

[9] Alonzo Church, 'Ontological Commitment', *Journal of Philosophy*, vol. 55 (1958), pp. 1008–14.

the activities of seeking and finding. These activities can be carried out in a meaningful way only if some underlying field of search is understood as being given. (This requirement was already commented on in the preceding chapter.) Any use of quantifiers thus presupposes (if I am right) that such a field of search exists, and is given. This is the case even if we do not use quantifiers to assert the existence of any particular member of the field of search. The commitment to *all* the values of our bound variables which Quine envisages can now be interpreted as a commitment to them as a field of search, which is on my view in fact presupposed by all use of quantifiers. Thus we can see more clearly the 'cash value' of the distinction between asserting the existence of certain entities and being committed to their existence through the use of the variables of quantification.

The connection between quantification and the concepts of seeking and finding may also help to show that Quine's criterion of ontic commitment is much more closely related to certain traditional and almost commonsensical ideas than one first realizes on the basis of the paradoxical-sounding formulation 'to be is to be a value of a bound variable'. It implies, presupposing that the main thesis of Chapter III above is correct, that we are committed to the existence of only those entities of which we can in principle say 'Now we have found one' or 'Now we have found it'. The objects to whose existence we are committed are in other words the potential objects of our activities of seeking and finding. If this makes Quine's criterion sound much less surprising, perhaps it also makes it more plausible. In the light of the observations made in the preceding chapter, this criterion also turns out to be closely related to the ideas on existence put forward by such diverse writers as Stephen Toulmin and G. E. Moore in his famous 'Proof of an External World'. What these philosophers do is also to emphasize in effect the conceptual connection between the 'real' existence of certain entities and our being able to say of them 'Now we have found one' or perhaps '*There* is one!'—i.e., their capacity of functioning as (potential) objects of search.

V

QUANTIFIERS, LANGUAGE-GAMES, AND TRANSCENDENTAL ARGUMENTS

1. *A Kantian approach to epistemology and to the philosophy of language*

IN recent years, we have witnessed something of a revival of interest in Kant's epistemology and metaphysics among analytical philosophers.[1] However, I hope I am not doing injustice to the philosophers who are responsible for this revival if I say that their efforts have not on the whole been crowned by unqualified success. Or perhaps I should rather say that we have been given interesting general suggestions concerning the interpretation of Kant and concerning his relevance to the contemporary scene rather than sharp, definite results in either direction. If so, there may be a deeper reason for this lack of success (or only partial success). One of the focal ideas in much of the best philosophy in the Kantian tradition—a German would speak here of *Transzendentalphilosophie*—has been to emphasize the human activities through which we obtain our knowledge and the contribution of these activities to the total structure of human knowledge. Occasionally, philosophers of this persuasion have even maintained that we can have full-fledged knowledge, such as synthetic knowledge *a priori*, only of these activities and of what is brought about by ourselves in the course of them.[2] 'Reason has insight only into that which it produces after a plan of its own', Kant writes in his *Critique of Pure Reason* (B xiii).

We do not have to go as far as this, however, in order to find the processes through which we obtain information about the objects of our knowledge both interesting and important. Yet

---

[1] Cf. the useful survey paper by M. J. Scott-Taggart, 'Recent Work on the Philosophy of Kant', in *Kant Studies To-Day*, ed. by Lewis White Beck (Open Court, La Salle, Illinois, 1969).

[2] I have tried to survey this tradition briefly in my essay, 'Tieto on valtaa', in Jaakko Hintikka, *Tieto on valtaa ja muita aatehistoriallisia esseitä* (WSOY, Porvoo, 1969), pp. 19–34. Cf. also my paper, 'Kant's "New Method of Thought" and his Theory of Mathematics', *Ajatus*, vol. 27 (1965), pp. 37–47.

most of the sharp conceptual tools of recent philosophy are much better suited for dealing with the structure of already-acquired information—the structure of theories, the structure of explanation, and so on—than the activities by means of which it is gathered. The 'transcendental' point of view which focuses on the human activities which are basically involved in our obtaining whatever information we have is notoriously absent from recent philosophizing.

This somewhat one-sided epistemological interest is connected with, and partly caused by, a parallel neglect in the logical analysis of language. There the study of the relations of our language—or anybody's language, for that matter—to the reality which it speaks of has either been left unattended or else has only been discussed in terms of unanalysed 'interpretations', 'valuations', 'name relations', or comparable unanalysed static ies between language and the world.[3] Even though it is obvious that these are not natural relations but are only created by and sustained through certain human activities and human institutions, very little systematic work has been done on these vital connecting links between language and reality. In saying this, I am not forgetting the rich Wittgensteinian literature on those 'language-games' which are supposed to give the expressions of our language their meanings. However, I am disregarding these language-games because of the unsystematic character of most current discussions about them.

2. *A game-theoretical interpretation of quantifiers*

In this chapter, I shall try to show that even quite modest systematic efforts in this direction can lead to interesting insights into central Kantian problems. I shall take as my theme one rather small-scale attempt to discuss in precise terms some of those activities that serve to connect, in some idealized but precise sense, certain parts of our language with the world. The expressions I want to find language-games for are the usual quantifiers 'for at least one' and 'for every', in symbols '(Ex)' and '(Ux)'. I have discussed them in relation to the problems at hand

---

[3] Cf. the last few pages of my paper, 'Logic and Philosophy', in *Contemporary Philosophy—La Philosophie contemporaine*, vol. 1, ed. by R. Klibansky (La Nuova Italia Editrice, Florence, 1968), pp. 3–30.

in an earlier chapter of this book.[4] The upshot there was what I have called the game-theoretical interpretation of quantifiers. It turns out that in this case the 'language-games' which give our words their basic meanings are not only games in the vague undifferentiated Wittgensteinian sense but also games in the precise sense of the mathematical theory of games. Of course, I am not claiming any radical novelty for this idea. Rather, I want to suggest that this interpretation is merely a clarification and explication of ideas which we all associate with quantifiers, albeit usually tacitly and in a confused fashion. With these—and certain other—qualifications in mind, I want to suggest that the primary meanings of quantifiers, and *ipso facto* the content of the ideas of existence and universality they express, is to be sought by examining these games.

For a motivation and a defence of this game-theoretical interpretation, the reader is referred back to Chapter III of this book. Since I want to discuss this interpretation in the present chapter, I nevertheless have to recall briefly what it is all about. For this purpose, I associate with each sentence F of an applied first-order (i.e., quantificational) language a two-person game. (F may contain, over and above predicates, individual variables and individual constants, the two quantifiers 'E' and 'U', as well as the connectives '&', 'v', and '$\sim$'.) The players we may call colloquially 'myself' and 'Nature'.[5] The game is one with perfect information, and it may be considered a zero-sum game.

Since we are dealing with an interpreted language, a domain D of individuals must be given on which all the relations and properties used in F are defined. At each stage of the game, a substitution-instance G of a (proper or improper) subformula of F is being considered. The game begins with F, and proceeds by the following rules:

(G.E) If G is of the form $(Ex)G_0$, I choose a member of D, give it a name, say 'n' (if it did not have one before). The game is continued with respect to $G_0(n/x)$.

Here $G_0(n/x)$ is of course the result of substituting 'n' for 'x' in G_0.

(G.U) If G is of the form $(Ux)G_0$, Nature likewise chooses a member of D.

[4] Chapter III above, originally published as 'Language-Games for Quantifiers', *American Philosophical Quarterly*, Monograph Series, No. 2: *Studies in Logical Theory* (Basil Blackwell, Oxford, 1968), pp. 46–72.

[5] Lorenzen speaks of a 'proponent' and an 'opponent'.

(G.v) If G is of the form $(G_1 \vee G_2)$, I choose G_1 or G_2, and the game is continued with respect to it.

(G.&) If G is of the form $(G_1 \ \& \ G_2)$, Nature likewise chooses G_1 or G_2.

(G.$\sim$) If G is of the form $\sim G_0$, the game is continued with respect to G_0 with the roles of the two players interchanged.

In a finite number of moves, an expression A of the form '$P(n_1, n_2,..., n_k)$' will be reached, where 'P' is a k-adic predicate defined on D. Since $n_1,..., n_k$ are members of D, A is either true or false. If it is true, I have won and Nature has lost; otherwise Nature has won and I have lost.

3. *Further comments on the game-theoretical interpretation of first-order logic*

A few comments may further clarify the nature of these games. Since every sentence of a first-order language can be brought (by means of De Morgan's Laws, the law of double negation, and the interconnection of the two quantifiers) to an equivalent form where negation-signs may only occur prefixed to atomic formulas we may omit (G.$\sim$) and allow the outcome of A to be an atomic sentence or the negation of an atomic sentence. In this way the exchange of roles could be avoided.

However, (G.$\sim$) is useful for another elimination. A strange and unrealistic feature of our games may seem to be due to the personification of Nature who must be thought of as actually choosing individuals if the game is to make sense. Now it is easy to rewrite all universal quantifiers '(Ux)' as '$\sim(Ex)\sim$' and all conjunctions $(G_1 \ \& \ G_2)$ as $\sim(\sim G_1 \vee \sim G_2)$. Then rules (G.U) and (G.&) become unnecessary, and no personification of Nature is needed. It goes without saying, however, that (G.$\sim$) is now absolutely vital.

It depends on one's purpose which of these formulations is the most natural one. In general, it is useful to preserve as much flexibility as possible.

The reason why this game-theoretical interpretation of quantifiers yields a full-fledged semantical theory of first-order logic is that the truth of F in D (with appropriate predicates defined on D) can be defined in terms of our games. It is easily seen that F is true in the usual sense if and only if I have a winning strategy in the associated game. Hence in our approach the truth of F in

D can simply be defined as the existence of such a winning strategy in a game on D. This definition assumes that truth and falsity have been defined for atomic sentences (and, possibly, for their negations), and serves to extend it for arbitrary truth-functions and for quantified sentences.

Since almost everything else can easily be defined as soon as we have the notion of truth at our disposal, the game-theoretical interpretation of quantifiers can serve (in principle) as a foundation of a semantical theory of first-order languages. Here we are more interested in the philosophical perspectives opened by the interpretation, however, than in technicalities. I cannot hope to exhaust even these philosophical applications here, but I can try to convey to the reader some idea of what is involved.

In the rule (G.E), we spoke of 'choosing' an individual. It is clear that in an actual play of these games this expression is not very happy. In order for me to win in a game, I usually cannot be content with an arbitrarily chosen member of D. Typically, I have to look around among the members of D for a suitable one. In brief, the step (G.E) involves essentially a *search* for an appropriate individual. Hence, the games we are dealing with are essentially games of seeking, and (we hope) finding, various kinds of individuals.

4. Quantificational games as 'games of exploring the world'. They presuppose an objectual interpretation of quantifiers

My aim in these games can also be described informally in very simple terms. If we start from the usual definition of truth, instead of defining this notion in game-theoretical terms, we can easily see how I must carry out my moves in order to win. I must choose them so as to make sure that not only the eventual outcome of the game (the sentence A) but also all the sentences which are reached in the course of the game are true (in the usual sense).

What this means is that the game I have described may be thought of as an attempt to *verify* F by searching for and finding suitable individuals in the 'world' D. From this point of view, the function of rule (G.U) can also be understood. In order to verify a generalization (universal sentence), I must assume the role of a devil's (or, strictly speaking, Nature's) advocate who is trying to find counter-examples to the generalization. If such a devil's advocate can always be defeated, I have won, i.e., verified the sentence.

Instead of speaking of verification and falsification I could have spoken of finding out which sentences of our language are true and which ones are false. Hence the language-games governed by the rules (G) can also be looked upon as the activities through which we (in principle) can gather the information about the world which is codifiable in first-order discourse. Here we are perhaps beginning to see the relevance of our games to Kant's transcendental questions. A first-order sentence becomes, as it were, a kind of prediction of what may happen in the game associated with it. This (somewhat imprecise) observation brings out the strong dependence of the meaning of quantified sentences on the language-game of seeking and finding.

In general, the informal view suggested by our observations is that the meaning of quantifiers lies in their role in guiding the processes ('games') of verifying (in principle) the sentences of our language. The primary meaning of quantifiers, in brief, is their use in the language-games of seeking and finding. A feeling for this may perhaps be engendered by expressing the existential quantifier by the locution 'one can find' and the universal quantifier accordingly by 'one cannot find —— not ——'. In some languages this would in fact result in idiomatic native expressions for quantifiers. In such languages, I submit, etymology reproduces ontology more faithfully than in English.

It is obvious that a great deal of idealization is normally involved in speaking of the activities of seeking and finding here. All human limitations have to be abstracted from. The searcher in question will have to be thought of, if not as omnipresent, then at least 'omni-nimble', free of all those limitations of access we humans are subject to.

For the purposes of the present chapter, these scattered hints will have to suffice as an explanation of what the game-theoretical interpretation involves. A couple of matters of principle must nevertheless be dealt with.

W. V. Quine has claimed that my game-theoretical interpretation of first-order sentences confers a kind of substitutional meaning to quantifiers.[6] This is a mistake whose reasons I

---

[6] W. V. Quine, 'Replies', in *Words and Objections: Essays on the Work of W. V.*

suspect to be more historical than topical. The demonstrable equivalence of our truth-definition with the usual (objectual) one already belies Quine's allegation. Another quick way of seeing the drastic difference between our interpretation and the substitutional one is to observe what assumptions we have to make in order to make sure that our interpretation agrees with the usual 'objectual' one, as compared with the assumptions one would have to make in order to force the substitutional interpretation to coincide with the objectual one. In the latter case, one would have to assume that each member of D has a name, and that there are no empty names around. In contrast, for the former purpose we do not have to assume anything about there already being names for anything in anyone's language. What we have to assume, say, for the purpose of explaining what the truth of a sentence with d layers of quantifiers amounts to, is merely that the speakers of our applied first-order language can give (in the course of a round of our game) names to any d members of D. This assumption is unaffected by the cardinality of D in the way the assumptions that a defender of the substitution instance interpretation needs are not. No fixed totality of names independent of the different strategies the players use is presupposed here.

The whole complex of problems about the different interpretations of quantifiers requires further attention. Here it nevertheless suffices to register the fact that we are on the side of the angels—or at least on the side of Quine and the objectual interpretation.

5. *Language-games of formal logic and the picture theory of language. Our rules* (G) *fill a gap in this theory*

Another important question here is the following. So far, I have only described to you what the truth (truth *simpliciter*) of an applied first-order sentence means in terms of the game-theoretical interpretation. I have not yet said anything about the role of the actual rules of logic—that is, rules for actually manipulating expressions for the purpose of uncovering *logical* truths, *logical* equivalences, *logical* inconsistencies, and so on—

Quine, ed. by Donald Davidson and Jaakko Hintikka (D. Reidel Publishing Company, Dordrecht, 1969), especially p. 314.

within the game-theoretical interpretation of quantifiers. A special poignancy is lent to this question by the fact that the rules of logic can be put to an extremely interesting general perspective from other points of view. As I have pointed out earlier in this book,[7] suitable rules for actually manipulating our formulas for the purpose of proving F may be thought of as governing attempts to describe, step by step, a counter-example to F. And even more: the rules may be thought of as recipes for trying to build, part by part, actual isomorphs ('pictures' in Wittgenstein's sense) to such counter-examples. Thus there obtains an extremely close relationship between the rules of logic and (an extension of) Wittgenstein's picture theory.

This relationship has already been seen to lead our attention away from typically Wittgensteinian ideas, however. It was shown above in Chapter II that the extension of Wittgenstein's theory which is required for the purpose of accounting success- fully for quantification theory at the same time destroys the usefulness of the picture theory for other purposes. It destroys all the interest of the picture theory as a realistic model of how first-order languages can actually be used. Two features of the extension cause this failure:

(i) The 'pictures' (model sets) associated with a sentence F are not given by F itself. They are only arrived at by starting from F and constructing 'pictures' (model sets) from it according to certain rules (of model set construction). Sentences, on this view, are not themselves pictures of states of affairs in which they would be true. They are recipes for constructing a number of alternative pictures.

(ii) The 'pictures' (model sets) involved are usually infinite, and an infinite number of them can usually be obtained from a given sentence F.

These facts make it clear that our actual understanding of first-order sentences cannot be based on their 'pictorial' charac- ter as Wittgenstein thought. In order to understand F, we just do not construct all the pictures to which F gives rise and com- pare them with the reality. For this, we typically do not have time (or memory-space) enough. Our actual understanding of first-order sentences must accordingly be based on some finite,

[7] See Chapter I and especially Chapter II.

step-by-step comparisons between the sentence F and the world rather than the (potentially) pictorial nature of F.

What the rules (G) of our games give you is precisely such a method of step-by-step confrontation between language and reality. They thus repair the defect which we found in our extension of the picture theory. It nevertheless remains to be seen whether, and if so how, our games will suggest an interesting general perspective on the role of logical proofs comparable to the perspective into which the (interpretationally greatly inferior) picture theory puts them.

6. *Games of searching and finding* v. *games of model set construction*

Such a perspective can easily be obtained. A set of rules for actually manipulating logical formulas may almost be read off from our game rules which of course themselves are of entirely different nature. In the rules (G), we are given a sentence F_0 and a domain D with the predicates of F_0 defined on it, and we are asked whether F_0 is true in D. Now in logic we are typically given F_0 and asked whether there is a D, again with certain appropriate relations and properties defined on it, such that F_0 will be true in D when its predicate symbols are interpreted as expressing these relations and properties.

One natural way of going about for the purpose of answering this question is to ask: if F_0 is to be true in D, that is, if I am to have a winning strategy in the associated game, what other sentences F must there be with the same property in relation to the same D? Assuming for a second that each member of D has a name 'n' $\in \mathcal{N}$, it is seen from the rules (G.E), (G.U), (G.v), and (G.&) that the totality μ of such sentences must satisfy the conditions that define a *model set*. These conditions are given above on pp. 10–11. Once again, we are assuming, for simplicity, that all negation-signs have been pushed into the sentences as far as they go.

Since a complete set of Herbrand-type rules for quantification theory may be obtained as (slightly modified) dual inverses of the rules for constructing model sets, we have connected in an extremely simple way our game rules with actual proof and disproof techniques for first-order logic. It is also clear that our rules for model set construction can be interpreted directly as rules for trying to construct an actual D with its relations and properties such that I would have a winning strategy in the game played on D. These rules are listed above on pp. 24–5 in an appendix to Chapter I. They are so simple and so important to my argument in the present chapter as to be worth listing again here. In them, λ is the set of sentences we have reached.

(A.E)   If $(Ex)G \in \lambda$ but not $G(n/x) \in \lambda$ for any free singular term (name) 'n', introduce a new singular constant 'm', and add $G(m/x)$ to λ.

This rule is often known as the rule of *existential instantiation*.

(A.U)   If $(Ux)G \in \lambda$, if 'n' occurs in the members of λ, and if not $G(n/x) \in \lambda$, add $G(n/x)$ to λ.

(A.v)   If $(G_1 \vee G_2) \in \lambda$ but neither $G_1 \in \lambda$ nor $G_2 \in \lambda$, add one of them to λ.

(A.&)   If $(G_1 \& G_2) \in \lambda$ but not both $G_1 \in \lambda$ and $G_2 \in \lambda$, add the missing one(s) to λ.

Here (A.v) gives rise to two different lines of construction which have to be examined separately. If all such construction branches lead to a violation of (C.$\sim$), F is inconsistent. This result may be said to establish the *soundness* of (A)-rules. Conversely, if F is inconsistent, this situation will arise after a finite number of construction steps, by choosing the order of application of the (A)-rules in a suitable way. (This result may be called the *completeness theorem* for (A)-rules.)

By inverting the direction of the process and by replacing all expressions by their negations, we obtain a simple proof procedure for first-order logic. This proof procedure is essentially a version of Herbrand-type proof methods.

This serves to connect our game-theoretical rules (G) with the rules of formal logic, for the rules (A) turn out to be nothing but inverses (duals) of a particularly simple set of proof rules for first-order logic.

7. *The function of the language-games of formal logic. The limits of their applicability*

Although the relationship between our game rules (G) and the model set construction rules (A) might thus appear almost trivially simple, it nevertheless deserves a few comments. The small differences that there are between the rules (G) and the rules (A) illustrate in fact very nicely certain misunderstandings which easily arise—and have in fact arisen—in the philosophy of logic. Many such misunderstandings can be traced to a failure to appreciate certain important features of the conceptual situation here.

What we must try to understand is primarily the relationship between two entirely different kinds of activities, viz. those governed by the rules (G) and those defined by the rules (A), respectively. Someone else might call both these activities 'language-games'. It is important to realize, however, that they are entirely different sorts of games. The former ones are 'outdoor games'. Each of them is played 'out there in the fields' among the entities (individuals belonging to the domain D) of which our applied first-order language speaks, and it consists of a sequence of searches for certain entities of this kind.

The latter ones—the games governed by the rules (A) of analysis—are 'indoor games', more specifically board games, played with pen and paper or with a piece of chalk and a blackboard. The objects we are dealing with are not the entities our language speaks of but sequences of symbols, and instead of searching for and finding suitable ones we create them with a stroke of the pen. (Cf., e.g., (A.E).) Furthermore, the activities governed by (A)-rules are not even real games in the sense that they do not involve any adversary.

The basic philosophical question here is due to the fact that games of the latter kind are obviously not vital to us in the sense the former ones—the actual transactions with the reality we are talking about—can be. Hence what we ask here is: how do the (A)-games help us in playing the (G)-games?

Even though this way of posing the question is natural enough, it is foreign to much of contemporary philosophy of logic. In it, the language-game of proving and disproving formulae is typically dealt with on its own as an independent unit, without any reference to the activities which serve to connect the sentences of an interpreted language with the reality which this language can serve to convey information about. Philosophers habitually ask, for instance, what 'intuitions' we have about logical truth and how well an axiomatization of logic serves to do justice to these alleged intuitions. Even some philosophers of logic who have approached logic in a game-theoretical spirit (e.g., Lorenzen)[8] have failed to connect their parlour games of 'challenges' and 'responses' with those activities we are engaged in when we are using language to some extra-linguistic purpose. I find this restriction to the one language-game of theorem-proving the original sin of much of the recent philosophy of logic, and a source of most of the indecision and confusion which is still found in this area.

On the positive side the insight that the language-games of formal logic are essentially tied, as far as the logic of existence and universality is concerned, to the language-games of searching and finding suggests something about the limits of applicability of the formal logic of quantification. Just because of this tie, quantificational logic is immediately applicable to a sphere of reality in so far as we can perform the activities of seeking and finding within it. Moreover, it applies directly to a class of objects only in so far as they are potential objects of searching and finding.

8. *Problems concerning the interrelation of the different games. Formal logic as a study of the best possible cases*

However, even when comparisons are made (explicitly or tacitly) between different language-games along the lines indicated, it is very easy to get confused and to forget that the comparison must be between the total language-games and not between the individual moves. This temptation is enhanced by the similarity between the corresponding (G)-rules and (A)-rules. For instance, it is easy to get perplexed if one starts comparing with each other the very similar-looking rules (G.E) and (A.E). The informal meaning of the former is easy to understand. Roughly speaking, it says that in order to verify an existentially quantified sentence one has to find a suitable (viz.

[8] See, e.g., P. Lorenzen, *Metamathematik* (Bibliographisches Institut, Mannheim, 1962); P. Lorenzen, 'Methodological Thinking', *Ratio*, vol. 7 (1965), pp. 35–60; P. Lorenzen, 'Ein dialogisches Konstruktivitätskriterium', in *Infinitistic Methods: Proceedings of the Symposium on Foundations of Mathematics, Warsaw* (Pergamon Press, London, and Państwowe Wydawnictwo Naukowe, Warszaw, 1961), pp. 193–200; K. Lorenz, 'Arithmetik und Logik als Spiele' (Dissertation, Kiel, 1961); Wolfgang Stegmüller, 'Remarks on the Completeness of Logical Systems Relative to the Validity-Concepts of P. Lorenzen and K. Lorenz', *Notre Dame Journal of Formal Logic*, vol. 5 (1964), pp. 81–112; K. Lorenz, 'Dialogspiele als semantische Grundlage von Logikkalkülen', *Archiv für mathematische Logik und Grundlagenforschung*, vol. 11 (1968), pp. 32–55 and 73–100.

true) substitution-instance of it. (More fully, one has to find an individual whose name yields, when substituted for the bound variable, a true substitution-instance.)

By contrast, in (A.E) we do not look for suitable individuals or even suitable substitution-instances at all. Rather, we introduce such a substitution-instance by a *fiat*. A *construction* takes the place of the activities of seeking and finding.

It is not immediately obvious what uses such arbitrary-looking acts of construction have in guiding our searches for suitable individuals. Prima facie, they may even seem completely useless for the purpose. They simply do not yield any instructions as to where to find the desired individuals. Moreover, they seem rather strange in their own right. In (A.E), we apparently introduce a representative of an individual—that is, a free singular term denoting it—without having found one. We seem to be anticipating a successful outcome of a process of search even when there is no guarantee of an eventual success. As some traditional philosophers might have expressed themselves here: how is it possible to use free singular terms in the absence of any objects they can refer to? What justification can there be for such a procedure? Why is the logical and mathematical knowledge we obtain by means of such anticipatory introductions of new symbols for individuals applicable to anything at all, let alone with *a priori* certainty, as we usually think of our logical truths as being applicable?

Questions arising from this problematic relation of (A.E) to the activities of seeking and finding have also led to more specific puzzles. Among them, there is the problem whether certain rules of logic, especially such rules of existential instruction as (A.E), involve reliance on 'arbitrary' or 'random' individuals, and if so, whether this notion of 'arbitrary' or 'random' individual is a legitimate one.[9] In an application of (A.E), we often do not—and sometimes cannot—have in mind any particular

---

[9] A discussion on this subject was carried out in *Analysis* some time ago; see, e.g., Nicholas Rescher, 'Can There Be Random Individuals?', *Analysis*, vol. 18 (1957–8), pp. 114–17; L. Goddar, 'Mr. Rescher on Random Individuals', i bid., vol. 19 (1958–9), pp. 18–20; J. L. Mackie, 'The Rules of Natural Deduction', ibid., pp. 27–35.

Although the terminology of 'random' or 'arbitrarily selected' individuals is not a very happy one, much more is at issue here than 'a reification of a notational device'.

individual *m* even when we know that there exist individuals satisfying *G*. Hence the universal validity of the rule seems to presuppose that *m* is an 'arbitrary' or 'random' individual satisfying this condition. This pseudo-problem has led to some amount of philosophical controversy.

These recent controversies are closely related to earlier discussions in the philosophy of logic and mathematics concerning the status of the so-called method of exposition or *ecthesis*, which to all practical purposes is just existential instantiation.[10]

Another way of getting oneself falsely puzzled about (A.E) is to observe that it has to all practical purposes the force of the principle of choice for finite sets of sets. Consequently, many of the general theoretical objections that have been levelled at the other cases of the principle of choice apply against (A.E), too.[11] In other words, much of first-order logic ought to be subject to the same doubts as the axiom of choice, if these sceptical objections are to be taken seriously.

The right way out of this kind of problem is to realize, first of all, that we should not be comparing individual applications of (G.E) and (A.E) but the whole language-games governed by the rules (G) and the rules (A), respectively. Moreover, it is important to recall that the language-game of formal logic (of quantification) gets its significance from its connection with the activities of seeking and finding, and in a sense reflects the structure of these activities. In a sense, the truths of logic hence also reflect only the structure of these human activities—or perhaps rather of the rules that govern them.

Secondly, the specific connection between the two language-games should be noted. In the former, I am trying to win in 'the game of exploring the world'. In the latter, I am asking whether

[10] Cf. E. W. Beth, 'Über Lockes "Allgemeines Dreieck" ', *Kant-Studien*, vol. 48 (1956–7), pp. 361–80; E. W. Beth, *La Crise de la raison et la logique* (Gauthier-Villars, Paris, 1957); E. W. Beth, 'The Problem of Locke–Berkeley', in E. W. Beth, *Aspects of Modern Logic* (D. Reidel Publishing Company, Dordrecht, 1970), pp. 42–62; Jaakko Hintikka, 'Kant on the Mathematical Method', in *Kant Studies To-Day*, ed. by Lewis White Beck (Open Court, La Salle, Illinois, 1969), pp. 117–40.

It seems to me that Beth, too, underestimates the depth of the problems that come up here.

[11] See, e.g., the doubts mentioned in R. L. Wilder, *Introduction to the Foundations of Mathematics* (John Wiley, New York, 1952). Some critics of the principle of choice have in fact extended their criticism to the finite case, unaware that they are in effect criticizing first-order logic and not set theory.

the world could be such that I can win in a game of this sort.
A positive answer to the latter question does not tell me much
about what will be happening in an actual play of a game of
seeking and finding, but a negative answer amounts to a rather
severe restriction of what my prospects in a 'game of exploring
the world' are. Hence the (A)-games of formal logic help me in
the (G)-games in that they show what my limits of freedom in
these games are. Moreover, from a closer examination of the
(A)-games I can also frequently find out that I can hope to win
in a type of (G)-game only by playing in certain ways, irrespective of what 'the state of nature' is, as a decision theorist would
say.

An example may make this clearer. We may in fact reconsider
our earlier sample argument (10)–(15) from Chapter II (p. 45)
in the light of the remarks. Consider, for the purpose, the following pair of statements:

(1)   '$(Ex)(Uy)R(x, y)$';
(2)   '$(Ex)(Uy) \sim R(y, x)$'.

In order to verify these two, we should have to find individuals a, b such that the following are true:

(3)   '$(Uy)R(a, y)$';
(4)   '$(Uy) \sim R(y, b)$'.

Of course, we do not know, sight unseen, whether such individuals can in fact be found. However, the game of formal logic
does not pretend to answer this question but rather to see
whether (1)–(2) can be verified in any case.

If (3)–(4) are to be the case, we must also have:

(5)   '$R(a, b)$';
(6)   '$\sim R(a, b)$'.

Intuitively, (5) and (6) say that what according to (3)–(4) holds
of *all* individuals holds of b and a, respectively.

Of course, (5) and (6) cannot both be true. Hence our little
argument shows that even if I should succeed in finding the
kinds of individuals I must look for, I cannot win in the game
associated with the conjunction of (1) and (2). It is of course no
accident that the argument (1)–(6) could be carried out by means
of our rules (A) of attempted model set construction, that is, that

(1)–(6) is really part and parcel of a suitable 'language-game of formal logic'.

This illustrates the way in which the language-games of formal logic expose the limits of what can be accomplished in the language-games of exploring the world, although they cannot predict in most cases what will actually happen in a game of the latter kind.

By way of a quick popularization of our observations it may be said that the language-games (A) of formal logic deal with the *best possible cases* that can arise in the corresponding 'outdoor' games (G). Just because we are in formal logic asking whether I *can* have—in suitable circumstances—a winning strategy in a certain outdoor game of seeking and finding or whether I am bound to fail 'come what may' against a clever enough opponent, it is pertinent to ask what I can accomplish in the best of circumstances, for nothing can be more suitable than they.

From this point of view the relation of (G.E) and (A.E) becomes crystal clear. The best situation one can hope to come upon in a game of searching and finding is one in which I always find the individuals I am searching for. What (A.E) says is in effect that this is the situation considered in the language-game of formal logic. If I can be defeated even in this optimal case, I am bound to be defeated in *any* circumstances.

From the same point of view, we can also understand the relation of (A.U) to (G.U). The foremost apparent puzzle here is due to the fact that (A.U) seemingly asks me to worry only about those members of our domain of individuals which are chosen earlier by myself in a play of a (G)-game. In other words, in (A.U) Nature's moves seem to be restricted in an inexplicable way to the choices I have already anticipated myself. The justification of this restriction may seem problematic till we realize that from the point of view of guarding oneself against counter-examples the optimal case is one in which I only have to worry about the individuals which I have myself needed at earlier stages of the game. Again, the point of an (A)-game is to set limits on the (G)-games by considering this 'best possible' situation in a (G)-game.

It is interesting to see that puzzles about the interrelation of the two types of language-games concern mainly the two quantifier-rules (A.E) and (A.U). Later in this book, it will be argued that it is the interplay of these two rules, and perhaps especially the use of the former, that makes many quantification theoretical inferences non-trivial. If we identify this non-triviality with a kind of syntheticity, we may even say that it is the use of existential instantiation that in the first place can make first order reasoning synthetic in a sense not unrelated to Kant's. (See Chapters VIII–IX below.)

9. Kant's 'transcendental question' concerning mathematics as a problem concerning existential instantiation

It still remains to bring our observations to bear on Kantian problems, as I promised in the beginning of this chapter. Such an application lies very close at hand, however, for I shall argue that Kant was led to his central doctrines concerning mathematics, space, and time by a line of thought closely related to the problem of justifying the rule of existential instantiation discussed above. Here problems naturally arising within the framework of our game-theoretical interpretation of the quantifiers actually overlap with questions Kant raises. Moreover, this overlap takes place in an area most vital to Kant's own thought. It is here that the role of our games of seeking and finding as knowledge-acquiring activities helps to build a bridge to Kantian doctrines where such activities are consistently emphasized.

This is best seen by considering the way Kant formulates his 'main transcendental question' about the possibility of mathematics in the *Prolegomena*.[12] In spite of the fact that Kant speaks of mathematical knowledge, it is not hard to see that what is at issue in his discussion here (as in so many other passages) is from the modern point of view as much quantificational logic as mathematics. (This point will be argued later in this book in greater detail.)

An outline of Kant's argument in the *Prolegomena* can be represented as follows: First, he recalls what in his view is the essence of the mathematical method. According to his own explanations, he saw this characteristic feature of the procedure of mathematicians in the use of what he called *constructions*. According to Kant, the 'first and highest' condition of the possibility of mathematical knowledge is that mathematics must be able to 'represent all its concepts *in concreto* and yet *a priori*, or, as it is

---

12 pp. 281–4 of the Academy Edition, vol. 4.

called, . . . to *construct* them'.[13] Now for Kant 'to *construct* a concept means to exhibit *a priori* the intuition which corresponds to the concept'. I have shown elsewhere that by an intuition Kant initially means nothing but a representative of an individual.[14] Hence this definition of construction means that Kant saw the essence of the mathematical method in the introduction of representatives of individuals which instantiate general concepts. Of such procedures, the rule of existential instantiation offers a paradigmatic case. (Compare step (i) of the appended outline of the Kantian argument, p. 118.)

Both in the 'constructions' Kant contemplated and in the applications of our rules (A.E) one introduces a representative of an individual (in Kant's terminology, an intuition, in our terminology, a free singular term) which does not refer to any known individual. As Kant puts it, the introduction of an individual takes place *a priori*. This gives rise to a problem, according to Kant. 'But with this step the difficulty seems rather to grow than to decrease. For now the question runs: *How is it possible to intuit anything* a priori? Intuition is a representation, such as would depend directly on the presence of the object. Hence it seems impossible to intuit anything *a priori* originally [in German, *ursprünglich*, that is to say, so as to give us the existence of the object in question], because the intuition would then have to take place without any object being present, either previously or now, to which it could refer, and so could not be an intuition. . . .'[15] From this we can see that Kant's problem is to all intents and purposes identical with the problem of the justifiability of the rule (A.E) of existential instantiation which we discussed earlier. In this rule, too, we seem to anticipate the existence of an individual before experience has provided us with one. (Compare the second stage of the appended arguments, p. 119.)

This creates a problem for Kant because he believed that mathematical knowledge is applicable to all experience *a priori*

[13] *Critique of Pure Reason*, A 713 = B 714.
[14] See 'On Kant's Notion of Intuition (*Anschauung*)', in *The First Critique: Reflections on Kant's Critique of Pure Reason*, ed. by Terence Penelhum and J. J. MacIntosh Wadsworth Publishing Company, Belmont, Cal., 1969), pp. 38–53, 'Kant on the Mathematical Method' (note 10 above), and Chapters VII–VIII of the present book.
[15] *Prolegomena*, § 8.

and with certainty—quite as much as we believe that our log
is necessarily applicable to all experience. For, we may ask, ho
can such firm knowledge be obtained by means of an anticip
tion of the existence of individual objects? (See the third sta
of the outline argument, p. 118.)

10. *Kant's attempted solution of his problem*

Kant's way of trying to solve this problem is closely connect
with the basic ideas of his philosophy. His 'New Method
Thought' was to assume that 'we can know *a priori* of things on
what we ourselves put into them'.[16]

This idea has a long and fascinating history which large
remains to be explored.[17] It is one of the tacit presuppositio
on which Kant is basing his 'transcendental arguments'. If the
arguments are to have deductive cogency, it must clearly
held that the *only* way in which we can account for our *a pri*
knowledge of certain things is to assume that somehow we ha
ourselves put the requisite properties and relations into them
(Cf. the use of the word 'only' at stages (iv) and (iv)* of t
appended outlines, pp. 118–19.)

This Kantian assumption is clearly highly interesting, wheth
it is correct or not. Prima facie, it seems highly dubious. We m
try to account for the possibility of our having knowledge
certain objects before having any direct experience of them (a
hence for the possibility of having knowledge of them *a priori*
a sense) in terms of innate ideas or evolutionary adaptatio
If this view is adopted, arguments based on Kant's assumpti
have no deductive cogency, but at best amount to inferences
the best explanation—a view in effect adopted by some of t
foremost Kantian scholars.

However, if knowledge *a priori* is taken to be conceptual kno
ledge, the situation is different. Then Kant's principle amou
to saying that we can have conceptually-guaranteed knowled
of certain things if and only if this knowledge is based on t
way in which we come to know them, and reflects the structu
of this process of coming to know them. Interpreted in this wa
the principle is still not obviously correct, but now it is in a
case a highly interesting and suggestive idea. I believe it has

[16] *Critique of Pure Reason*, B xviii.
[17] Cf. note 2 above.

great deal of value in conceptual analysis. This point is unfortunately too large to be argued here, however.

Kant's use of his assumption is seen clearly in his theory of space, time, and mathematics. Since mathematical knowledge was assumed by Kant to be *a priori*, this implies that only such properties and relations of individuals must be anticipated in mathematical constructions as we have ourselves put into objects, and the existence of only such individuals may be anticipated which have been created by ourselves. Now mathematical knowledge is assumed by Kant to apply to all experience (of individuals). But there is, according to Kant's assumptions, only one stage at which we can 'put properties and relations into objects' in coming to know all the different individuals of our experience. This stage is the process by means of which we become aware of individual objects in general. And this process is according to Kant *sensation*. Kant thought that all 'objects are *given* to us by means of sensibility, and it alone yields us *intuitions*', i.e., representations of individual objects.[18] Hence the relations and properties with which mathematical reasoning deals and which are anticipated in the *a priori* intuitions which a mathematician uses must have been created by ourselves in the process of sense perception. Only in this way Kant thinks that one can explain the possibility of the use of *a priori* intuitions (introduction of new individuals) in mathematical arguments. If the existence and properties of a triangle had no 'relation to you, the subject', then 'you could not add anything new (the figure) to your concepts (of three lines) as something which necessarily must be met with in the object, since this object is given antecedently to your knowledge and [on that view] not by means of it'. From this Kant concludes that the knowledge we gain through mathematical reasoning applies to objects only in so far as they are possible objects of sensation. He also concludes that the relations with which mathematical reasoning is concerned merely reflect the form (structure) of our sensibility.

11. *Kant's views evaluated*

This argument is represented in the outline on p. 118. How is it to be evaluated? We have already seen that no doctrines like Kant's theories of space and time are needed to explain the

[18] *Critique of Pure Reason*, A 19 = B 31.

Kant's argument concerning mathematics

(i) The essential feature of synthetic reasoning in mathematics is the introduction of new intuitions *a priori*.

(ii) In such an operation, we seem to anticipate the existence of an individual with certain properties before experience has provided us with one.

(iii) The results of such reasoning are nevertheless applicable to all experience *a priori* and with absolute necessity.

(iv) This is possible only if the knowledge which we gain by means of these anticipations of existence pertains to individuals only in so far as they are objects of the activities by means of which we come to know the existence of individual objects in general.

(v) The knowledge obtained in this way will then only reproduce the structure of the activities by means of which we come to know the existence of individual objects in general.

(vi) The activity by means of which we come to know the existence of individual objects is *sensation*.

(vii) Hence the knowledge gained by means of mathematical reasoning applies to objects only in so far as they are objects of sensation (sensible intuition).

(viii) Furthermore, the interrelations of the individuals introduced in mathematical reasoning (and hence also the interrelations of their representations or the corresponding intuitions) are due to the structure (form) of our sensibility, and reflect it.

Analogous argument concerning quantification theory

 (i)* The essential feature of synthetic reasoning in quantification theory is the use of the rule of existential instantiation.

 (ii)* In applying it, we seem to anticipate the existence of an individual with certain properties before experience has provided us with one.

(iii)* The results of such reasoning are nevertheless applicable to all experience *a priori* and logical necessity.

(iv)* This is possible only if the knowledge which we gain by means of these anticipations of existence pertains to individuals only in so far as they are objects of the activities by means of which we come to know the existence of individuals in general.

 (v)* The knowledge obtained in this way will then only reproduce the structure of the activities by means of which we come to know the existence of individuals in general.

(vi)* The activities by means of which we come to know the existence of individuals are the activities of *searching* and *finding*.

(vii)* Hence the knowledge we obtain in quantification theory applies to individuals only in so far as the activities of searching and finding can (in principle) be performed among them.

(viii)* Furthermore, the structure of quantificational arguments reflects the structure of the activities of searching and finding.

role of such rules as (A.E). Nothing very much hence seems to remain of Kant's conclusions. However, it is difficult to recast some of our observations in a form which is in a very deep sense similar to Kant's arguments. These arguments represent a highly interesting line of thought with which one might profitably compare a similar argument which one could try to carry out in terms of quantifiers (second part of the outline). In particular, it seems to me very interesting to try to explain the necessity and strict universality of our logical reasoning in the way Kant strives to explain the necessity and universality of our mathematical knowledge. It seems to me justified to say that in so far as it is a conceptual certainty that our logic applies to all experience, then there must be a conceptual tie between our logical concepts and the ways in which we come to have our experience. In the case of the concepts of existence and universality, which constitute the subject matter of quantification theory, the relevant experiences are the ones on which our knowledge of the existence of individuals turns. Quantifiers must in other words be essentially connected with the processes by means of which we come to know the existence of individual objects. Now Kant thought that the only process of this kind is sense-perception. However, I have already argued that this view is wrong. I pointed out in Chapter III that it is misleading to say that we come to know the existence of all individual objects by means of sense-perception.[19] Saying this overlooks entirely the role which our active attempts to find suitable objects play in the genesis of our knowledge of individual existence. Direct observation may be thought of as a 'trivial case' of successful search, but the language-games of seeking and finding cannot be reduced to direct observation. Hence we must say that the processes through which we become aware of the existence of individual objects in general are the activities of seeking and finding, not the process of sense-perception. Hence what Kant ought to have concluded was something rather different from his actual conclusions. He was wrong in concluding that quantificational modes of inference are intimately connected with the mode of operation of our faculty of sense-perception. What he ought to have concluded is that quantificational modes of argument are bound up with the structure of our activities of seeking

---

[19] 'Language-Games for Quantifiers' (note 4 above).

and finding. This bond between them does in fact hold, and it is just what I have tried to spell out in the early parts of this chapter.

Kant was thus wrong in his attempt to connect all intuitions (in his sense of the word) with sense-perception. The connection which he thought there was between sensibility and *a posteriori* intuitions does not exist, and as a consequence the argument of Kant's which we have been considering and by means of which he tried to connect the use of *a priori* intuitions in mathematics with the form of our sensibility is fallacious.

12. *A parallel argument for quantifiers. Revisions are needed in Kant's system*

However, we have seen that this argument (which is essentially the argument which Kant calls 'the transcendental exposition of the concepts of space and time') can be recast so as to become a kind of 'a transcendental exposition of quantifiers'. This strange name is appropriate because Kant explains its meaning by saying that he understands 'by a transcendental exposition the explanation of a concept, as a principle from which the possibility of other *a priori* synthetic knowledge can be understood'. For what we have obtained is just a modified argument which purports to show that quantificational arguments, including arguments which are synthetic in what I take to be the best modern reconstruction of Kant's notion, apply to all experience. If I do not embrace this argument as wholeheartedly as Kant accepts his, this is merely because I am not fully convinced of the truth of one of its premisses. I am not sure whether we should really say that quantificational arguments apply to all experience. But if this assumption is made, I do not see why this 'transcendental exposition of quantifiers', or some closely similar argument, should not be fully acceptable. We have already seen that the main conclusions (vii)* and (viii)* of the parallel argument reflect insights into the interrelations of the language-games of formal logic and the (G)-games of searching and finding.

It would be interesting to see what further changes are necessitated in Kant's philosophy by the switch from Kant's argument concerning mathematics to our argument concerning quantifiers. It seems to me that interesting light could be thrown on some of Kant's doctrines in this way. It would take us too far, however, to mention more than a single example here. It will be obvious, for instance, that Kant's concept of *Ding an sich* will have to be modified profoundly. Instead of saying with Kant that we can know individual objects only in so far as they are potential objects of sense-perception we shall have to say merely that we cannot use quantifiers to describe a class of individual things without considering them as potential objects of searching and finding. I made a number of remarks in Chapter III[20] concerning the conditions on which this is the case. In this way, these earlier remarks can be fitted into a semi-Kantian framework.

In this direction there is plenty of room for much further work, and so there is in the systematic questions which our observations pose.

[20] Note 4 above.

VI

AN ANALYSIS OF ANALYTICITY

1. Analyticity and analysis

A FEW years ago an anthology of philosophical literature was published which covered most of the different periods of Western thought. The volume dealing with our own time was entitled 'The Age of Analysis'.[1] The aptness of the title is liable to be challenged by some philosophers, especially continental ones. No one is likely to deny, however, that the concept of analysis, together with its cognates, is important enough to deserve a careful conceptual analysis of its own. Nevertheless no fully satisfactory discussion of this concept seems to exist. What is especially needed is in my view a distinction between the different senses which the notions of analysis and analyticity have had in philosophy. An essay towards such a distinction will be made in this chapter.

I shall confine my remarks to the dichotomy between analytic and synthetic truths (propositions, sentences, judgements, arguments, etc.) which has often figured prominently in recent as well as traditional philosophy. Other members of this family of concepts will not be discussed systematically.

The lively discussion concerning the distinction between analytic and synthetic truths which started around 1950 and which has barely begun to subside will not be commented on systematically, either.[2] I shall rather try to provide a larger conceptual and historical framework for judging the older as well as newer issues to which this distinction has given rise.

---

[1] *The Great Ages of Western Philosophy*, vol. 6: *The Age of Analysis*, ed. by Morton G. White (The New American Library, New York, 1957).

[2] This discussion was initiated mainly by Quine and White; see W. V. Quine, *From a Logical Point of View* (Harvard University Press, Cambridge, Mass., 1953); and Morton G. White, *Toward Reunion in Philosophy* (Harvard University Press, Cambridge, Mass., 1955). Cf. also the interesting evaluation of the early stages of the discussion by Hilary Putnam in *Minnesota Studies in the Philosophy of Science*, vol. 3, ed. by Herbert Feigl and Grover Maxwell (University of Minnesota Press, Minneapolis, 1962), pp. 358–97, especially 359–60.

The distinction between analytic and synthetic was brought to prominence in philosophy by Immanuel Kant.[3] For this reason, we shall consider the several senses in which these concepts may be understood against the backdrop of his use of them.

The history of the notion of analyticity up to and including Kant will be studied somewhat more closely in later chapters of this book, especially in Chapters VIII and IX. Here I shall mainly try to exhibit the systematic interrelations of the different senses of analyticity irrespective of the historical context in which these senses were first developed.

A useful point of view is suggested to us by the connection of the term 'analyticity' with the word 'analysis'. Whatever analytic truths are or may be, originally they were truths that could be established by the sole means of analysis. In Kant, this connection is still very much alive. The terms 'analysis' and 'synthesis' occur in his critical writings earlier than the corresponding adjectives, and he feels called upon to explain their meaning in some detail. Most of the subsequent senses of analyticity can also be correlated with appropriate senses of analysis. We may thus approach the concept of analyticity by asking: what does this analysis amount to in different cases? What exactly is being analysed in these different analyses?

In order to make our ideas definite we shall first consider the concept of analyticity as it applies to one step of argument. Subsequently, the results of our considerations are easily extended to other contexts in which one can speak of analyticity and syntheticity (e.g., to proofs and to truths that can be established by means of such proofs). From this point of view, an argument step is analytic if (and only if) the conclusion is obtained by merely analysing what the premisses give us. A common traditional formulation of this basic idea is to say that the conclusion of an analytic argument step expresses something one was already thinking of in the premisses, however confusedly, or to say that one cannot conceive of the premisses clearly and distinctly without already thinking of the conclusion.[4] Part of

---

[3] He did it rather self-consciously, calling the distinction 'classical' and 'vast'; see *Prolegomena*, §§ 3, 5 (pp. 270 and 276 of vol. 4 of the Academy Edition of Kant's works).

[4] Cf. Kant's words in the *Prolegomena*, § 2 (p. 266 of the Academy Edition): 'Analytic judgements say nothing in the predicate that was not already thought in the concept of the subject, though not so clearly and with the same consciousness';

what I shall be doing is to see what logical and epistemological counterparts such quasi-psychological formulations may have.

But what is it that the premisses of an argument give us? What is it that we think of when we contemplate the premisses? Different answers to this question will give us the different senses of analyticity we want to consider.

2. *Analysis of concepts*

A premiss is a sentence (proposition, judgement, etc.—the differences which there may be between these and other similar entities need not detain us here). What is it that a sentence gives us? There is a time-honoured type of answer to this question according to which a sentence expresses a judgement, a thought, or perhaps a proposition. On this view these are in turn obtained by relating a number of *ideas* or *concepts* to each other. Hence what a premiss or some other kind of a sentence presents to us is in the last analysis a number of concepts put together in some definite way.

Various versions of this general idea were current in the seventeenth, eighteenth, and nineteenth centuries.[5] The idea still has not completely lost its hold of philosophers (or of linguists). For instance, it seems to lurk in the background of much of the discussion G. E. Moore and others have conducted concerning the nature of philosophical analysis.[6]

This view of the nature of sentences and propositions suggests one particular interpretation of analyticity. If what the premisses give us is a number of interrelated concepts, then the analyticity of an analytic step of argument can only mean that in it one

also cf. *Critique of Pure Reason*, A 6 = B 10, and B 17 ('A' and 'B' refer here to the first and second edition of *Kritik der reinen Vernunft*). Descartes's remarks on the nature of necessary connection between ideas in the *Regulae* (Rule XII) are closely similar. Cf. also Thomas Aquinas, *Summa Theologica* I, 2, 1. (For this reference I am indebted to Dr. P. Weingartner.)

[5] Cf., e.g., *Port-Royal Logic* (Part II, Ch. 1), where a proposition or a judgement is characterized as a comparison of ideas; Locke, *Essay* (Book IV, Ch. 1, § 1), where knowledge is said to consist of 'perception of the connexion of and agreement, or disagreement and repugnancy of any of our ideas'.

[6] Cf., e.g., Moore's remarks on the way in which an expression for an *analysans* of a given concept or a given proposition (the *analysandum*) should not only explicitly mention the concepts by means of which the *analysandum* is analysed but also explicitly mention the way in which they are combined in this *analysandum*. See 'A Reply to My Critics' in *The Philosophy of G. E. Moore*, ed. by P. A. Schilpp (The Library of Living Philosophers, Open Court Publishing Company, La Salle, Illinois, 1942), especially pp. 666–7.

merely analyses these concepts and their mutual relations. A sentence is analytic if it can be established by an argument in which we are merely taking apart the different concepts which are used in the sentence, and their interrelations, without introducing any new concepts or any new interrelations. In other words, a sentence is analytically true if and only if its truth can be established by the sole means of conceptual analysis, without recourse to experience. In this way, analytic truth becomes identified with conceptual truth.[7] This sense of analyticity (or, rather, a group of senses which can be obtained from it by developing it further) will be referred to in what follows as sense I.[8]

Apart from differences in detail, this sense of analyticity has dominated recent discussion. This sense is betrayed by the characterizations contemporary philosophers have given of their notion of analytic truth, such as conceptual truth, truth in the sole virtue of the meanings of words,[9] truth *ex vi terminorum*, and so on.[10] This sense of analyticity has also been employed by some philosophers who probably would not accept the derivation of this sense from the basic idea of analysis which I have just sketched.

Thus the criticisms that have been levelled against a dichotomy between analytic and synthetic truth in recent discussion, too, pertain mainly to sense I. These criticisms show at the very least that this sense is somewhat vague. Whatever one is inclined to say and to think of concepts or ideas and of the other entities

[7] It also becomes associated rather closely with *a priori* truth. If one uses the sense of analyticity which we are here approaching, it is not easy to avoid identifying by definition analytic truth with *a priori* truth. In fact, at least one contemporary philosopher has made this identification well-nigh explicitly. (See Arthur Pap, *Semantics and Necessary Truth* (Yale University Press, New Haven, Conn., 1958), p. 423.) To my mind, this already suggests that something is wrong with the prevalent contemporary sense of analyticity, for whether synthetic truths *a priori* exist or not, their non-existence ought not to be a matter of mere definition. From a historical point of view, it would probably be more appropriate to call conceptual truths *a priori* truths, and to reserve the term 'analytic' for other purposes.

[8] A list of the different senses of analyticity we are trying to explicate is given in an appendix at the end of this chapter.

[9] In so far as there are such entities at all. Some philosophers have thought that they have discerned here a confusion between 'being meaningful' or 'having meaning' and 'having *a* meaning', only the last of which expressions commits us to the existence of meanings as separate entities.

[10] Cf., e.g., Pap's definition of implicit analyticity in op. cit. (note 7 above), p. 423.

that can serve as meanings of our words, one is bound to admit that they are abstract entities which are often rather difficult to grasp clearly and inconvenient to deal with. Partly for this reason, philosophers have sought to develop further sense I of analyticity. Often it is thought that the way in which a concept should be specified is by giving it a definition. Often it is also thought that the results of our conceptual analyses can always be formulated as definitions of the concepts in question. On either view, an analytic truth in the sense of a conceptual truth will mean a truth which hinges solely on the definitions of the concepts it involves. This leads one to an interpretation of analytic truth as definitory truth. This variant of sense I of analyticity will be designated as sense I (a).

But what exactly does one mean by saying that the truth of a sentence turns solely on definitions? Usually one does not mean that the sentence in question is itself a definition or a substitution-instance of a definition. Normally one is likely to mean, it seems to me, that the sentence in question is logically implied by a definition or a number of definitions. Thus we reach a somewhat more explicit variant of sense I which we can call I (b): a sentence is analytic if and only if it is logically implied by the definitions of the terms it contains.

This sense of analyticity is based on an assumption which should be brought to light at once. It is a reasonable meaning of analyticity only if all relations of logical implication are themselves analytic. Otherwise the analyticity of definitions might not carry over to the logical consequences of these definitions. Now relations of logical consequence undoubtedly seem to be analytic in the unanalysed sense I, that is to say, they seem to be based solely on the meanings of logical terms.[11] But it does not follow that they are analytic in the other senses of the word which will be discussed later. It does not even follow that the logical truths on which these consequence relations are based are analytic in sense I (a), that is to say, based solely on the definitions of logical terms. This has sometimes been asserted, but the justification and the precise meaning of this claim escapes me.

---

[11] The arguments of the intuitionists might seem to throw some doubt even on this point. I do not think that they turn out really to do so on closer analysis; but even if they should do so, it will only strengthen my hand here.

What philosophers have usually done in this situation is to assume that logical truths are analytic and then to use them in order to catch the rest of analytic truths. The definition o analyticity which was given by Gottlob Frege is typical in thi respect. According to Frege, a truth is analytic if and only if i can be justified by the sole means of 'general logical laws and . . definitions'.[12] This sense of analyticity will be called sense I (c)

Some recent philosophers have been unhappy with the notion of definition, however, and have sought to replace it by a con cept which would be less technical and more closely connected with the actual workings of language. It is not very difficult to find candidates for this role. One obvious requirement we have to impose on definitions is that the *definiens* and the *definiendum* have the same meaning, that they are synonyms. Even though it is not obvious that this notion is clearer than the concept o definition, one may try to use it in defining analyticity. Thus one may follow W. V. Quine and identify the class of analytic truths with the class that includes all logical truths plus what ever truths one can obtain from them by replacing synonyms by synonyms.[13] (Sense I (d) of analyticity.)

3. *The insufficiency of the sense I of analyticity*

Kant's statements show certain similarities between his notion of analyticity and the group of senses just explained. Analyticity was closely associated by Kant with logical truths and with definitions. According to some of his pronouncements, a truth is analytic if it can be established by the sole means of the principles of contradiction and of identity.[14]

---

[12] Gottlob Frege, *Die Grundlagen der Arithmetik* (Wilhelm Koebner, Breslau, 1884). Tr. by J. L. Austin (Basil Blackwell, Oxford, 1950), as: *The Foundations of Arithmetic*. (See pp. 99–101.)

[13] W. V. Quine, op. cit. (note 2 above), pp. 22–3. Quine does not believe that the distinction he thus makes is satisfactorily motivated, however.

[14] See *Critique of Pure Reason*, A 150–3 = B 190–2 (tr. by Norman Kemp Smith, Macmillan, London, 1929, pp. 189–91), where Kant writes: 'For, if the judgement is analytic, . . . its truth can always be adequately known in accordance with the principle of contradiction.' This principle 'belongs only to logic; it holds of knowledge . . . irrespective of content'. For the connection between logical truth and analyticity in Kant, see also Konrad Marc-Wogau, 'Kants Lehre von dem analytischen Urteil', *Theoria*, vol. 17 (1951), pp. 140–54, especially pp. 152–3. For the connection between analytic truth and definition in Kant, it may be observed that for Kant analytic judgement merely made explicit what we actually (albeit confusedly) think in a certain concept. Now according to Kant 'what I am actually

This similarity is largely an illusion, however, whose causes will be briefly commented on later. However vague and equivocal Kant's notion of analyticity may have been, it was scarcely intended to comprise all conceptual truths. On the contrary, more than once Kant explicitly countenances truths which are conceptual and nevertheless 'synthetic. Commenting on the reasons for the syntheticity of mathematical truths, Kant says that in a synthetic judgement we sometimes 'are required to join in thought a certain predicate to a given concept, and *this necessity is inherent in the concepts themselves*' (my italics). This does not make the judgement analytic, Kant says, for the decisive question 'is not what we *ought to* join in thought to the given concept, but what we *actually* think in it, even if only obscurely' (the italics are now Kant's).[15]

These quotations show that Kant's notion of analyticity is fundamentally different from the analyticity of those modern thinkers who simply equate analytic truth with conceptual truth. It follows from their definitions of analyticity that a truth is analytic

thinking in my concept of a triangle . . . is nothing but the mere definition' (*Critique of Pure Reason*, A 718 = B 746). Thus analytic truth is virtually identified by Kant with truth based solely on definitions.

[15] The quotation is from the *Critique of Pure Reason* (B 17, pp. 53–4 of the Kemp Smith translation). In the preface to the second edition (B xii, p. 19 of the translation) Kant explains in the same vein what he calls 'the true geometrical method' discovered by one of the Presocratics by saying that this method 'was not to inspect what he discerned either in the figure, or in the bare concept of it, and from this, as it were, to read off its properties; but to bring out what was necessarily implied in the concepts that he had himself formed *a priori*, and had put into the figure in the construction by which he presented it to himself'. This is interesting also because it shows that a widespread interpretation of Kant's theory of the mathematical method is mistaken. When Kant said that geometrical arguments are based on the use of intuitions he did not mean in the first place that in a geometrical argument one has to construct a figure and inspect it in order to find out its properties by means of one's geometrical imagination or 'intuition', as many contemporary philosophers seem to assume that Kant meant. Such an appeal to geometrical imagination is virtually forbidden by Kant. In fact, the quotation continues as follows: 'If he is to know anything with *a priori* certainty he must not ascribe to the figure anything save what necessarily follows from what he has himself set into it in accordance with his concept.' In *Critique of Pure Reason*, A 716 = B 744, Kant indicates that a geometrical proof is 'a chain of inferences' which follow necessarily 'from the universal conditions of the construction'. It is also instructive to note that when Frege introduced his sense of analyticity he was well aware of departing from Kant's usage. In fact, he pointed out explicitly that he was broadening the scope of the term as compared with Kant's sense. (Op. cit., pp. 99–100.) Frege's commendable caution has not always been maintained by his successors.

if we can come by it as soon as we have all the concepts it
involves. Now any truth which turns on necessities inherent in
certain concepts is obviously analytic in this sense; however,
some such truths are explicitly called synthetic by Kant. This
historical fact should already make us chary of sense I of analyticity. An examination of the usage of some other traditional
philosophers would likewise show that their intentions are not
very well served by an explication of the notion of analyticity
along the lines of sense I.[16]

There are also ample topical reasons for being dissatisfied
with the senses of analyticity which we have encountered so far.
They are undermined by two types of difficulty neither of which
has been eliminated so far. On the one hand, one may doubt
whether any of the senses I (a)–(d) really serves its purpose, that
is to say, exhausts the field of the vaguer but perhaps more
intuitive sense I (analytic truth as conceptual truth). On the
other hand, one may find the way in which this broader sense I
itself was arrived at unsatisfactory and therefore want to replace
it by some altogether different sense.

In discussing the former point, we must specify the import of
the suggested definition I (d) of analyticity in somewhat greater
detail. (This definition is chosen for consideration here because
it seems to be the most important current definition of analyticity.) Each of the relations of synonymy with which it deals has
to be understood as holding between some one term on the one
hand and with an explanatory expression on the other. We may
of course also speak of relations of synonymy between such larger
expressions as sentences. But if such synonymies are admitted to
the characterization I (d) of analyticity, the connection between
this sense and the senses I (b)–(c) is lost, for it is inadmissible
to speak of definitions of sentences. Furthermore, if arbitrary

---

[16] It is clear that John Locke would have recoiled from the idea that all conceptual truth is analytic. It is true that Locke did not use the terms 'analytic truth'
and 'analytic proposition'. However, he did use the notion of a trifling proposition
which he described in a manner closely reminiscent of Kant's comments on analytic
judgements. Locke did not think that all the truths that are due to conceptual
necessities are trifling. On the contrary, he indicates that in addition to the merely
verbal certainty which we have of trifling propositions we can also 'know the truth
of, and so may be certain in propositions, which affirm something of another, which
is a necessary consequence of its precise complex idea, but not contained in it'. Such
a truth is, according to Locke, 'a real truth, and conveys with it instructive real
knowledge', and is therefore not trifling. (*Essay*, Book IV, Ch. 8, § 8.)

ynonymies were considered in I (d), this definition would be
o wide as to be worthless. For instance, the question whether
a given sentence F_1 analytically implies another sentence F_2 is
clearly tantamount to the question whether F_1 & F_2 says the
ame thing as F_1 alone, or whether it adds something to it, in
other words, whether the sentences F_1 and $(F_1$ & $F_2)$ are synonymous. Hence in answering questions of synonymy in the wider
ense of the word we should frequently be *ipso facto* answering
questions of analyticity directly; and hence the notion of
ynonymy would scarcely help us in answering questions of
analyticity. In fact, most perpetrators of sense I (d) seem to have
understood the notion of synonymy mentioned in it in the
narrower sense, that is to say, as a relation between terms and
not between sentences.[17]

But if the sense I (d) of analyticity is understood in this way,
t becomes very questionable whether it catches all conceptual
truths, in other words, whether it catches all the truths analytic
n the broader sense I. Examples to the contrary seem to be
offered *inter alia* by the studies which are known as epistemic
ogic and deontic logic.[18] They have brought to light many
nteresting and sometimes rather subtle laws governing such
concepts as knowledge, belief (or opinion), obligation, and permission. Nevertheless these laws are not laws of logic in any
usual sense of the word (whence the claim of these studies to the
itle of epistemic or deontic *logic* has sometimes been challenged).
On the one hand, it is natural to say that these laws depend
solely on the meanings of the terms 'knows that', 'believes that',
'ought to', and 'is permitted to', which are not logical terms in
the normal sense of the word. On the other hand, nothing suggests that these laws could somehow be reduced to the laws
of normal quantificational logic by replacing some particular
terms occurring in them by synonymous terms. Nor does there
seem to be much evidence to show that they could be reduced
to those systems of modal logic which are supposed to formulate

[17] As far as I can see, this is the way in which Quine has intended definition I (d)
to be understood.

[18] See, for instance, Risto Hilpinen, ed., *Deontic Logic: Introductory and Systematic
Readings* (D. Reidel Publishing Company, Dordrecht, 1971); Jaakko Hintikka,
Knowledge and Belief (Cornell University Press, Ithaca, N.Y., 1962); Jaakko Hintikka,
Models for Modalities: Selected Essays (D. Reidel Publishing Company, Dordrecht,
1969).

the logical behaviour of the notions of logical necessity and logical possibility. On the contrary, a closer study of the situation reveals subtle differences between these modal logics and epistemic logic. The laws studied by the latter therefore seem to be analytic in the broader and vaguer sense I but not in the more precise sense I (d). Similar remarks apply also to senses I (b)–(c).[19]

The more general sense I is itself already suspect, however. The connection of this sense with the notion of analysis (and therefore its claim to the term 'analyticity') seems to be based on rather weak grounds.[20] The connecting link was the assumption that what a sentence or proposition primarily gives us is a number of interrelated concepts or ideas. This way of thinking is perhaps not so much wrong as over-simplified. It is over-simplified because it overlooks the variety of ways in which our concepts may contribute to the formation of a meaningful sentence (or proposition, if you want). Because of this variety, it is also difficult to quote any very general reasons why the view of propositions as bunches of concepts is misleading. Propositional connectives and quantifiers already show us, however, how over-simplified this view is in one respect. It is natural to say that each of the connectives and quantifiers expresses a concept. These concepts have familiar names of their own: negation, conjunction, disjunction, existence, and universality. However, the

[19] In an important article (see note 2 above), Hilary Putnam makes certain interesting points which may be compared with the ones just made. Although Putnam expresses himself differently, one of his main theses might perhaps be expressed by saying that many important terms do not take their meaning from definitions or from relations of synonymy but from the role they play in several non-logical laws. This is not unlike the observations just made. The moral Putnam draws from his examples is different from mine, however. He finds the traditional distinction between analytic and synthetic truths along the lines of our definitions I (c) or (d) relatively unimportant, but he nevertheless seems to be happy with trying to explicate it along these lines. The moral I want to extract from examples of an entirely different kind is that sense I (d) of analyticity is unsatisfactory in that it does not even catch all conceptual truths; and I think that this moral could also be drawn from examples rather like Putnam's.

[20] I do not want to deny that one can simply identify analytic truth with conceptual truth and be perfectly happy. It seems to me, however, that such a notion of conceptual truth does not have any claim to the term '*analytic* truth' nor to any connection with the notion of analyticity used by such classical philosophers as Kant until it has been connected with the notion of analysis in some way or other. The notion of conceptual truth is by itself not very clear, either; and if one wants to explicate it, the most useful sense of analyticity may very well turn out to be the sense IV later to be defined rather than I (c) or (d).

way in which they co-operate in the construction of sentences out of simpler elements does not fit the picture which the view we are criticizing presents to us.

A brief glimpse of the way in which the concepts of negation, conjunction, disjunction, existence, and universality can be used to build propositions already shows that they are not simple building-blocks which can only be used once in a given sentence, as one and the same brick can only be used once in building a house. The logical concepts just mentioned are of the nature of *operators* which can be used again and again in one and the same sentence. In fact, from the five logical concepts plus a single two-place relation one can already build an infinity of non-equivalent sentences. Thus a quantificational sentence cannot be specified simply by specifying which concepts occur in it and how these concepts themselves are related to each other. We have to discuss the interrelations of the different occurrences of these operator-like concepts.

Other concepts violate in other ways the simple 'building-block' model of propositions which underlies sense I of analyticity. Philosophers have spoken of 'relations of ideas' or 'relations of concepts' ever since Plato became fascinated in the *Sophist* with the συμπλοκὴ εἰδῶν. This terminology hides more problems than they usually realize, however. The logic of quantification already shows us one way in which this terminology and the way of thinking on which it is based is misleading.

4. *Analysis of sentences*

What happens if we take seriously the operator-like character of our basic logical notions? An answer may be formulated by saying that in considering a sentence it is not very useful simply to consider the 'relations of the ideas' occurring in it. We have to widen our point of view: we have to take into account the history of the sentence in question, i.e., the way in which it has been constructed from atomic sentences (and identities, if they are used in our sentences). The rules which govern this construction are in the case of quantification theory the usual rules of formation. They bring out the operator-like character of the basic concepts of quantification theory.

What kind of notion of analyticity do we arrive at if we say that what a premiss of a step of inference primarily gives us is a sentence with a formational history? Considering a quantificational sentence from the point of view of its structure, what can it mean to say that in a step of argument one is 'merely analysing' it? An answer lies close at hand. In a step from F_1 to F_2 we are 'merely analysing' F_1 if (and only if) F_2 is part of F_1. And this relation of being a part of a sentence can be explained by saying that F_2 is a part of F_1 if and only if it occurred or could have occurred as a stage of the formational history of F_1. Speaking more precisely, we may say that F_2 is a part of F_1 in the relevant sense of the word if and only if it is a *subsentence* of F_1. This notion is defined recursively by inverting the usual rules of formation for quantification theory:

(S.A) An atomic sentence has no subsentences.

(S.$\sim$) The subsentences of $\sim F$ are F and the subsentences of F.

(S.&)–(S.v) The subsentences of $(F_1 \,\&\, F_2)$ and of $(F_1 \,\mathsf{v}\, F_2)$ are F_1 and F_2 and their subsentences.

(S.E)–(S.U) The subsentences of $(Ex)F$ and of $(Ux)F$ are all the sentences of the form $F(a/x)$ as well as all their subsentences.

This definition is of course relative to some given set of free singular terms from which the term a mentioned in (S.E) and in (S.U) is to be chosen.

I am using the letters 'x', 'y',... as bound individual variables, and the letters 'a', 'b',... as placeholders for free singular terms. $F(a/x)$ is the result of replacing 'x' everywhere in F by 'a'.

We can now say that in a sense an argument step is analytic if (and only if) its conclusion is a subsentence of one of the premises (or identical with one of them). This sense of analyticity will be called sense II.

This sense can be extended from one-step arguments to longer proofs in more ways than one. One possibility is to say that a proof is analytic if and only if all its steps are analytic in sense II. (Sense II (a) of analyticity.) A much more interesting sense is obtained, however, by considering a proof from the vantage point of both its premises and its conclusion. In this sense, a proof of F_2 from F_1 is analytic if and only if all the intermediate stages of the proof are sentences each of which is a subsentence of either F_1 or F_2. (Sense II (b).) A quantificational sentence is finally analytic if and only if it can be proved analytically in sense II (b) from propositional tautologies of the form $(A \vee \sim A)$ (where A is an atomic sentence), or from a conjunction of such tautologies. Analogously, a quantificational sentence is analytically inconsistent if and only if one can derive from it a disjunction of sentences of the form $(A \& \sim A)$ (A atomic) by an argument which is analytic in sense II (b).

This group of senses of analyticity is here studied almost exclusively in quantification theory. There is no obstacle in principle, however, why it could not be extended beyond quantification theory.

This kind of notion of analyticity has not attracted much attention. I have encountered it only in some pertinent comments by E. W. Beth and William Craig.[21] It has a great deal of interest, however. The requirement which it puts on proofs is closely related to the subformula property which has figured importantly in the development of the logical techniques known as natural deduction methods.[22] In fact, one may say that one of the main achievements of the natural deduction methods has been to enable us to make all quantificational proofs analytic in sense II (b). This sense of analyticity is therefore connected very closely with the development of the systematic theory of quantification.

The possibility of making quantificational proofs analytic in the sense we are now considering is closely related with the possibility of dispensing with unrestricted applications of *tertium non datur* in quantificational proofs. The question whether this is possible in higher-order logics (impredicative ones) is an

[21] E. W. Beth, 'Semantic Entailment and Formal Derivability', *Mededelingen van de Koninklijke Nederlandse Akademie van Wetenschappen*, Afd. Letterkunde, N.S., vol. 18, No. 13 (North-Holland Publishing Company, Amsterdam, 1955); E. W. Beth, *The Foundations of Mathematics* (North-Holland Publishing Company, Amsterdam, 1959; see p. 193 for 'the ideal of a purely analytic method'). There is a sense in which Craig's 'linear reasoning' is also a realization of the same or a closely related ideal of 'purely analytic procedure'; see William Craig, 'Linear Reasoning', *Journal of Symbolic Logic*, vol. 22 (1957), pp. 250–68, and 'Bases for First-Order Theories and Subtheories', ibid., vol. 25 (1960), pp. 97–142.

[22] See, e.g., G. Gentzen, 'Untersuchungen über das logische Schließen', *Mathematische Zeitschrift*, vol. 39 (1934), pp. 176–210 and 405–31, reprinted in English translation in *The Collected Papers of Gerhard Gentzen*, ed. by M. E. Szabo (North-Holland Publishing Company, Amsterdam, 1969); Dag Prawitz, *Natural Deduction: A Proof-Theoretical Study*, Stockholm Studies in Philosophy, vol. 3 (Almqvist & Wiksell, Stockholm, 1965).

important problem which remained unsolved for some fifteen years.[23]

5. *Analysis of complexes of individuals*

Although sense II of analyticity thus deserves more attention than it has so far received from philosophers, it still does not catch some of the most important intentions of those traditional philosophers who employed the distinction between analytic and synthetic. We can bring out these intentions, however, in the same way as we have arrived at the earlier senses of analyticity, namely, by asking: What is it that a premiss gives us to be analysed? Perhaps the most concrete answer to this question is to say that it gives us a number of individuals to be considered. If this answer is accepted, then a step of argument is analytic if and only if it does not introduce any new individuals. For if such new individuals have to be considered, we clearly are not any more 'merely analysing' what the premiss gave us. Accordingly, the following definition of analyticity may be proposed:

III An argument step is analytic if and only if it does not introduce any new individuals into the discussion.

An argument step may be analytic in sense II and yet synthetic in sense III, for even if it takes us from a more complicated sentence to a less complicated one it may nevertheless introduce individuals which had not been referred to before. The new sense III therefore differs from sense II.

This new notion of analyticity is in many respects a clear and concrete one. In sense I of analyticity, we were enjoined not to go beyond a number of given concepts. In sense III, we are asked not to transcend a number of given individuals. The new sense can be understood better than the old one to the extent the notion of an individual object can be understood better than

---

[23] The problem was first proposed by G. Takeuti in 'On a Generalized Logic Calculus', *Japanese Journal of Mathematics*, vol. 23 (1953), pp. 39–96, and subsequently studied by him in several papers. Its semantical implications were brought out by Kurt Schütte in 'Syntactical and Semantical Properties of Simple Type Theory', *Journal of Symbolic Logic*, vol. 25 (1960, published in 1962), pp. 305–26. It was solved for the general case (without the assumption of extensionality) by Dag Prawitz and independently by Takahashi. See Dag Prawitz, 'Hauptsatz for Higher Order Logic', *Journal of Symbolic Logic*, vol. 33 (1968), pp. 452–7, and Moto-o Takahashi, 'A Proof of Cut-Elimination Theorem in Simple Type-Theory' *Journal of the Mathematical Society of Japan*, vol. 19 (1967), pp. 399–410.

that of a general concept.[24] In the old sense, we were concerned with the analysis of concepts; here we are concerned with the analysis of concrete complexes of individuals. This sense of 'conceptual' analysis does not seem to be completely new. Their professions to the contrary notwithstanding, philosophers who have been practising conceptual analysis have not always restricted themselves to discussing interrelations of general concepts but have resorted to mentioning individuals. To use as an example what ought to be the most thoroughly analysed concept in literature, if a brother is defined as a male child of the same parents, we make use of the interrelations of concrete individuals: *a* is a brother of *b* if and only if *a* is a male and if there are two individuals *x* and *y* such that *x* and *y* are parents of both *a* and *b*. Here the concept of a brother is analysed by means of the concepts of a male and of a parent *together with* the existence of the individuals *x* and *y*.

Sense III approximates rather closely Kant's notion of analyticity. Kant understood this sense as implying that inter-individual inferences concerning existence are impossible by purely analytic means. In other words, he held the following principle:

III (a) An analytic step of argument cannot carry us from the existence of an individual to the existence of a different individual.

Kant's writings show that inferences violating III (a) were in his view virtually paradigmatic instances of synthetic modes of reasoning.[25] Time and again he returns to the problem which

---

[24] I do not want to pin my point on any ontological distinction between individuals and entities of other kinds, however. What I am trying to establish is a criterion for distinguishing synthetic modes of argument from analytic ones in a quantificational language. Hence my 'individuals' may for my immediate purposes be any entities that can serve as values of the bound variables of quantification. I am at the moment not inquiring into the conditions on which an entity can serve this purpose.

[25] See Kant's comments on Hume's problem, especially in the *Prolegomena* (see the references given in note 27 below and also pp. 370–1 of the Academy Edition) and in the *Critique of Practical Reason*. Statement III (a) is a partial formulation of the general conclusion Kant wants to derive from Hume's discussion of the problem of causality. It is only a partial formulation for two reasons. First, Kant is also concerned with inferences from the existence of an individual to the *non-existence* of another individual. Secondly, he is also interested in inferences from a fact to the existence of another (different) fact. That III (a) is in any case part of what Kant means is shown especially clearly by his formulations in the *Critique of Practical*

he takes to be a generalization of the Humean problem of
causality and which he once formulates as follows: 'Wie soll ich
es verstehen, daß weil Etwas ist, etwas anderes sei?'[26] He goes
on to point out that this cannot take place 'durch den Satz des
Widerspruchs', that is, analytically.[27] From the *Prolegomena* it
appears that Kant took his own main problem of the justifiability of synthetic *a priori* truths to be a generalization of the
problem of justifying inferences synthetic in sense III (a).[28]

6. *Quantifiers as introducing individuals*

One of the principal aims of this chapter and of its sequels is
to make clear this sense III of analyticity and to develop it
further. In order to do so, we must ask: how are individuals
imported into our considerations and arguments? Part of an
answer is obvious: individuals are introduced into our reasoning
by free singular terms. They are not the only expressions, however, which invite us to consider individuals, not even if we
restrict our attention to quantification theory. Perhaps the most
straightforward way of seeing this is to recall the most accurate
translations that can be given of quantifiers in ordinary language. The existential quantifier '(Ex)' should be read somewhat
as follows: 'there is at least one individual (call it x) such that',
and the universal quantifier '(Ux)' should be read: 'each individual (call it x) is such that'. These translations make it clear that
although the bound variable 'x' does not stand for any particular

Reason, where he explains Hume's position as follows: 'Nun ist es, sagt er, unmöglich,
die Verbindung, die zwischen einem Dinge und einem anderen (oder einer
Bestimmung und einer anderen, ganz von ihr verschiedenen), wenn sie nicht in der
Wahrnehmung gegeben werden, a priori und als notwendig zu erkennen.' The
whole concept of a cause (Kant goes on to expound Hume) is based on a custom,
'gewisse Dinge oder ihre Bestimmungen öfters neben- oder nacheinander *ihrer
Existenz nach* als sich beigesellet wahrzunehmen' (Part I, Book 1, Erstes Hauptstück,
§ 2; my italics). Cf. also Kant's final remarks in his *Prolegomena*: 'I cannot bring
forth from the concept of one thing the concept of another thing the existence
(*Dasein*) of which is necessarily connected with the first. . . .'

[26] See the Academy Edition of Kant's works, vol. 2, pp. 202–3.

[27] This formulation presupposes some amount of hindsight, for when writing the
passage in question Kant had not yet developed fully his notion of analyticity.
However, my point is confirmed by Kant's later works.

[28] See the preface, section II (p. 257 and p. 260 of the Academy Edition); and
compare § 3 (pp. 277–8), where Kant's generalization on Hume's problem turns
out to give rise to his own basic question: how are synthetic propositions *a priori*
possible?

individual, each quantifier invites us to consider one individual in addition to the other ones which may have been introduced earlier.

One way of illustrating this function of quantifiers is to recall the figures by means of which we ordinarily illustrate geometrical propositions, for instance, theorems of elementary geometry.[29] Although these theorems usually assert something about *all* triangles, *all* circles, or *all* geometrical entities of some other sort, each of them can be illustrated by means of a figure which has only a finite number of geometrical entities explicitly represented. This number is determined in the way just mentioned: Each quantifier typically brings one geometrical entity (of the sort over which the associated bound variable ranges) into the figure.

Here we can see an additional reason for saying that it often is an over-simplification to consider propositions as structured collections of concepts. In such formulations the term 'concept' is often restricted to *general* concepts only. And when it is not so restricted, what is being considered in addition to general concepts is usually a separate class of 'individual concepts', whatever these are or may be. No member of this tradition seems to have paid much attention to the fact that some of our most general concepts, viz. the concepts of existence and universality, which are regimented by the two quantifiers, contain in their most common use (viz. that codified in first-order languages) an unmistakable reference to individuals, however unspecified these individuals may be.

How profoundly this fact is likely to affect the point of view of some traditional philosophers is perhaps best seen by considering Kant's conceptual apparatus. Kant contrasted general concepts (which he often called simply *Begriffe* or concepts) to representations of individual objects which he called *intuitions* (*Anschauungen*). As I have argued elsewhere, by definition these intuitions comprise simply everything which represents an individual.[30] If

---

[29] This geometrical paradigm appears to be one of the historical antecedents of Kant's distinction between the analytic and the synthetic; see the papers referred to in note 38 to Chapter I above, as well as 'Kantin oppi matematiikasta' (in Finnish), *Ajatus*, vol. 22 (1959), pp. 5–85.

[30] See the papers referred to in note 38 to Chapter I above, especially 'On Kant's Notion of Intuition'. For evidence, cf., e.g., *Critique of Pure Reason*, A 320 = B 376–7; *Prolegomena*, § 8 (p. 282 of the Academy Edition); Kant's lectures on logic, § 1.

we follow Kant's terminology, we are thus led to say that quantifiers do not deal with general concepts only but contain an intuitive element. What we are accustomed to call the logic of quantification in its general form would not have been logic at all for Kant, for according to Kant logic dealt with general concepts only. Quantification theory, Kant would have been forced to say, hinges on non-logical, 'intuitive' methods. Of course, saying this is not much more than another way of saying that typically quantificational modes of inference would have been called by Kant mathematical rather than logical.[31]

The intimate relation of quantifiers and of the variables bound to them to free singular terms is shown by the fact that for many purposes quantifiers may be omitted and the variables bound to them replaced by suitable free singular terms. Of course, this is just what one tries to do in applying natural deduction methods. Roughly speaking, there usually is little to choose between a free singular term and a variable which is bound to a quantifier whose scope comprises the whole formula (with the possible exception of a string of initial quantifiers), in the sense that the logical operations one is allowed to perform are to most intents and purposes exactly the same in the two cases. Hence we must conclude that if individuals are introduced into one's logical arguments by free singular terms, they are likewise introduced by quantifiers, too. What really distinguishes a bound variable from a free singular term, one might almost say, is not so much its being bound to a quantifier as its being restricted by the scope of the quantifier.

This restriction has also the effect that parallel quantifiers (i.e., quantifiers whose scopes do not overlap) cannot be said to add to the number of individuals we have to consider in their relation to one another. They may introduce new cases to be considered, but they do not complicate the complexes of individuals we have to take into account.

Since a bound variable does not refer to any particular individual it does not make sense to ask whether an argument step which involves quantifiers introduces new individuals into the argument. We may ask, however, whether it adds to the number

---

[31] In general, Kant drew the boundary between logic and mathematics in a way different from our way of drawing it. Cf. note 38 to Chapter I above, especially the paper 'Kant on the Mathematical Method' referred to there.

of individuals we are considering in their relation to each other in the premisses. If it does, the argument step is synthetic in a sense closely related to sense III—we shall call it sense III (b)—because then we cannot be simply analysing in the conclusion a complex of individuals which was already being considered in the premiss.

On the basis of what has been said, it is not difficult to see how the maximal number of individuals we are considering in their relation to each other in a quantificational sentence is determined. What are the individuals which we may consider in a certain part of a quantificational sentence, say between a certain pair of parentheses? There are two kinds of such individuals: (1) the individuals referred to by the different free singular terms of the sentence; (2) the individuals which we are invited to consider by the different quantifiers within the scope of which we are moving.[32] Accordingly, the desired maximal number of individuals that we may consider together in a certain sentence F is obtained as a sum of two numbers: (i) the number of the free singular terms of F; (ii) the maximal number of quantifiers whose scopes have a common part in F.

This sum will be called the *degree* of F. The second of its *addenda* will be called the *depth* of F. This notion admits of several alternative explanations. It may be defined as the maximum of the lengths of nested sequences of quantifiers in F. Somewhat more popularly, it might be said to be the number of different layers of quantifiers in F at its deepest. The depth $d(F)$ of F could also be defined recursively as follows: $d(F) = 0$ whenever F is atomic (or an identity); $d(F_1 \& F_2) = d(F_1 \vee F_2) =$ the greater

[32] The following acute objection has been made against this point by Hector-Neri Castañeda: this number is not always the maximal number of *different* individuals introduced by the quantifiers, for the values of different bound variables may coincide even though the scopes of the quantifiers to which they are bound overlap. This objection loses its point, however, if it is assumed that our quantifiers are subjected to what I have called the (strongly) exclusive interpretation or assumed that the degree of a sentence is measured only after it has been transformed into a form in which its quantifiers are subject to this interpretation; for this interpretation amounts to requiring just that the values of variables bound to nested quantifiers must be different. (Concerning this interpretation and concerning the possibility of the transformation just mentioned, see my paper on 'Identity, Variables, and Impredicative Definitions', *Journal of Symbolic Logic*, vol. 22 (1957), pp. 225–45.) In most cases, a distinction between the two interpretations of quantifiers makes little difference, however, and in any case virtually nothing in this chapter or in its sequel will turn on it.

of the numbers $d(F_1)$ and $d(F_2)$; $d[(Ex)F(x/a)] = d[(Ux)F(x/a)] = d(F)+1.$[33]

A deeper justification for equating the degree of a quantificational sentence with the number of individuals considered in it in their relation to each other ensues from the game-theoretical interpretation of first-order languages outlined in Chapter III above. It is natural to understand by the latter number (the maximal number of individuals related to each other in a given sentence F) the maximal number of individuals considered in any given round of the game associated with F. On the game-theoretical interpretation of quantifiers, this is precisely the greatest number of individuals that F forces us to consider together. But this number is easily seen to equal the degree of F.

Moreover, this relationship between the lengths of sequences of individuals considered in the game associated with F and the degree of F can be preserved even after the notion of degree is sharpened as indicated in note 33 above. This necessitates

[33] What is given in the text is not the only way of understanding the notion of depth, nor the sharpest way of understanding it. This notion is based on the idea of 'considering individuals in their relation to each other'. When exactly are the individuals, which two quantifiers invite us to consider, related to each other in a sentence? The definition in the text is based on the assumption that this is the case as soon as the quantifiers in question are nested, i.e., as soon as the scope of one of them is included within the scope of the other. It is obvious, however, that the individuals that nested quantifiers introduce into our considerations may not be related to each other in any direct or indirect way in the sentence F in question. Hence a sharper definition may be obtained by considering only such bound variables x_1, x_k as invite us to consider individuals that are related to each other in the sentence in the sense that there is a sequence of bound variables $x_1, x_2,...,x_{k-1},$ x_k with the following properties: for each $i = 1, 2,..., k-1$, x_i and x_{i+1} occur in the same atomic subsentence or identity of F; each variable x_i is bound to a quantifier occurring within the scope of the wider of the two quantifiers to which x_1 and x_k are bound. Let us call such variables and the quantifiers to which they are bound *connected*. (It may be assumed for simplicity that different quantifiers have typographically different variables bound to them in F.) The maximal number of nested *and* connected quantifiers in F is now called the depth of F.

The two aspects of this definition reflect the intuitive content of the notion of depth. The requirement that we consider only connected variables reflects the idea that only individuals that are related to each other are counted. The fact that only nested variables are considered only reflects the idea that parallel quantifiers do not count. The difference between the old definition and the new one is in a sense inessential. Clearly, the new depth of each quantificational sentence is smaller than or equal to its old depth. Moreover, it may be shown that for each sentence F there is an effectively constructible equivalent sentence whose old depth equals the new depth of F. However, in spite of the small difference between them, for many purposes the sharper new definition is preferable to the old one.

certain changes in our game rules which nevertheless are entirely natural.

The connection between the notion of depth and the idea of the number of individuals we are considering together has a neat formal counterpart. If it is required (as we have done and as it is natural to do) that quantifiers with overlapping scopes should always have different variables bound to them, then the depth of a sentence is the minimum to which we can reduce the number of different bound variables of F by renaming them in the usual way. It is, in other words, just the number of different bound individual symbols we need in F.[34]

For quantification theory, we may thus reformulate the sense III (b) of analyticity in a more explicit way as follows:

III (c) An argument step is analytic if and only if the degree of the conclusion is smaller than or equal to the degree of at least one of the premisses.

7. *Further explanations*

It should be made clear that the number of individuals one is considering in their relation to each other in a sentence has little to do with the number of individuals that are asserted to exist in the world by the sentence. When I say that each number has a successor I am in some sense speaking of all numbers. I am not considering them all in their relation to one another, however. I am not saying anything about the interrelations of any two arbitrarily chosen numbers, although something may follow from what I say concerning their interrelations. I am in an obvious sense of the word considering only two individuals at one and the same time: an arbitrary number and its successor. Likewise in saying that a relation is transitive, I am in a sense speaking of its whole field, but I am relating only three members of the field to each other at one and the same time.

Sense III (c) of analyticity may be applied to longer arguments in the same two ways as sense II. We may say that a proof

---

[34] The intuitive meaning of the degree of a sentence as the number of individuals we are considering at one and the same time in it is straightforward enough to have caught already the eye of C. S. Peirce, at least in a simple special case. In his *Collected Papers* (note 22 to Chapter II above), vol. 3, section 392, we read: 'The algebra of Boole affords a language by which anything may be expressed which can be said without speaking of more than one individual at the time.'

is analytic if and only if all its steps are analytic in sense III (c). This will be designated as sense III (d) of analyticity. A much more important sense of analyticity is obtained, however, by disregarding the direction of the argument. In this sense—we shall call it sense III (e)—a proof of F_2 from F_1 is analytic if and only if the degree of each of the intermediate stages is smaller than, or equal to, the degree of either F_1 or F_2. That this sense is more natural than sense III (d) is suggested by the fact that by contrapositing all the steps of a proof of F_2 from F_1 we obtain a proof of $\sim F_1$ from $\sim F_2$. In sense III (e) the old and the new proofs are synthetic or analytic simultaneously, as one seems to be entitled to expect on the basis of the fact that the difference between the two proofs seems inessential for our purposes. In sense III (d), however, one of them may be synthetic and the other analytic, which seems rather odd.

A logical truth of quantification theory may be called analytic if it can be proved without making use of sentences of a degree higher than that of the sentence to be proved. In other words, a logical truth of quantification theory is analytic if and only if it can be proved from propositional tautologies of the same degree analytically in sense III (e). A sentence is analytically inconsistent if and only if its inconsistency may be proved without using intermediate stages whose degree would be higher than its own degree. In other words, a sentence is analytically inconsistent if and only if a propositional contradiction of the same degree can be derived from it analytically in sense III (e).

In many of the senses we have defined, the analyticity of a logical truth or the possibility of deriving a sentence from another analytically depends on the underlying selection of axioms and of rules of proof. In order to specify these senses of analyticity more closely, we shall therefore have to say more about the selection of axioms and of rules of inference. Only when the principles of this selection are described more carefully can we say that we have fully defined the relevant senses of analyticity.[35] I shall return to this problem in Chapter VIII below.

[35] We shall not attempt, however, to derive a definition of the class of logical truths from any sense of analyticity. We shall take it for granted that the class of all the logical truths of quantification theory has already been defined, and we inquire into its relation to the several senses of analyticity. Likewise, we shall take for granted the usual ways of axiomatizing quantification theory, and inquire into

The senses III (c)–(e) of analyticity are variations of one and the same basic idea III. Between them, they offer a close reconstruction of Kant's notion of analyticity as he used it in his philosophy of mathematics. I shall later try to explain in more detail how Kant came to use this notion of analyticity and of syntheticity. Here I shall only recall that for Kant the essence of the mathematical method was the use of constructions, i.e., the introduction of representatives of individuals as distinguished from general concepts, and that was also what in his view made mathematical arguments synthetic.[36] Thus Kant in effect explained the synthetic character of mathematical modes of reasoning by pointing out that they are synthetic in our sense III.

We shall return to sense III of analyticity and to its relation to Kant's philosophy of mathematics later, especially in Chapter VIII. The most challenging question which has to be left

their status with respect to the different ways of distinguishing between analytic and synthetic.

[36] Kant defined construction as the introduction or 'exhibition' *a priori* of an intuition which corresponds to a general concept. (See *Critique of Pure Reason*, 713 = B 741.) As we have already observed, by an intuition Kant meant in the first place the representative of an individual. Hence a construction is for him the introduction (*a priori*) of a representative of an individual to illustrate a general concept. For additional evidence for this interpretation, see *Prolegomena*, § 7 (p. 281 of the Academy Edition) and the literature mentioned in note 38 to Chapter I above. This interpretation may seem far-fetched and even paradoxical. Perhaps the easiest way of realizing how natural it in fact is, is to ascertain that its most surprising feature is found without any ambiguity in Kant's pre-critical writings. In his 'Untersuchungen über die Deutlichkeit der Grundsätze der natürlichen Theologie und Moral' (1764) Kant had already claimed that mathematicians always consider general concepts *in concreto*, that is to say, by means of their individual instances. It is to be noted that this explicit doctrine is formulated without using the problematic concept of an intuition, and is therefore free of all the ambiguities of this difficult concept. There is no reason to doubt that Kant's statement in the *Critique of Pure Reason* that in mathematical reasoning one typically employs intuitions to represent general concepts is intended to formulate in the first place the very same pre-critical theory, no matter what superstructure Kant subsequently had built on the top of it. The models on which this theory of Kant's was based will be commented on briefly in Chapter IX below. Further evidence for this kind of interpretation is also found in the works of E. W. Beth, to which I am in many ways greatly indebted. Among them, one has to mention 'Kants Einteilung der Urteile in analytische und synthetische', *Algemeen Nederlands Tijdschrift voor Wijsbegeerte en Psychologie*, vol. 46 (1953–4), pp. 253–64; 'Critical Epochs in the Development of the Theory of Science', *British Journal for the Philosophy of Science*, vol. 1 (1950), pp. 27–42; *La Crise de la raison et la logique* (Gauthier-Villars, Paris, 1957); 'Über Lockes "Allgemeines Dreieck"', *Kant-Studien*, vol. 48 (1956–7), pp. 361–80; *The Foundations of Mathematics* (North-Holland Publishing Company, Amsterdam, 1959), pp. 41–7.

suspended here is the question: was Kant right? Are the modes o argument which Kant thought of as being typically mathemat: cal but which we now classify as belonging to quantificatio theory really synthetic in sense III, as Kant thought? To th question I shall also return in later chapters of this book.

8. *Analyticity* v. *information*

It remains to mention one more sense of analyticity. It can b obtained by asking the same question as gave us the other sense of analyticity, viz. the question: what does the premiss of a inference give us? Perhaps the most natural answer is to say tha it gives us a certain amount of information. On this view a ste of inference is analytic if it does not increase this informatior i.e., if the information carried by the conclusion is no greate than the information carried by the premisses. A sentence i analytic in this sense if it does not convey any information. It i natural to call such a sentence a tautology. This variant o analytic truth may therefore be labelled analytic truth in th sense of tautological truth. It will also be called analyticity i sense IV. It will be examined in some detail in the next chapter

Even without any detailed discussion it is obvious enough tha this sense of analyticity has played an important role in philo sophical literature. Kant already called analytic judgement merely 'explicative' (*Erläuterungsurteile*) and identified syntheti ones with judgements which extend the scope of our knowledg (*Erweiterungsurteile*).[37] Earlier, we found that at other times Kan also came fairly close to sense III of analyticity. His notion o analyticity may therefore be characterized as a mixture of thes two senses. It was already noted that the apparent similarit between his usage and our sense I of analyticity is largely a illusion, in spite of the fact that this aspect of Kant's views ha often been emphasized in recent expositions. His notion o analyticity differs from the prevalent modern one more tha many writers have realized.

In recent times, philosophers have also frequently asserte that logical and perhaps also mathematical truths are in som sense 'empty' or 'tautological'. The sense involved has no always been made very clear, however. If we had to characteriz the current notion of analyticity very briefly, it may be calle

[37] *Prolegomena*, § 2 (p. 255 of the Academy Edition); *Critique of Pure Reason*, B 17–19

compound of senses I and IV, although different writers have ⊂ressed the two elements differently.

This compound notion is not without difficulties. The un--arity of sense I and the difficulties of making it clear have ⊏ready been registered. The relation of the two senses has not ⊏en understood very clearly, either. Sometimes they have been ⊃nnected in an erroneous way. It is plausible to say that while ⊏ue) analytic sentences are true in the sole virtue of the mean--gs of the terms they involve, true synthetic sentences are true ⊔ virtue of matters of fact also. It may also seem plausible to ⊃nclude from this that in the same way as synthetic sentences ⊃nvey information concerning matters of fact, in the same way ⊓alytic sentences convey information concerning the meanings ⌐our terms or other conceptual matters. Their apparent empti--⊇ss is merely emptiness of non-linguistic information. In par--cular, this idea has been suggested as an explanation of the fact ⊔at logical and mathematical sentences have some unmistak--⊃le informative function in spite of being tautologies in the ⊏nse of conveying no information concerning matters of fact. ⌐has been suggested that the information they carry is really ⊃nceptual or perhaps linguistic.[38]

This line of thought appears to me unsatisfactory.[39] The prob--⊓ of clarifying sense IV of analyticity is primarily a problem ⌐ clarifying the notion of information-content on which it is ⊔sed. In so far as this clarification can be achieved, it seems to ⊔e, sentences analytic in sense IV turn out not to have any ⊓formation-content to them, linguistic or otherwise. There may ⊏ a sense in which analytic sentences serve to illustrate concep--⊔al relationships, but the sense in which they convey informa--⊃n concerning such relationships has never been spelled out

[38] See, e.g., A. J. Ayer, *Language, Truth, and Logic* (Gollancz, London, 1936, ⊂ond ed., 1946; reprinted by Dover Publications, New York), pp. 79–80: 'When ⊇ say that analytic propositions are devoid of factual content . . . we are not ⊇gesting that they are senseless. For . . . they do enlighten us by illustrating the ⊓y in which we use certain symbols. . . . We see, then, that there is a sense in ⊓ich analytic propositions do give us new knowledge. They call attention to ⊔guistic usages. . . .'

[39] Some of this unsatisfactoriness appears already from the fact that the mathe--⊓tical truths which are best suited for illuminating the basic concepts of a ⊓thematical theory are normally rather trivial, while the results which a mathe--⊓tician would consider interesting and informative are seldom useful for illustrat--g how the symbols which occur in them are used.

with sufficient clarity. It seems to me, moreover, that in so fa as this informative function of analytic sentences can be clarifie and studied, the useful sense of analyticity is III rather than The sense in which non-trivial mathematical results conve information even though they can be proved in quantificatio theory is a significant and important philosophical problem, bu I think that it is best approached by asking whether they ar analytic or synthetic in sense III. This is one of the things w shall keep in mind when we study senses III and IV of analyt city (in the inverse order) a little more closely. If and when the and the other possible senses of analyticity have been satisfa torily charted we shall perhaps have a somewhat better right call our philosophical age the age of analysis.

9. *Different senses of analyticity*

I Analytic truths are true in the sole virtue of the meanin of the terms they contain. (Analytic truth as conceptual truth

I (a) Analytic truth is based solely on the definitions of term

I (b) Analytic truths comprise definitions and their logic consequences.

I (c) Analytic are those truths which can be proved by th sole means of general logical laws and definitions (Frege).

I (d) Analytic truths comprise the truths of logic and all th truths that can be reduced to them by substituting synonyms fo synonyms (Quine).

II A (valid) argument step is analytic if the conclusion is subsentence of one of the premisses.

II (a) An argument is analytic if all its steps are analytic sense II.

II (b) A (valid) proof of the sentence F_1 from the sentence is analytic if all the sentences occurring as intermediate stag of this proof are subsentences of either F_0 or F_1.

III A (valid) argument step is analytic if it does not introdu new individuals into the discussion.

III (a) An analytic argument cannot lead from the existen of an individual to the existence of a different individual (Kan

III (b) A (valid) argument step is analytic if it does not i crease the number of individuals one is considering in the relation to each other.

III (c) A (valid) argument step is analytic if the degree of th conclusion is no greater than the degree of at least one of the premisses.

III (d) An argument is analytic if all its steps are analytic in sense III (c).

III (e) A (valid) proof of the sentence F_1 from F_0 is analytic if none of the sentences occurring as intermediate stages of this proof has a higher degree than F_0 and F_1.

IV A (valid) argument step is analytic if the information carried by the conclusion is no greater than the information carried by the premisses. (Analytic truth as tautological truth.)

(In this list 'if' is to be read 'if and only if'.)

VII

ARE LOGICAL TRUTHS TAUTOLOGIES?

1. *The ups and downs of the concept of tautology*

THE title of this chapter suggests a period-piece. The period in question is the twenties of this century. Inspired by the ideas Ludwig Wittgenstein had put forward in the *Tractatus Logico-Philosophicus*, many philosophers then employed the concept of tautology and sought to apply it more widely than Wittgenstein had done or in a way different from his.[1] A typical question asked by such philosophers was whether the truths of this or that part of logic or of mathematics are tautologies or not.

These questions can be understood as questions of analyticity in sense IV, as explained in the preceding chapter. In this sense, a sentence is analytic if and only if it conveys no factual information concerning the subject-matter of which it apparently speaks, and an inference (say from F_1 to F_2) is analytic if and only if it does not increase the information of our sentences, that is to say, if and only if the factual information conveyed by F_2 is smaller than or equal to the information conveyed by F_1.[2] In order to avoid confusion with the other senses of analyticity, I shall here speak simply of tautologies and of tautological inference.

I shall overlook the fact that the term 'tautology' does not sit as happily with analytic sentences as it does with analytic infer-

---

[1] Ludwig Wittgenstein, *Tractatus Logico-Philosophicus* (Routledge & Kegan Paul, London, 1922); cf., e.g., F. P. Ramsey, *The Foundations of Mathematics* (Routledge & Kegan Paul, London, 1931, especially the title essay); Hans Hahn, *Logik, Mathematik und Naturerkennen* (Springer, Vienna, 1933).

[2] Strictly speaking, it ought to be required that the information conveyed by F_2 is contained in the information conveyed by F_1 (instead of requiring only that the amount of the former is smaller than or equal to the amount of the latter). We take it for granted, however, that this stricter requirement is satisfied for all the types of inference we are here interested in as soon as the weaker one is satisfied. It is important to note that we are not here trying to derive a definition or a characterization of logical inferences from the requirement that they are tautological. We assume that we know what logical inferences and logical truths are, and merely inquire into the question whether they are tautologies in some reasonable sense of the word. (Cf. note 35 to Chapter VI above.)

ences. A tautological sentence is not tautological in the literal sense of being a pleonasm. It is, rather, empty or 'nugatory' in the sense of saying nothing.

Why did the notion of tautology enjoy the currency it enjoyed in the twenties and why have most philosophers subsequently been disenchanted with it? This question is not asked here only or primarily because of its historical interest. We are not here concerned with the motives of individual philosophers, but with those features of the concept of a tautology which originally promised a great deal but which have since disappointed many philosophers. So conceived, our question turns out to have considerable topical interest.[3]

2. *Semantic information in propositional logic*

One reason for the popularity of the concept of tautology was probably its success in the limited area of propositional logic where Wittgenstein had primarily used it. There the situation can be described very aptly by saying that the truths of this part of logic are as many tautologies. In propositional logic, we really seem to have a good grasp of the factors which determine the amount of information which a sentence carries and which justify Wittgenstein's claim that the truths of propositional logic are tautologies, i.e., carry no information at all.

In order to enable you to see the situation clearly, I must briefly sketch the way in which the notions of information and of tautology can be brought to bear on propositional logic. A second reason why I must cover this familiar ground is that I have to introduce a certain amount of notation for later use. In order to conform to current terminology, I shall from now on speak of *semantic information* instead of 'information-content' or 'information'.

Broadly speaking, the concepts of semantic information and of tautology can be brought to bear on propositional logic because in this part of logic we can always list all the possible worlds (possible states of affairs, possible courses of events) that can be described by means of certain definite resources of

---

[3] We are not asking whether the philosophers who used or rejected the concept of tautology were aware of the underlying justification for their enthusiasm or for their disappointment. Much of this justification was not spelled out until considerably later.

expression. In propositional logic, such means of expression normally comprise a number of unanalysed sentences (atomic sentences) plus a number of suitably chosen propositional connectives, for which we shall here employ the connectives '$\sim$', '&', 'v'. Given these, the relevant 'possible worlds' are described by certain conjunctions which we shall call, following a time-honoured precedent established by Boole, the *constituents* of propositional logic.[4] If we are given the atomic sentences F_1, F_2,..., F_k, then a constituent contains as a member, for each $i = 1, 2,..., k$, either F_i or $\sim F_i$. It contains no other members. For instance, if $k = 2$, $F_1 = $ 'it is raining', and $F_2 = $ 'the wind is blowing', then constituents are the following sentences:

'it is raining and the wind is blowing',
'it is raining but the wind is not blowing',
'it is not raining but the wind is blowing',
'it is not raining nor is the wind blowing'.,

It is intuitively obvious that these are all the possibilities concerning the weather that can be specified by means of the two unanalysed sentences 'it is raining' and 'the wind is blowing'.

Given the atomic sentences F_1, F_2,..., F_k, I shall designate an arbitrary constituent by:

$$(1) \qquad \prod_{i=1}^{i=k} F_i$$

or, more simply, by: $\prod\limits_{i=1} F_i$ or, still more simply, by $\prod F$. There are obviously just 2^k constituents. Different constituents are distinguished from each other by attaching subscripts to them. I shall assume that these subscripts run consecutively from 1 to 2^k. This makes it possible to use the same kind of notation repeatedly in representing one and the same sentence, as I shall do in the sequel.

In propositional logic, every consistent sentence has a normal form (complete disjunctive normal form) in which it is a disjunction of some (or all) of the constituents (formed from the atomic sentences which occur in it). What this means may be explained informally as follows: in propositional logic, each consistent sentence admits some of the possibilities listed by the constituents

[4] Cf. George Boole, *An Investigation of the Laws of Thought* (Walton and Maberly, London, 1854), p. 75 (Ch. V, sec. 11).

and excludes the rest. It is true if one of the admitted possibilities is realized, false if one of the excluded ones comes about. A logically false (inconsistent) sentence may be said to exclude all the possibilities, whereas a logical truth of propositional logic admits all of them. Conversely, a sentence which admits all the possibilities is logically true.

Now in an obvious sense a sentence is the more informative the more possibilities it excludes. If you do not see this at once, try thinking of the different possibilities as so many contingencies you have to be prepared to meet. The more alternatives you can rule out, the more narrowly you can restrict the scope of your preparations, and the more you can say that you know about the subject matter at hand.

As a sort of rough measure of the information which a sentence carries, we may therefore use the number of possibilities it excludes, in other words, the number of constituents missing from its normal form. Somewhat more general ways of measuring the semantic information of a sentence are obtained by first assigning a 'weight' p_j to each constituent $\prod_j F$, in such a way that each p_j is between one and zero and that the sum of all the weights p_j is one. Each such number p_j may be thought of as the probability *a priori* that the state of affairs or course of events described by $\prod_j F$ is realized. Then the sum of the weights of the constituents missing from the normal form of a sentence serves as a measure of the semantic information of the sentence.[5]

For various special purposes one may want to select this measure differently. Among the candidates for the role there is the measure given by the function

$$(2) \qquad \log_2\left(\frac{1}{1-s}\right) = -\log_2 p$$

where s is the semantic information just defined and p the sum of the weights of the constituents in the normal form of F.

Independently of the choice between these particular measures, it is seen that there is in any case exactly one class of sentences which do not carry any semantic information at all. They are the sentences which admit all the alternatives and

---

[5] For certain purposes, we may want to have this sum multiplied by a number which depends on k before we admit it as a measure of semantic information. The simplest choice would be to choose k itself as this factor.

hence exclude none of them. Their emptiness is also obvious from an intuitive point of view. They are the sentences whose import does not save us from being prepared for all the possible contingencies anyway. (As Wittgenstein says in *Tractatus* 4.461, 'I know nothing about the weather when I know that it is either raining or not raining.') And as we saw four paragraphs ago, these empty sentences are exactly the logically true sentences of propositional logic. The truths of propositional logic are therefore tautologies; they do not carry any information. Similarly, it is easily seen that in the logically valid inferences of propositional logic the information carried by the conclusion is smaller than or at most equal to the information carried by the premisses.

The term 'tautology' thus characterizes very aptly the truths and inferences of propositional logic. One reason for its one-time appeal to philosophers was undoubtedly its success in this limited area.[6]

One implicit reason for the decline of its appeal is equally undoubtedly the difficulty of generalizing it in a satisfactory way to other parts of logic.[7] In discussing this difficulty, quantification theory will again constitute a convenient testing ground for the different views that have been put forward.

3. *Semantic information in first-order logic: Carnap's approach*

It is not that philosophers have not tried to generalize the notion of semantic information. The most impressive generalization is undoubtedly the theory of semantic information which has been developed by Carnap and Bar-Hillel on the basis of Carnap's theory of inductive probability.[8] The defects which

[6] The exact character of this success was not formulated at the time, however. The first philosopher to emphasize the connection between the information (content) of a sentence and the number of possibilities it rules out was probably Karl R. Popper; see his *Logik der Forschung* (Springer, Vienna, 1934, translated with additional notes and appendices as *Logic of Scientific Discovery* (Hutchinson, London, 1959), section 35 and *passim*.

[7] There have been a great many generalizations of the notion of tautology, but few of them have succeeded in retaining any semblance of a connection between the generalized notion and the idea that a tautology somehow admits all the alternatives that there are and hence does not convey any information, provided the number of these alternatives is to be finite. For an attempted generalization in which this connection is not severed, see G. H. von Wright, *Logical Studies* (Routledge and Kegan Paul, London, 1957), first essay, originally published separately under the title *Form and Content in Logic* (Cambridge University Press, 1949).

[8] Yehoshua Bar-Hillel and Rudolf Carnap, 'Semantic Information', *British Journal of the Philosophy of Science*, vol. 4 (1953), pp. 147–57; Rudolf Carnap and

seem to attach to this generalization perhaps illustrate the underlying reasons for many philosophers' disillusionment with the notion of tautology.

I assume that the reader is somewhat familiar with the basic ideas of Carnap's approach.[9] To express the matter very briefly, Carnap uses the concept of a state-description as an explication of the notion of a 'description of a possible world'. Now for many purposes there are only inessential differences between the notions of a state-description and of a constituent. Each constituent may be thought of as the conjunction of all the members of some state-description. Hence what Carnap does is in effect to extend to other parts of logic the same approach which was just used in propositional logic. In order to specify this approach completely one has to specify the set of atomic sentences which are being presupposed. This set is in Carnap's approach specified in the simple and obvious way. Given a set of free singular terms and predicate symbols, the relevant set of atomic sentences consists simply of all the atomic sentences which can be formed from these free singular terms and predicate symbols. In what follows, it is normally assumed (when dealing with Carnapian methods) that some fixed set of free singular terms and of predicate symbols has been given as the basis of the discussion.

This suffices to indicate the main features of Carnap's approach to the notion of semantic information, for in other respects the crucial concepts may be developed essentially in the same way as we did above in the case of propositional logic. There is, however, one important further feature of Carnap's theory which remains to be considered. This contribution of Carnap's consists of a particular way of assigning *a priori* probabilities to the states of affairs described by the different state-descriptions.[10] In a nutshell, this way of assigning probabilities

Yehoshua Bar-Hillel, 'An Outline of a Theory of Semantic Information', *M.I.T. Research Laboratory in Electronics*, Technical Report no. 247, 1953; reprinted in Y. Bar-Hillel, *Language and Information* (Addison-Wesley and The Jerusalem Academic Press, Reading, Mass., Palo Alto, Cal., London, and Jerusalem, 1964).

[9] Rudolf Carnap, *Meaning and Necessity* (The University of Chicago Press, Chicago, 1947; second ed. 1956); *Logical Foundations of Probability* (The University of Chicago Press, Chicago, 1950; second ed. 1963).

[10] See *Logical Foundations of Probability*, Carnap's remarks on m^* and c^*, pp. 294–6 and elsewhere. It must be added that Carnap has subsequently modified his position concerning the choice of measure function, and that my discussion here therefore pertains only to Carnap's position in 1950 as far as this problem is concerned.

amounts to considering as equiprobable, not the different states of affairs listed by the state-descriptions, but rather the different structures these states of affairs may exhibit. Each of these structures is described by a disjunction of all the state-descriptions which can be transformed into each other by permuting free singular terms. Each such disjunction is called by Carnap a *structure-description*. In other words, we may say that transformability into each other by an arbitrary permutation of free singular terms defines an equivalence relation on the set of all state-descriptions with fixed free singular terms and predicate symbols. The disjunction of all the members of some equivalence class is a structure-description. Each structure-description is given the same weight by Carnap, and this weight is then divided evenly among all the members of the structure-description in question, i.e., divided evenly among all the state-descriptions that make it true. Since the number of such state-descriptions is different for different structure-descriptions, not all state-descriptions will have the same weight.

Intuitively, it may be said that in this approach one is not considering in the first place the different states of affairs when one is assigning weights to state-descriptions.[11] One is primarily considering the different *kinds of* states of affairs; and one is giving an equal probability to all these different kinds of states of affairs ('kinds of possible worlds'). However, this does not yet fully specify Carnap's approach, for this notion of 'a kind of possible world' can still be interpreted in different ways (as we shall see). Carnap in effect interprets it as a possible world with a given structure, in other words, a possible world determined up to a permutation of the individuals.

Given all this, the semantic information which a sentence carries may be defined essentially in the same way as it was defined in propositional logic. Given a state-description μ, each quantificational sentence whose predicate symbols and free singular terms all occur in the members of μ will be either true or false in the world completely described by μ. In the first case the sentence may be said to admit of the alternative described by the state-description in question, in the latter case to exclude

[11] This way of explaining (or illustrating) Carnap's choice of a measure function (i.e., the assignment of *a priori* probabilities) is not found in Carnap's writings, and I do not claim that it fully represents his intentions.

it. The semantic information which a sentence carries may be defined simply as the sum of the weights of all the state-descriptions which it excludes. Various alternative measures are of course also possible here, measures which might, e.g., be generalizations of (2) in the same way as the measure just defined is a generalization of the measure we originally defined for propositional logic.

It is important to realize that all these definitions of semantic information are relative to a list of all the different states of affairs that can be described by means of certain definite resources of expression and therefore also relative to these resources of expression themselves. In other words, they are all relative to a given set of free singular terms and predicate symbols or, if you prefer, relative to a given fixed set of individuals and predicates. The individuals in question are all the individuals that together constitute the universe of discourse which we are presupposing.

4. *The shortcomings of Carnapian ideas*

Why is this characterization of the notion of semantic information (together with the associated notion of zero information, i.e., the notion of tautology) less than satisfactory? Some logicians are probably inclined to argue that it is in fact satisfactory. They are likely to argue that the disillusionment with the notion of tautology which the attitude of most philosophers towards this notion seems to betray is not due to an objective evaluation of the situation. It seems to me, however, that Carnap's approach is in fact burdened by grave defects which to some extent justify the suspicions of the generalizability of the notion of semantic information along Carnapian lines.

We have to be careful here, however. I am willing to admit and to argue that many widespread charges against Carnap's approach do not really reflect on its significance.[12] The apparent dependence of this approach on the logical independence of the predicates (and individuals) we are dealing with, and the doubts which have been expressed concerning the status of the 'semantic rules' or 'meaning postulates' which have been employed for the purpose of dispensing with this dependence, are cases in

[12] For examples of such criticism, see the works referred to in note 2 to the preceding chapter.

point. There are more serious things to be said against it, however. The main point may be expressed as follows: formally speaking, the whole approach, including the notion of a state-description, is relative to a given set of free singular terms. (It is also relative to a set of predicates, but that fact is of lesser importance.) Informally speaking, the possible worlds or possible kinds of worlds which Carnap contemplates are specified by specifying the individuals there are in the world in question. In order to describe such a world, we must know all its individuals; moreover, we must know that they are all the individuals there are in the world in question. In order to say what such a description looks like, we have to know how many individuals there are, i.e., what the size of our universe of discourse is. If a new individual is added to the system, most of the approach is thrown out of gear. For instance, the semantic information which is assigned to a sentence often changes. In this respect, one can level against Carnap's approach one of the well-known charges which Max Black has levelled against Tarski's semantical theory of truth.[13]

As a consequence, we cannot apply the approach to any situation which would be even approximately realistic, for in most actual applications we do not know the whole of the universe we are studying. This is philosophically pernicious not because it shows that Carnap's approach is without applications. It may still have some applications, and even if it had none, it might perhaps still serve as a simplified model which clarifies the nature of certain aspects of our scientific enterprise. The defects I indicated are philosophically pernicious, however, in that they tend to misrepresent in a certain sense the whole nature of this scientific enterprise. Part of this enterprise is to come to know the universe in which we live, and a part of this task is to find out what individuals there are in the world and how many they are. In so far as logic is intended to help this enterprise, or to serve to clarify its nature, we cannot start from a situation in which we have not only exhausted the individuals of the universe of discourse but have also come to know that we have done so or in which we have at the very least come to know

---

[13] Max Black, 'The Semantic Definition of Truth', *Analysis*, vol. 8 (1947–8); reprinted in *Philosophy and Analysis*, ed. by Margaret Macdonald (Basil Blackwell, Oxford, 1954), pp. 245–60.

the number of all existing individuals. If it were true, as some Carnapians have implied, that we do not really have a fully specified language until we have specified the domain of individuals, then cosmologists could not speak a fully specified language until they had already completed an important part of their task. In Carnap's semantics there is no room for the discovery of new individuals or for their introduction into our reasoning, in spite of the fact that this is part and parcel of the work, not only of cosmologists, but of many other scientists as well.

This difficulty is more general than the difficulties which the infinity of one's domain of individuals may cause. The source of trouble is not the possible infinity of the domain but rather the dependence of many of Carnap's key concepts on the size of the universe, finite or infinite. For instance, the 'kinds of possible worlds' (meaning non-isomorphic possible worlds) which are central in his approach depend on the size of the domain. (There are more and more of them when the size grows.) Many of the awkward consequences of letting the domain become infinite already make their appearance in almost as damaging a manner in a fairly large finite universe.

Again, the difficulties I am trying to describe are not just difficulties in writing out the different state-descriptions, whether these difficulties are thought of as caused by the large size of our universe of discourse or by our ignorance of the exact number of individuals it contains. They are brought out by the general theoretical problems into which Carnap's approach runs and which can usually be traced to the dependence of his concepts on the underlying selection of individuals. These theoretical problems have little to do with the practical impossibility of spelling out the state-descriptions one by one.

Here it suffices to mention only the most striking difficulty. On Carnap's definitions, the probability (*a posteriori* probability, Carnap's 'degree of confirmation') of each universally quantified sentence which is not logically true becomes less and less when the number of individuals in the domain increases, and becomes zero as this number goes on to infinity.[14] In a

---

[14] Carnap, *Logical Foundations of Probability*, pp. 570–5. Subsequently, Carnap has developed a different explication of inductive probability for which this undesirable result does not hold. It is mentioned, but not discussed, in § 26 of Carnap's reply

sufficiently large domain each factual generalization is thus as improbable as you may wish. Correspondingly, the semantic information of each existential sentence which is not logically false becomes vanishingly small as the size of the universe increases without limit. Of course this is exactly the opposite of what one would expect on intuitive grounds, for the larger the universe, the harder it is to find an individual of the desired kind there, and the more informative is therefore a sentence which affirms the existence of such an individual.

This alone suffices to show that the results which Carnap's approach yields cannot be accepted as they stand as a satisfactory definition of semantic information for the whole of quantification theory. The improvements which have been published by Carnap himself, by John Kemeny, and by others, do not alter the picture substantially.[15]

5. *Semantic information in first-order logic: constituents as descriptions of kinds of worlds*

Can we do better than this? Can we free the notion of semantic information from the fetters of the notion of a domain of individuals? In order to do so, we have to describe an exhaustive set of possible worlds or, rather, possible kinds of worlds without mentioning explicitly all the individuals these worlds contain. The notion of a state-description is ruled out by these requirements.

Expressed more precisely, the question is whether we can list all the possible kinds of worlds that can be described by means of given resources of expression. As usual, we shall use quantification theory (first-order logic) as a test case.

Now in quantification theory the answer to this question

---

to his critics in *The Philosophy of Rudolf Carnap*, ed. by P. A. Schilpp (The Library of Living Philosophers, Open Court Publishing Company, La Salle, Ill., 1964). It should also be added that Carnap requires in *Logical Foundations of Probability* that the probabilities of *singular* statements must be independent of the size of the domain (see pp. 290–2). However, general and existential statements have no such independence in his system.

[15] Cf. Rudolf Carnap, 'Meaning Postulates', *Philosophical Studies*, vol. 3 (1952), pp. 65–73; Y. Bar-Hillel, 'A Note on State-Descriptions', *Philosophical Studies*, vol. 2 (1951), pp. 72–5; John Kemeny, 'Extension of the Methods of Inductive Logic', *Philosophical Studies*, vol. 3 (1952), pp. 38–42; John Kemeny, 'A Logical Measure Function', *Journal of Symbolic Logic*, vol. 18 (1953), pp. 289–308. Cf. also note 14 above for an unpublished improvement by Carnap.

depends on the meaning we assign to the phrase 'given resources of expression'. If these resources are limited only by restricting our attention to a finite number of predicates and free singular terms but not by imposing any limitations on the use of quantifiers and sentential connectives, there is in most cases no hope of compiling a list of the desired kind, provided it has to be finite.

If further restrictions are introduced, however, the answer is different. In the preceding chapter, the concept of the degree of a quantificational sentence was introduced. Formally speaking, the degree of F is the number of the free singular terms of F plus the numbers of layers of quantifiers F contains (the depth of F). Informally speaking, the degree of F is the maximum number of individuals considered together at one and the same time in F. The notion of a degree thus has a very intuitive meaning. In view of the intuitiveness of the notion of the degree of a sentence it is not unnatural to restrict it. But if a restriction is imposed on this characteristic parameter of quantificational sentences, the situation is in most respects the same as it is in propositional logic. If we consider all the sentences that can be built out of a given finite number of predicates and free singular terms and which have a degree smaller than a given finite number, then there exists a way of listing all the different kinds of worlds that can be described by means of these resources of expression. If all these restrictions are observed, each consistent sentence again has a normal form in which it is a disjunction of a finite number of sentences we shall again call *constituents*. These constituents describe the different kinds of possible worlds that can be specified under the restrictions in question. By listing them, we in effect list these possible kinds of worlds as well. The existence of this normal form means that each sentence again admits of some of the possible worlds and excludes the rest, in the same way as in propositional logic.

These normal forms may be called *distributive normal forms*. It is not a part of my purpose here to study their properties in any detail. Their nature and some of their most important characteristics have been discussed elsewhere, although not yet as fully as they seem to deserve.[16]

---

[16] See Chapter XI below as well as the following works of mine: 'Distributive Normal Forms and Deductive Interpolation', *Zeitschrift für mathematische Logik und*

The constituents of which the distributive normal forms consist serve much better than Carnap's structure-descriptions the purposes for which the latter were cast for. They are also in a sense descriptions of *kinds of* possible worlds, although this sense is different from the sense in which this expression applies to structure-descriptions. The principal difference is that our descriptions of possible worlds can be specified independently of any one particular domain of individuals. Mainly for this reason, they seem to be free from most of the defects from which Carnap's concepts suffer. We can develop an interesting concept of inductive probability by using constituents in the same way Carnap uses his structure-descriptions.[17] If a domain of individuals (i.e., a set of free singular terms) is given in addition to a set of predicate symbols, then the weight of a constituent may be divided evenly among the state-descriptions which make it true (in the monadic case) or as evenly as is compatible with the assignment of weights to other constituents (in the polyadic case). The resulting concept of inductive probability is such that a universally quantified sentence normally has a non-zero probability (although it is not logically true) even in an infinite domain of individuals. In fact, the *a priori* probability of every sentence containing only such free singular terms as are already included within those 'means of expression' employed in certain constituents is independent of the size of the universe. Moreover, it may be shown that the inductive probability of a generalization increases in certain typical cases as the number of observed confirming instances grows (provided of course that no disconfirming instances are observed).[18]

Grundlagen der Mathematik, vol. 10 (1964), pp. 185–91; 'Distributive Normal Forms in the Calculus of Predicates', in the series *Acta Philosophica Fennica*, vol. 6 (1953); 'Are Logical Truths Analytic?', *Philosophical Review*, vol. 74 (1965), pp. 178–203. It may be added that the transformability of each sentence of a given depth into a distributive normal form with the same depth holds also when the notion of depth is modified as indicated in note 32 to Chapter VI above.

[17] See my papers, 'Towards a Theory of Inductive Generalization', in *Proceedings of the 1964 International Congress of Logic, Methodology, and Philosophy of Science*, ed. by Yehoshua Bar-Hillel (North-Holland Publishing Company, Amsterdam, 1965), pp. 274–88, 'A Two-Dimensional Continuum of Inductive Methods', in *Aspects of Inductive Logic*, ed. by Jaakko Hintikka and Patrick Suppes (North-Holland Publishing Company, Amsterdam, 1966), pp. 113–32, and 'Induction by Enumeration and Induction by Elimination', in *The Problem of Inductive Logic*, ed. by Imre Lakatos (North-Holland Publishing Company, Amsterdam, 1968), pp. 191–216.

[18] This is shown in the papers referred to in the preceding note for the monadic

From these inductive probabilities one can obtain a measure of semantic information in the same way as before. The simplest definition would be to take the sum of the *a priori* probabilities of those constituents (with the same free singular terms and predicate symbols, and with the same depth) missing from the normal form of a sentence as a measure of the semantic information of this sentence.[19] This measure of information is free from the defects that were noted in connection with Carnap's approach.

In terms of distributive normal forms, we may also define certain measures of *logical simplicity* and relate them in an interesting way to the notions of semantic information and inductive probability. These possibilities of development have not been utilized yet, but they promise interesting insights into a number of problems. We cannot investigate them here, however.

6. *The structure of constituents*

There are two questions which we nevertheless have to take up. First of all, we have to make sure that the new constituents really list all the different possibilities concerning the world that we can specify after we have restricted our resources of expression in the way we have done, and that they list all these possibilities in a sense as clear-cut as the one in which the constituents of propositional logic do so. Secondly, we have to examine whether the logical truths of quantification theory are related to these generalized constituents in the same way as the logical truths of propositional logic. In short, we have to examine whether the logical truths of quantification theory are tautologies in the sense obtained from our new measure of semantic information as a special case (zero information).

I think that the first point can be sufficiently established by considering, by way of example, some of the simplest kinds of

case. Although other cases have not yet been studied in detail, there is no reason to expect that they would change the picture substantially. An important qualification is needed here, however: the observed instances must eventually eliminate all the competing simpler generalizations. A second qualification concerning the kind of generalization we are considering is also needed.

[19] This definition could be developed in many different directions. One possible development is to try to take into account the structure of the different constituents that are present in the normal form of a sentence or missing from it.

quantificational constituents. If there are no free singular terms present and if we have merely a number of monadic (one-place) predicate symbols $P_i(x)$ $(i = 1, 2,..., m)$ the constituents will have the following form:

$$(3) \qquad \prod_{k=1}^{k=2^m} (Ex) \prod_{i=1}^{i=m} {}_k P_i(x).$$

This is in a clear-cut sense a description of one kind of a 'possible world'. It is easy to see how this description is accomplished. First, we list all the possible kinds of individuals that can be specified by means of the predicate symbols $P_i(x)$. This is what the conjunctions

$$(4) \qquad \prod_{i=1}^{} {}_k P_i(x) = C_k(x)$$

$(k = 1, 2,..., 2^m)$ do. Then we specify, for each such kind of individual, whether individuals of that kind exist or not. It is perhaps not entirely surprising that everything we can say by the sole means of the predicate symbols $P_i(x)$, of quantifiers, and of sentential connectives, is a disjunction of such descriptions of kinds of possible worlds.

An example perhaps makes the situation clearer. If $m = 2$, that is to say, if we have but two monadic predicate symbols, and if these predicates are expressed by 'red' and 'round', then the different kinds of individuals listed by the different conjunctions (4) are the following:

(5)   'x is red and round',
               'x is red but not round',
               'x is round but not red',
               'x is neither red nor round'.

These are obviously all the different kinds of individuals specifiable by means of the two predicate expressions 'red' and 'round'. Each different kind of possible world that can be described by means of these predicate expressions is specified by indicating, for each kind of individual (5), whether there are such individuals in the world in question. The following are thus examples of such descriptions of possible worlds:

(6)   'There are individuals which are red and round, there are no individuals which are red but not round, there are individuals which are round but not red,

and there are no individuals which are neither red nor round';

(7) 'There are no individuals which are red and round, there are individuals which are red but not round, there are no individuals which are round but not red, and there are no individuals which are neither red nor round'.

We can also see a handy way of paraphrasing a constituent like (3). Instead of listing all the different kinds of individuals that are exemplified and also listing the kinds of individuals that do not exist, it suffices to list the kinds of existing individuals and simply to add that they are *all* the kinds of individuals in existence. This means that each constituent of the form (3) can be rewritten so as to be of the form

(8) $(Ex)C_1(x) \ \& \ (Ex)C_2(x) \ \& \ ... \ \& \ (Ex)C_n(x)$
$\& \ (Ux)(C_1(x) \lor C_2(x) \lor ... \lor C_n(x)),$

where $\{C_i(x)\}$ $(i = 1, 2,..., n)$ is some subset of the set of all conjunctions (4). It can be shown that all the constituents of quantification theory can be similarly rewritten.

For instance, (6) may obviously be rewritten as follows:

(6)* 'There are individuals which are red and round as well as individuals which are round but not red, and every individual is either red and round or else round but not red',

and (7) may be rewritten as follows:

(7)* 'There are individuals which are red but not round, and every individual is red but not round.'

The second example illustrates the fact that the kind of rewriting we are dealing with often simplifies the constituent in question considerably.

In order to gain more insight into the structure of our constituents, let us assume that we are given a number of dyadic (two-place) predicate symbols $R_i(x, y)$ $(i = 1, 2,..., r)$ but no other predicates nor any free singular terms, and that the degree of our sentences is at most 2. Then the constituents are still of form (8). In fact, (8) may be said to be the general form of those constituents which do not contain free singular terms. The definition of the conjunctions $C_i(x)$ has to be changed from case to case, however. Each $C_i(x)$ is now rather like (8):

(9) $(Ey)C'_1(x,y)$ & $(Ey)C'_2(x,y)$ & ... & $(Ey)C'_s(x,y)$

$$\& \ (Uy)(C'_1(x,y) \lor C'_2(x,y) \lor ... \lor C'_s(x,y)) \ \& \ \prod_{i=}^{i=r} R_i(x,x).$$

Here each $C'(x,y)$ is of the form

$$\prod_{i=1}^{i=r} R_i(x,y) \ \& \ \prod_{i=1}^{i=r} R_i(y,x) \ \& \ \prod_{i=1}^{i=r} R_i(y,y).$$

The intuitive meaning of (9) is not very difficult to appreciate. What goes into it is that we first list all the different ways in which an individual y may be related to a given fixed individual, say x. This is what the different conjunctions $C'(x,y)$ are good for. Then we specify, for individuals y related to x in each of these different ways, whether individuals of that particular kind exist or not. This is what the bulk of (9) (apart from its last part) accomplishes. We also specify, in the last part of (9), how the fixed individual x is related to itself.

The statement above that (9) can play the same role in (8) as the expressions $C_i(x)$ played in it before thus amounts to saying that if the process just described is carried out in all the different ways, we obtain an exhaustive list of all the possible kinds of individuals x that we may specify by means of the predicate symbols we have at our disposal plus one layer of quantifiers. What remains to be done is therefore just what happens in (8): we run once again through the list of all the possible kinds of individuals x and indicate which of them are exemplified and which ones are not. In this way, we obtain a description of one possible kind of world, in so far as it can be described by means of the resources to which we have restricted ourselves.

What happens in (9) may also be described as follows: we take a list of all the complex relations (predicate-expressions with two argument-places) that may obtain between two individuals and that can be specified without using quantifiers, and we construct out of them a list of all the possible complex properties (predicate-expressions with one argument-place) that an individual may have and that can be specified by means of one layer of quantifiers. It is a straightforward task to generalize this: In the same way we may start from the list of all the possible complex relations that may obtain between $n+1$ individuals and that can be specified by m layers of quantifiers, and construct out of them a list of all the different complex relations that can obtain between n individuals and that can be described by means of $m+1$ layers of quantifiers. In this way we can in fact obtain a recursive definition of constituents in general, for in the case $m = 0$ we have simply constituents in the sense of propositional logic. (Such a definition is of course relative to a given finite list of predicates and free individual symbols.)

These examples perhaps suffice to show that the constituents of quantification theory really do give us a systematic list of all the different possibilities concerning the world that we can specify by the means of expression to which we have restricted ourselves, and that they do this in as clear-cut a sense as the constituents of propositional logic. In most other respects, too, the situation in quantification theory is the same as it is in propositional logic. We can assign weights to the different constituents and define measures of inductive probability and of semantic information in the same way as before. There is a minor complication here in that we have to see to it that when a constituent is expanded into a disjunction of deeper constituents (we shall call them its *subordinate* constituents) the sum of the weights of these subordinate constituents equals the weight of the original constituent. There is no difficulty in principle of doing so, however.

7. *Inconsistent constituents*

There is one important exception to this general similarity between quantification theory and propositional logic, however. This one major difference between the two cases is the fact that in quantification theory some constituents are inconsistent, a contingency which never arises in propositional logic.

We have to make a minor qualification here. Inconsistent constituents begin to appear only when the degree of constituents is two or more. When it is one, the situation is to all intents and purposes exactly the same as in propositional logic. This case arises, e.g., in monadic quantification theory, that is to say, when all the predicates we are dealing with are one-place (monadic) predicates.[20] Monadic quantification theory thus

---

[20] The tautological character of the logical truths of monadic quantification theory has been brought out very clearly by von Wright (op. cit., note 7 above).

constitutes an interesting special case. In it everything works out exactly in the same way as in propositional logic. The truths of monadic quantification theory are tautologies in the same sense as the truths of propositional logic. This is interesting because it already shows that the notion of a tautology has in any case an interesting application outside propositional logic.

Returning to the general case, the question we have to ask there is whether the presence of inconsistent constituents makes the situation essentially different from what it is in propositional logic. Are all the logical truths of quantification theory tautologies? We shall see later that it is not useful to insist on an unqualified answer to this question. What is important is to realize that there is at least one clear-cut sense in which the answer is affirmative. In this chapter I am trying to catch and to bring out this sense of a tautology. In the next one I shall try to outline a different sense.

At first blush, however, the presence of inconsistent constituents seems to make an essential difference no matter how we look at the situation. The existence of inconsistent constituents means that a sentence may be logically true even though its distributive normal form does not contain all the constituents, provided that the missing constituents are all inconsistent. Thus it may appear that the truths of quantification theory need not be tautologies in the sense of admitting all the alternatives that we can specify with respect to the world. It suffices for them to admit all the alternatives specified by the consistent constituents.

An answer lies close at hand. We suggested defining a tautology as a sentence which admits of all the possibilities that there are with respect to the world. Now it is perfectly natural to say that an inconsistent constituent does not specify a genuine possibility concerning the world it seems to be speaking of. It only appears to describe a possible world; however, under closer scrutiny it turns out not to describe any such thing. Just because an inconsistent constituent is inconsistent, the state of affairs it purports to describe can never be realized. There is therefore no need for any sentence to exclude it. Hence a necessary and sufficient condition for a sentence of quantification theory to admit of all the (really) possible kinds of worlds, i.e., to be a tautology, is that its distributive normal form contains all the *consistent* constituents. And it is readily seen that all the truths of quantification theory really are tautologies in this sense.

This way out of the difficulty may seem far too simple. As far as the notion of semantic information is concerned, it amounts to assigning a zero weight to all the inconsistent constituents by a *fiat*. Our way out can be greatly strengthened, however, by means of further arguments.

8. *Constituents as jigsaw puzzles*

Here I shall give but one such argument. I shall first give it the form of an analogy, and subsequently indicate how it may be strengthened. If we are given a constituent, it may be said, we are not yet given a genuine picture of a possible state of affairs. We are given nothing that directly shows how the world must be in order for it to be true. We are given, rather, a way of constructing such a picture—a way which is rather like a jigsaw puzzle. In fact, from (8) you can see that being given a constituent is very much like being given an unlimited supply of a finite number of different kinds of pieces of a jigsaw puzzle, with the instructions (i) that at least one piece of each kind has to be made use of, and (ii) that no other kinds of pieces may be used. An attempt to construct 'a picture of a possible state of affairs' in accordance with these instructions may fail. Then the jigsaw puzzle does not give us any picture of reality. It cannot be used to convey information concerning the state of the world. We cannot give it to somebody and say 'This is what the world is like' and hope to convey any real information to him in the way we could if we had given him instead a ready-made picture of the world or even a jigsaw puzzle which in fact can be completed so as to form a genuine picture. In a similar way, it may be suggested, an inconsistent constituent does not describe a genuine possibility as to what the world may be like; it only appears to describe one. Hence its presence or absence in the normal forms makes no real difference. No knowledge of the reality of which the sentences in question speak is needed to rule it out.

This analogy between constituents and jigsaw puzzles can be converted into something more like a genuine argument. It may be pointed out that it is a very good analogy in that it reproduces rather well the reasons why a constituent may fail to be consistent.

In order to see two such reasons, we may consider the sentences (8) and (9), and assume that the latter occurs as a part of the former. Both (8) and (9) are lists of all the kinds of individuals that there are. In the first list these individuals are classified absolutely, in the second with respect to the given individual *x*. Nevertheless, the two lists have to be compatible for every sentence of the form (9) which occurs in (8), i.e., for every such individual *x* as is asserted to exist by (8): every individual which exists according to the absolute list has to find a place in the relative list of each existing individual, and vice versa.[21] These two requirements are not always met. If they are not met, (8) is inconsistent. If the former is violated, (8) may be shown to be inconsistent essentially by one application of the exchange theorem

$$(Ex)(Uy)P(x, y) \supset (Ux)(Ey)P(y, x).$$

If the latter is violated, it may similarly be shown to be inconsistent essentially by one application of the exchange theorem

$$(Ex)(Ey)P(x, y) \supset (Ex)(Ey)P(y, x).$$

These two are essentially the only ways in which a constituent can turn out to be inconsistent. (There is a third one, but it is in a certain sense trivial.)[22] Of course, this cannot mean that every constituent which is not inconsistent for one of these two reasons is thereby shown to be consistent. Often the failure of a constituent to meet the two requirements is implicit and only becomes explicit when the constituent in question is expanded into a disjunction of several constituents of a higher degree. For

---

[21] The members of the absolute list are the 'kinds of pieces' of my jigsaw puzzle analogy. Each member of the absolute list specifies a relative list, which may be compared to a list of all the different gaps such a piece leaves to be filled.

[22] The two requirements are the conditions (A)–(B) explained below in Chapter XI, 'Distributive Normal Forms in First-Order Logic' (section 10; cf. note 16 above). The third requirement mentioned is the condition (C) explained in the same chapter. Its lesser importance is illustrated by the fact that we can dispense with it altogether if we use an exclusive interpretation of quantifiers, as is explained in Chapter XI. In other respects, the difference between the two interpretations of quantifiers (cf. note 31 to Chapter VI) does not make much difference to what I have said in the present chapter. The only difference that ought to be made explicit is that when we are using an exclusive interpretation there is no need to require that a member of the absolute list be compatible with itself, whereas this has to be required if we use an inclusive interpretation.

some finite degree, all these higher degree constituents will then be inconsistent for one of our two reasons.

Here the jigsaw puzzle analogy serves us remarkably well. The two reasons for which some constituents are inconsistent may be illustrated by comparing each one of my constituents to a jigsaw puzzle which can fail to yield a coherent picture for two reasons: either there are two pieces (or, rather, kinds of pieces) which are incompatible in the sense that they cannot be fitted into one and the same picture, or else one of the pieces leaves a gap which is such that it cannot be filled by any of the different kinds of pieces that we have at our disposal. The former case is comparable to that of a member of the absolute list which cannot find a place in the relative list of one of its fellow members. The two members of the absolute list (my 'two pieces of the jigsaw puzzle') are then incompatible. The latter case illustrates that of a member of some relative list which cannot find a niche in the absolute list. This relative list itself is then comparable with a piece of jigsaw puzzle leaving an unremovable gap.

There is a complication here in that we sometimes have to expand the given constituent into a disjunction of several constituents of a higher degree before it can be seen to be inconsistent. But this is merely comparable to the fact that we sometimes have to carry an attempted construction of a jigsaw puzzle to a certain extent before it can be seen that it is impossible to complete for one of the two reasons which I have just mentioned.

Hence the analogy I have explained fits the facts quite well. Moreover, it may be argued that it is in fact somewhat more than a mere analogy. It was argued above in Chapter II that something like the well-known picture theory of language can be extended to quantification theory.[23] According to this theory, a quantificational sentence does not itself show how the reality of which it speaks is constituted. The sentence itself does not reflect the structure of the reality of which it speaks. Rather, it

[23] By a picture, I mean here an 'isomorphic representation' roughly in the same sense as Erik Stenius in his book *Wittgenstein's 'Tractatus'* (Basil Blackwell, Oxford, 1960). It is not very difficult to show that Carnap's state-descriptions can be understood as such representations. Moreover, what I have called 'model sets' of quantificational sentences can be similarly conceived of as isomorphic representations of reality such as it would be if they were true. (For model sets, see Chapter I above, and my 'Form and Content in Quantification Theory', *Acta Philosophica Fennica*, vol. 8 (1955), pp. 5–55.)

is a starting-point for certain picture constructions, the end-products of which are pictures of reality in the sense of the picture theory of language. What most directly shows the meaning of a sentence are these alternative pictures to which it gives rise. And these picture constructions are in the special case of constituents precisely the processes which I have compared to jigsaw puzzle constructions.[24]

The results of Chapter II serve to reinforce the point I am making here. They show that the jigsaw puzzle analogy is in a certain respect a faithful account of how our language works, in that they show that sentences (of an applied first-order language) can be understood as recipes for constructing pictures of the world, just as the jigsaw puzzle analogy brings out. Of course, this is the whole story of the situation only in so far as we are only interested in the function of our (first-order) language in depicting the world. Fortunately, this function is precisely what is at issue when such notions as tautology are considered. Hence the results of Chapter II apply here with full force.

There is another direction in which the jigsaw puzzle analogy turns out to be more than a mere expository device. Hao Wang has shown how the decision problems which arise in first-order logic can be converted into what he calls domino problems. These are sets of questions concerning the completability of what I find difficult not to call logicians' jigsaw puzzles. Each question asks whether it is possible to pave the whole two-dimensional Euclidean plane with square dominoes under restrictions closely reminiscent of the puzzles described earlier in the present chapter. Speaking of dominoes means of course that the adjacent sides of the tiles must match. Over and above this, it is required that the dominoes used must be drawn from a finite list of different kinds of dominoes and that at least one domino of each of these finite number of kinds must be used. These are obviously the natural counterparts to the restrictions discussed above.[25]

---

[24] From section 16 of Chapter XI below, one can see what form the conditions that define a model set assume in the special case of constituents (as well as certain closely related expressions called attributive constituents). The connection between these special conditions and the informal idea of a jigsaw puzzle construction is so clear as not to need further explanation.

[25] For details, see Hao Wang, 'Remarks on Machines, Sets, and the Decision Problem', in *Formal Systems and Recursive Functions*, ed. by J. N. Crossley and M. A. E. Dummett (North-Holland Publishing Company, Amsterdam, 1965), pp. 304–20; A. S. Kahr, Edward F. Moore, and Hao Wang, 'Entscheidungsproblem

There are in fact intrinsic connections between the different completability questions Wang asks and the satisfiability questions which I have in this chapter compared to jigsaw puzzles.

9. *Logical truths are tautologies (in a sense)*

In any case, there appear to be good reasons for answering the question which figures as the title of this chapter affirmatively, at least in so far as quantification theory (first-order logic) is concerned. The logical truths of quantification theory can be shown to be tautologies. The interest of this answer does not lie primarily in the argument I have given for it. As so often is the case in philosophy, the main interest of one's answer lies in making explicit and clear the concepts one is employing, in our case the notions of semantic information and of analytic truth in the sense of tautological truth. I have already expressed the belief that, in the form which I have given to them, these notions will turn out to have other uses as well.

In so far as you still feel dissatisfaction with my answer, one reason for this dissatisfaction is likely to be just the way in which I have understood the crucial notions of semantic information and analyticity. Is not this way somewhat arbitrary? Was my decision to assign a zero probability to all inconsistent constituents only one of many alternative courses?

In short: are there perhaps other ways of understanding the notions of semantic information and analyticity? There certainly are, and part of our intellectual discomfort may perhaps be eliminated by investigating these alternative ways of looking at the concepts of information and analyticity. This is (among other things) what I shall try to do in the next few chapters.

Reduced to the AEA Case', *Proceedings of the National Academy of Sciences* (USA), vol. 48 (1962), pp. 365–77; Robert Berger, *The Undecidability of the Domino Problem* (Memoirs of the American Mathematical Society, No. 66, Providence, R.I., 1966).

VIII

KANT VINDICATED

1. *Constituents and existential inference*

IN Chapter VI above, a number of different senses of analyticity were examined. Some of these senses are familiar but vague,
some unfamiliar but fairly sharp, at least in the limited area of
quantification theory (first-order logic) where they were considered. Among the latter, there is a sense or a group of senses
in which an argument step is analytic if and only if it does not
introduce any new individuals into our reasoning. In this sense,
an inference is analytic if in it one merely analyses the interrelations of the individuals which are already mentioned in the
premisses, without 'going beyond' them in the sense of considering other individuals. This group of senses was listed as sense III
of analyticity. It has several variants, the most important ones
of which were called III (a)–(e). In formulating them, we made
use of the notion of a degree of a quantificational sentence. Intuitively speaking, the degree of a quantificational sentence is the
maximal number of individuals we are considering together in
their relation to each other in any one part of the sentence in
question. Formally speaking, it is the sum of two numbers one
of which is the number of its different free singular terms and
the other (called its depth) the number of the different layers of
quantifiers it contains.[1]

In the present chapter this group of senses will be studied in
somewhat greater detail. A starting-point is offered by what was
found in the preceding chapter. It was pointed out there that
every consistent quantificational sentence has a distributive
normal form in which it is a disjunction of certain conjunctions
called constituents. This normal form is a generalization of what
is known as the complete disjunctive normal form of proposi-

---

[1] The possibilities of sharpening the definition of depth that were pointed out
in note 32 to Chapter VI above are also relevant here.

tional logic. Each constituent which does not have any free singular terms was seen to have the following structure:

(1) $$(Ex)C_1(x) \ \& \ (Ex)C_2(x) \ \& \ ... \ \& \ (Ex)C_n(x) \ \&$$
$$\& \ (Ux)(C_1(x) \lor C_2(x) \lor ... \lor C_n(x))$$

where each $C_i(x)$ again has a similar structure (unless the depth of the constituent in question is one). This structure is in fact representative of the structure of constituents in general. In the general case, the only additional member of conjunction (1) is a conjunction of negated or un-negated atomic sentences. Furthermore, in the general case free singular terms may be present in the sentences $C_i(x)$.

The main difference between the distributive normal forms of propositional logic and of monadic (one-place) quantification theory on the one hand and the general case (constituents of depth two or more) on the other is that in the general case some of the constituents are inconsistent. This fact is at once seen to be relevant to one of our senses of analyticity. If (1) is inconsistent, its negation is logically true. This negation is readily seen to be equivalent to the following sentence:

(2) $$((Ex)C_1(x) \ \& \ (Ex)C_2(x) \ \& \ ... \ \& \ (Ex)C_n(x))$$
$$\supset (Ex)(\sim C_1(x) \ \& \ \sim C_2(x) \ \& \ ... \ \& \ \sim C_n(x)).$$

Now what does (2) say? It says that if there exist individuals of certain kinds, $C_1, C_2,..., C_n$, then there also exists an individual which belongs to none of these kinds. But this means that (2) enables us to infer the existence of an individual of a certain kind from the existence of a number of individuals which are necessarily different from it, having as they do different properties. In other words, (2) authorizes an interindividual existential inference. This inference, and hence also sentence (2), is thus synthetic in sense III (a). This sense was seen to be characteristic of Kant. For Kant, every inconsistency of a constituent is thus an almost paradigmatic example of a synthetic truth, in spite of the fact that this inconsistency is entirely a matter of quantificational logic. Conversely, it may be shown that behind every logical truth of form (2) there lies (apart from certain trivial exceptions) the inconsistency of at least one constituent.[2] Hence we may say fairly accurately that a truth is synthetic in sense

---

[2] By a logical truth of form (2) I mean of course a logical truth in which the

III (a) if and only if it turns on the elimination of inconsistent constituents. In this sense, many important truths of quantificational logic are therefore synthetic.

In order to avoid misunderstanding, it is important to notice that the inconsistency of (1) is largely independent of the possible inconsistency of the sentences $C_i(x)$ which occur in (1). The inconsistency of (1) thus is usually not of a trivial variety, due to the inconsistency of one of the component constituents. Of course, it may happen that one of the sentences $C_i(x)$ is inconsistent; then (1) is also inconsistent. But this will only mean that a constituent of a lesser depth (with a greater number of free singular terms) is already inconsistent. If its inconsistency is of the trivial variety, we may push further towards shallower and shallower constituents until we come to one which is inconsistent although it contains no inconsistent constituents of lesser depth. Hence the trivial cases in which one of the sentences $C_i(x)$ occurring in (1) is already inconsistent are in fact parasitic on the non-trivial cases, which may therefore be considered as typical.

Nevertheless, implication (2) is sometimes logically true merely because its antecedent conjunction is logically false. Then a number of sentences of the form $(Ex)C_i(x)$ occurring in (1) will be logically incompatible. Let us assume that $(Ex)C_1(x),..., (Ex)C_m(x)$ are not incompatible but that they become incompatible if $(Ex)C_{m+1}(x)$ is added to them. Then the implication

$$(3) \qquad ((Ex)C_1(x) \text{ \& } ... \text{ \& } (Ex)C_m(x)) \supset \sim(Ex)C_{m+1}(x)$$

is logically true although its antecedent is not inconsistent. Kant's pronouncements show that for him (3) would also have been an instance of synthetic truth.[3] Hence this special case does not really make much difference here. We could have said instead of III (a) that an analytic argument cannot lead from the existence of an individual (or a number of individuals) to

sentences $C_i(x)$ occurring in (2) are arbitrary sentences whose only free singular term is x.

[3] See note 24 to Chapter VI above, and the passages in Kant referred to there, especially Kant's 'allgemeine Anmerkung' at the end of *Versuch, den Begriff der negativen Größen in die Weltweisheit einzuführen* of the year 1763. These passages show that for Kant an inference from the existence of certain individuals to the *non*-existence of a different individual is as problematic as an inference to the existence of such an individual.

the existence *or non-existence* of a different individual. This would have been in accordance with Kant's intentions, and it would have brought us even closer to the inconsistency of constituents than III (a).

2. *Non-trivial elimination of constituents is a synthetic procedure*

Thus there obtains in any case a clear-cut connection between sense III (a) of analytic and synthetic on the one hand and the inconsistency of some constituents on the other. This is not the only interesting connection between our observations in the preceding chapter and the different variants of sense III of analyticity. A process was there described by means of which each inconsistent constituent may be shown to be inconsistent. It consists of expanding the given constituent into a disjunction of constituents with the same predicate symbols and free singular terms but with an ever-increasing depth. All the constituents that arise during this process are said to be *subordinate* to the original one, and the process itself is called an *expansion* process. If certain simple criteria of inconsistency are applied to all the constituents which arise during this process, then for each inconsistent constituent there is a depth such that all its subordinate constituents of this depth are inconsistent by these criteria.[4] The applicability of these criteria can in each case be mechanically tested. The reason why this does not yield a decision procedure is that there usually is no way of knowing how far one has to expand a given constituent in order to bring out the inconsistency that may lurk there.

Most of the steps of this process are innocent-looking. What we use in the expansion process are simply the rules for converting a sentence into its distributive normal form, plus some rule which has the effect of increasing the depth of constituents so as to add a new layer of quantifiers while the free singular terms remain the same. The addition of any trivially redundant part to a constituent serves this purpose as long as it increases the depth of the constituent by one. Because of this triviality, one is

---

[4] The criteria of inconsistency considered in the preceding chapter are in effect the criteria (A)–(B) (and, to a smaller extent, (C)) discussed below in section 10 of Chapter XI. These criteria can be derived from certain simpler criteria, however, which may therefore be considered as the basic ones for our purposes. They are the criteria (D)–(E) and (C) (or, if we presuppose an exclusive interpretation of the quantifiers, (D)–(E) only) discussed in section 12 of Chapter XI.

tempted to say that each stage thus differs from its predecessor only in that it has a greater depth, and hence a greater degree.

Now what does this increase in degree mean? As we saw, it means increasing the number of the individuals one is considering in their relation to each other. Increasing this number is by III (b) or III (d) the mark of a synthetic procedure. The expansion process, by means of which inconsistent constituents may be shown to be inconsistent, is thus a synthetic procedure in these two senses. It follows that the resulting method of proof from premises, which one easily obtains in terms of the distributive normal forms and their expansions, is synthetic in sense III (e).[5] Likewise, the corresponding proof procedure, which we obtain as the dual of the disproof procedure given to us by the expansion process, is synthetic in the sense that not all logical truths can be proved analytically in sense III (e) from propositional tautologies of their own degree. In brief, the proof and disproof procedures which we obtain in this way are normally synthetic. The only case in which they are not synthetic arises when a proof does not turn on the elimination of any inconsistent constituents, or, alternatively (here we have some room for choosing our concepts in different ways), when a proof does not turn on the elimination of inconsistent constituents by means of first raising their depth. The latter of these two courses brings out more faithfully than the former the spirit of such characterizations of analyticity as III (b).

3. *The inevitability of synthetic elements in first-order logic*

Is this syntheticity of quantificational proofs perhaps an accidental peculiarity of the expansion procedure? It seems to me that it is not. Here, as in so many other cases, distributive normal forms merely bring out in an accentuated form features which belong to all quantificational sentences, albeit usually in a less explicit form. In fact, it may be shown that in a certain sense the observations we made concerning distributive normal forms, and concerning the ways in which they are naturally proved and disproved, bring out an unavoidable feature of all

---

[5] This procedure operates as follows: in order to derive F_2 from F_1, we transform them into their respective normal forms. Each of these normal forms may be assumed to contain all the free singular terms occurring in F_1 or in F_2. Then F_2 can be proved from F_1 if and only if the expansion of the normal form of the former will at some depth contain the expansion of the normal form of the latter, when constituents inconsistent by our criteria are omitted from the expansion.

complete systems of proof in quantification theory. In so far as these systems are in a certain sense natural, they must all of them allow the proving and disproving of sentences by means of sentences of a higher degree.

The sense of naturalness which is involved here has some interest of its own. What do we 'naturally' mean by an axiom and by a rule of inference (or of proof)?

Usually, the notion of an axiom in its widest sense is identified with that of a recursive one-place predicate of the Gödel numbers of the formulae or sentences in question, and the notion of a rule of inference is likewise identified with that of a recursive two-place predicate of the same Gödel numbers.[6] It has not been pointed out, to the best of my knowledge, that this identification does not do full justice to what we are likely to mean by an axiom and by a rule of inference. Speaking intuitively, what we are willing to call axioms and rules of inference must depend only on what the sentences in question say. Now the Gödel number of a sentence obviously depends on many other things besides this. It depends also on what are obviously purely notational features of the sentence in question. For instance, the number of repetitions of a member of a conjunction does not in any relevant sense make a difference to what the sentence in question says, but it will of course make a difference to its Gödel number. More generally, a rule of inference should not depend on purely propositional transformations of the sentences in question or of their parts.[7] In fact, it seems to me that a much better approximation towards what we really want to call a rule of inference can be obtained just by requiring this kind of invariance. A two-place predicate of the Gödel numbers of sentences (formulae) qualifies for a rule of inference only if it can be extended (taken to hold between more pairs of sentences) without affecting the resulting provability relations so as to become invariant with respect to changes in which a truth-function

[6] For simplicity, we assume here that quantification theory has to be formulated in terms of inference rules in which exactly one conclusion is always inferred from exactly one premiss. Although the most common axiomatizations of quantification theory are not of this form, they can easily be converted into it. Likewise, our discussion can easily be freed from this restriction.

[7] It is assumed here and in the sequel that a purely propositional transformation means the replacement of a truth-function of certain atomic or quantified sentences by a tautologically equivalent truth-function of *the same sentences*. The introduction of new arguments into truth-functions is in other words ruled out.

of certain sentences or subsentences is replaced by a tauto
logically equivalent truth-function of the same sentences o
subsentences.[8] Moreover, by the same token it must b
generalizable so as to become invariant with respect to permuta
tions of free singular terms. Furthermore, it may be require
that it does not introduce new predicates. Similar requirement
may be imposed on the notion of axiom. We shall call axiom
and rules of inference satisfying these requirements *natural*
axioms and rules of inference.

Is it possible in quantification theory to have a complet
system of natural rules of inference (for proofs from assumptions
analytic in sense III (e)? Is it possible to have a system of natura
rules of inference which would enable us to prove all the logica
truths of quantification theory without using sentences of
degree higher than that of the sentence to be proved? That i
to say, can they be proved analytically in sense III (e)? In shor
are the logical truths of quantification theory analytic i
sense III (e)?

The answer to all these questions is no. The details of th
proof of this answer will not be given here, however. It will hav
to suffice to indicate some of the main ideas. If we conside
sentences as equivalent whenever they can be transformed int
each other by purely propositional transformations of them
selves and of a number of their subsentences, then there is onl
a finite number of equivalence classes provided one conside
sentences whose depth is smaller than a given finite numbe
and whose free singular terms and predicate symbols all ha
from a given finite set of symbols. (Assume that the depth is
and the number of free singular terms t. Then the finitude i
easily proved by induction on d.) One representative of eac
class is easily constructed. It may be considered as a kind c

---

[8] This may also be expressed as follows: A two-place recursive relation R giv
us a natural rule of inference if and only if there is a similar relation R' with th
following properties: (1) Whenever xRy, then also $xR'y$; (2) the ancestral of R hol
between two numbers if and only if the ancestral of R' holds between them; (3)
x and x' are the respective Gödel numbers of two sentences which can be tran
formed into each other by purely propositional transformations of themselves an
of their subsentences, then $xR'y$ whenever $x'R'y$ and $zR'x$ whenever $zR'x'$. Th
notion of ancestral is here understood in the usual way: the ancestral of a relatio
R holds between x and y if and only if there is a finite number of individua
$z_1, z_2,..., z_{k-1}, z_k$ such that $z_1 = x$, $z_k = y$, and that the relation R holds betwee
z_i and z_{i+1} ($i = 1, 2,..., k-1$).

'normal form' of the members of this class. We shall call this their *primitive* normal form.

Suppose now that there is a recursive proof predicate which never adds new free singular terms to our sentences and which is such that all proofs can be carried out analytically in sense III (e). If it is a natural proof predicate in our sense, then it holds between two sentences if and only if it holds between their primitive normal forms. In order to test whether it holds between two sentences we can simply test whether it holds between their primitive normal forms. Hence in order to test whether a chain of such proof predicates can be constructed between F_1 and F_2 (i.e., whether the ancestral[9] of the proof predicate holds between them) we can test whether such a chain can be constructed between their normal forms through other normal forms. From the analyticity requirement it follows that these intermediate normal forms must have all their free singular terms among those occurring in F_1 or F_2, and must have a degree smaller than or equal to that of F_1 and F_2. However, the number of such primitive normal forms is finite. There is therefore only a finite number of possible intermediate stages, and there also is an effective test for the existence of a chain of proof predicates leading from F_1 to F_2. Hence there is a mechanical test for the provability of F_2 from F_1. However, in that case the provability relation which our proof predicate gives us cannot be both sound and complete, for if it were, we would have a decision method for the whole of quantification theory.[10]

By means of a supplementary argument it may be shown that the assumption that the proof predicate does not introduce any new free singular terms can be omitted if we require that the proof predicate is symmetric with respect to the different free singular terms.[11] Hence all the proofs of quantification theory

[9] See note 8 above.

[10] The soundness of a formal rule of inference means that F_2 can be inferred from F_1 *only when* F_2 is a consequence of F_1 in the usual semantical sense of the word. The completeness of a rule of inference means that F_2 can be inferred from F_1 in one step or more *always when* it is a (semantical) consequence of F_1.

[11] From the symmetry requirement it readily follows that we can always make do with a fixed finite set of free singular terms in the intermediate stages of our proof from assumptions. Hence there again is only a finite number of normal forms that can act as possible intermediate stages in a proof from F_1 to F_2. Then our proof predicate cannot give us a complete method of proofs from premises for the same reason as before.

cannot be carried out by the sole means of natural rules of inference analytic in sense III (e).

A rule of inference which is natural in the sense just defined, i.e., which can be extended (without affecting provability relations) so as to become dependent only on the primitive normal forms of the sentences in question, can also be extended (possibly by strengthening it somewhat but never inadmissibly) so as to become dependent only on their *distributive* normal forms.[12] In a sense, to require that a rule of inference be a natural one is tantamount to requiring that it depend only on the distributive normal forms of the sentences in question.

It is of some interest to note that the existence of a distributive normal form, which was the major reason for saying that logical truths of quantification theory are analytic in sense IV, now turns out to be closely connected with the reason why the same truths are synthetic in another sense (not captured by natural rules of inference analytic in sense III (e)).

We can now vindicate Kant. What he meant when he held that mathematical arguments are normally synthetic was quite right. By mathematical arguments he primarily meant modes of reasoning which are now treated in quantification theory. But it was just seen that many quantificational modes of reasoning are inevitably synthetic in a natural sense of the word. This sense is, moreover, closely related to Kant's intentions, for it was pointed out in Chapter VI above that the group of senses III of analyticity may be taken to be a very good reconstruction of Kant's notion of analyticity as he used it in his philosophy of mathematics.

---

[12] Let us assume that we are given a rule of inference R which depends only on the primitive normal form of our sentences. We may then define (in two steps) a new rule of inference R' as follows: (A) Infer a distributive normal form D_2 from another normal form D_1 by R' if and only if there are primitive normal forms P_1 and P_2 such that (1) D_1 is the distributive normal form of P_1, D_2 the distributive normal form of P_2; that (2) the predicates and free singular terms of D_1 and P_1 as well as those of D_2 and P_2 are the same; and that (3) P_2 can be inferred from P_1 by R. (B) Infer a sentence F_2 from another sentence F_1 by R' if and only if the distributive normal form of the former can be inferred from the distributive normal form of the latter by (A). Then this new rule of inference R' is sound if R is. (This is what is meant in the text by saying that the extension is never inadmissible.) Its applicability can be effectively tested. By definition, R' depends only on the distributive normal forms of the sentences in question. Hence it accomplishes what it was claimed to be possible to accomplish.

4. *Other proof procedures*

Before considering further the philosophical and historical implications of our results, it is advisable to see more fully what they imply. Do the current systems of rules for quantification theory really contain rules which make the resulting proofs synthetic in sense III (e)?

Most of them obviously do. There are certain types of rules of inference, however, which prima facie seem to go against what has been said. For instance, the rules of inference used in the inferential methods known as methods of *natural deduction*[13] usually do not lead from a formula to another formula by way of formulae of higher degree. How does this square with my contention that complete systems of rules of inference have to contain rules synthetic in sense III (c)?

The answer is that the rules of natural deduction do not all satisfy the requirement of being invariant with respect to permutations of free singular terms.[14] When in a system of natural deduction one goes from $(Ex)F$ to an expression of the form $F(a/x)$ (i.e., F with 'x' replaced by 'a'), the legitimacy of this step depends on the choice of the free singular term 'a'. The usual requirement is that 'a' must not coincide with any of the free singular terms occurring earlier in the proof, that it must be a *new* term. Hence this step depends, not just on the sentence (formula) $(Ex)F$, but also on all the free singular terms which do not occur in it but which occur at earlier stages of the proof. If their number is added to the degree of $(Ex)F$, we have a parameter which is a more realistic measure of the number of individuals we are considering in the step of proof in question. Of this number it can be shown that it must be allowed to exceed the degrees of the starting-point and the end point of a natural deduction. If the methods of natural deduction are forced to conform with the requirement I set up for rules of inference in an intuitively acceptable sense, it is thus seen that they contain synthetic elements in the same sense as the other methods of proof in quantification theory.

We may consider, as an example, the method which I have

[13] See note 22 to Chapter VI.
[14] There is almost a verbal contradiction here: the methods of natural deduction (in the usual sense of the term) give us our prime examples of unnatural rules of inference (in the sense in which we are here using the term).

outlined elsewhere and called the method of model set construction.[15] It is conveniently presented in the form of a disproof procedure. This procedure is formulated so as to apply to sets of sentences, not only to individual sentences. As in natural deduction methods, we have to consider here the degree of such a set and not just the degree of individual sentences. Here the degree of a finite set of sentences may be defined simply as the degree of the conjunction of all its members. Of the two quantificational rules for operating with sets of sentences, the rule (A.U) does not affect the degree of the sets involved. The only 'synthetic' rule is (A.E), the rule which may be called a rule of existential instantiation or existential specification. It enables us to adjoin $F(a/x)$ to a set μ provided that $(Ex)F \in \mu$ and that a is a *new* free singular term. This is the rule which makes the model set constructions synthetic.[16] Its connection with the basic idea of sense III of analytic and synthetic is obvious enough: this rule always introduces a new individual into the argument.

In fact, there appears to be a close connection between the applications of this rule and the increase of depth in the expansion process described earlier, although the details of this connection are in need of closer study. The possibility of disproving a sentence without using (A.E) (except in certain relatively trivial cases) by means of our rules for model set construction is related to the possibility of disproving it by showing that all the constituents of its normal form are inconsistent by a set of especially simple criteria of consistency, without having to add to their depth. These criteria are described in some detail in Chapter XI below.[17] Here it must suffice to say that they require in effect that no obvious inconsistency must result by omitting

---

[15] See above, Chapter I, sections 3–5, and the literature mentioned in note 14 to Chapter I.

[16] If the definition of depth is made sharper along the lines of note 32 to Chapter VI above, this statement will need a qualification. Intuitively speaking, the new individual which is introduced by (A.E) will not be initially related to the old ones in the way which would justify us in saying that the number of individuals considered together in their relation to each other is increased. Such a relation is established only through subsequent applications of the rule (A.U). However, this does not diminish the central role of the rule (A.E) in introducing new individuals into discussion. Although it is now the rule (A.U) and not the rule (A.E) that strictly speaking raises the degree of our sets of sentences, we would soon run out of applications of (A.U) without intermittent uses of (A.E).

[17] See pp. 260–6. The criteria in question are the criteria (D)–(E) and (C) mentioned in note 4 above.

parts of a constituent. Constituents inconsistent by these criteria will be called *trivially inconsistent*. These criteria are more basic than the ones indicated above in the preceding chapter. The criteria given in the preceding chapter are in fact obtained as derived criteria when the criteria of trivial inconsistency are applied after having first increased the depth of the normal form in question by one.[18]

One of the most interesting and important senses of analytic and synthetic is obtained by stipulating that a sentence is synthetically inconsistent if and only if its disproof (by means of its distributive normal form and of the expansion process) turns on the elimination of non-trivially inconsistent constituents. This sense of analytic and synthetic is very closely connected with sense III (a) of these notions. One difference between this new sense and sense III (a) is that III (a) did not allow us to distinguish between trivial and non-trivial inconsistency of constituents. Furthermore, the original definition of sense III (a) did not tell us whether we should consider the steps by means of which a sentence is transformed into its normal form, and the steps by means of which its normal form is expanded, as being unanalysable in the sense that the definition of III (a) can be applied to it directly.

Similarly, a sentence F_2 may be said to follow from F_1 analytically if and only if the distributive normal form of F_1 will become a part of the normal form of F_2 as soon as trivially inconsistent constituents are eliminated from it. (The normal forms in question are thought of as containing all the free singular terms occurring either in F_1 or in F_2 and as having the depth of the deeper of the two sentences F_1 and F_2.) Similar characterizations can be given of analyticity in all the other important contexts.

5. *Sense III of analyticity related to a notion of information*

The sense of analytic and synthetic we obtain in this way will be called the *explicit form of sense* III of these notions. It can be developed further in more than one direction. First, we may try to make the syntheticity of a synthetic disproof (by means of the expansion process) a matter of degree.[19] If in disproving F by

[18] Cf. note 4 above.
[19] Cf. Chapter XI, last few pages. In a similar way we may also obtain a measure of how deeply entangled the different predicates and free singular terms with each

means of the expansion process, we have to add n new layers of quantifiers (increase the depth of the normal form by n) before all the constituents of the expansion are trivially inconsistent, then the disproof may be said to be synthetic to the nth degree. Analyticity will be syntheticity of degree zero. Inconsistency in virtue of the criteria explained last time (by means of the jigsaw puzzle analogy) will be synthetic inconsistency of degree one. This notion is easily extended from disproofs to proofs and to proofs from premisses.[20]

The explicit form of sense III may also be connected with the concepts of information and of tautology, although with information and tautology in a sense different from the one studied in the preceding chapter. There it was assumed that a weight between zero and one is assigned to each *consistent* constituent (with given fixed predicates and free singular terms) in such a way that the sum of all the weights is one. (Of course, it has to be required also that the weight of a constituent equals the total weight of all its subordinate constituents of each given depth.) Presupposing some such assignment, we studied certain ways of defining the semantic information of a sentence with the same free singular terms, the same predicate symbols, and the same depth as these constituents. The concept of semantic information we defined there may be called *depth information*. A different concept of information is obtained in the same way if we start from a similar assignment of weights to *all* the constituents with fixed free singular terms, fixed predicate symbols, and a fixed depth, instead of an assignment in which only consistent constituents are considered. Only *trivially* inconsistent constituents will now be given a zero weight. This new notion of information may be called *surface information*. It may again be measured in a variety of ways analogous to the ways in which depth information may be measured. The difference between these ways is not of the same importance as the difference between surface information and depth information. Perhaps the most important consequence of the difference between their respective definitions is

other are in a given sentence; cf. my paper, 'Distributive Normal Forms and Deductive Interpolation', *Zeitschrift für mathematische Logik und Grundlagen der Mathematik*, vol. 10 (1964), pp. 185-91.

[20] The degree of syntheticity of an argument appears to be connected with the degree of its 'non-triviality' in a natural sense of a word, although it is not yet easy to see how good a measure it is.

that surface information can be increased by logical (deductive) inferences. This observation already hints at the great philosophical interest of the notion of surface information for the philosophy of logic. This notion will be examined in a slightly different setting in Chapter X below.

The notion of a surface information seems to have other interesting uses. For instance, it appears to be closely related to such notions as 'saying', 'asserting', and 'meaning'. What a sentence 'says' or 'asserts' must be closely connected with the information it conveys. This information cannot be depth information, however, for a speaker certainly cannot be said to 'assert' something that only very distantly follows from the sentence he has uttered. It is much more natural to relate it to the surface information of his sentence. Furthermore, from a given sentence one can tell how much surface information it conveys, whereas it is readily seen that there usually is no recursive method of computing the amount of depth information a sentence carries.[21] Hence what a man 'says' can scarcely be related to depth information, for a man may normally be said to know how much information he is giving to others explicitly, although he may not always be able to anticipate the amount of information someone else may be able to deduce logically from what he says.

In this way, the requirement which was imposed earlier in this lecture on natural rules of inference receives a deeper justification. This restriction was motivated by the applicability of a natural rule of inference having to depend only on what the sentence in question says, not on its purely notational features. This sense of 'what the sentence in question says' cannot be identified with the depth information of the sentence. Because this information usually cannot be measured recursively, we shall not be able to obtain feasible rules of inference in this way. But if this notion of saying is related to surface information, we obtain just the restriction that was imposed on natural rules of inference. For then our intuitive requirement will mean that the applicability of a rule of inference must depend only on the

---

[21] In order to compute this amount, we should have to have a method of telling which constituents are consistent and which ones are not. It is seen very soon that having such a method would be tantamount to having a decision method for quantification theory, which is known to be impossible.

distributive normal form of the sentences in question (minus trivially inconsistent constituents). And it has been pointed out already that this is equivalent to the original interpretation we gave to the requirement of naturalness. This interpretation, and the resulting notion of a natural rule of inference, thus turn out to be much less *ad hoc* than perhaps they appeared at first.

In this way we can also relate the explicit form of sense III of analyticity to the old requirement that the conclusion of an analytic argument step merely repeats in a different form something that was already said in the premisses. If 'saying' is here understood with reference to surface information, this is exactly what happens with our explicit form of sense III of analyticity. What this means is that sense III of analyticity turns out to be nothing but a variant of sense IV.

6. *Logical truths are not all surface tautologies*

The two notions of information yield as a special case (viz. zero information) two different notions of tautology. They will be called, not surprisingly, depth tautology and surface tautology. The former concept was discussed in the preceding chapter. The reader may have been bothered by the way in which I at that time dismissed all the inconsistent constituents in defining tautology (or, if you prefer, by the way in which I assigned to them a zero weight). Perhaps he felt that this dismissal was too cavalier, in spite of the justification given to it. Now we can see that there is no reason for apprehensions on this score. There are two alternative courses we can follow here. One of them leads to the notion of depth tautology, the other to the notion of surface tautology. What is important is not the spurious question which of the two courses is the correct one. What is important is to realize that there are two different notions here, both of which can be defined in a perfectly correct and natural manner, and to perceive the differences as well as the interrelations that obtain between them.

Among other things, the distinction between surface tautology and depth tautology necessitates a qualification to the answer which was given in the preceding chapter to the question: are logical truths tautologies? If we consider quantification theory as a test case once more, we can now answer it more fully than before: logical truths (of quantification theory) are all depth tautologies, but they are not all surface tautologies. The view of those philosophers who claimed that mathematical arguments are not analytic in the sense of not being merely 'explicative' thus admits of a partial vindication after all. For not even all those mathematical arguments that can be formalized in quantification theory are tautological in the sense of being surface tautologies.

In general, we see that the senses III and IV of analyticity have more in common than first meets the eye. If they are developed in a suitable direction, they are to some extent analogous. They may also have some interesting interconnections. For instance, if the weights that are assigned to the different constituents are distributed evenly (in the sense that the weight which a constituent of depth d has is always divided evenly among all the eligible subordinate constituents of depth $d+1$), then the depth information of a sentence is always greater than its surface information. If the distributive normal form of a sentence is expanded and if all the trivially inconsistent constituents are omitted as soon as they appear, the surface information of the expansion normally varies. When the depth goes on to infinity, the surface information of the expansion approaches the depth information of the sentence as a limit.

In any case, the two notions of information coincide in monadic quantification theory. This follows from the fact, noted in the preceding lecture, that no monadic constituents are inconsistent. This is interesting because almost all the examples of logical truths to which pre-Fregean philosophers paid close attention belonged to monadic quantification theory, which comprises all of traditional syllogistic (non-modal syllogistic) as a part. The fact that the notions of surface tautology and depth tautology coincide in this area has probably encouraged the idea that logical truths are tautologies or non-informative also in senses stronger than our sense IV.

Those who realized (more or less clearly) that there are valid logical implications which are not tautologies in the sense of not being surface tautologies could have reacted to this observation in different ways. One possibility is illustrated by Kant. In effect, it consisted in restricting the field of logical truths to monadic quantification theory (traditional syllogistic), and in classifying all the other quantificational modes of reasoning as mathematical. If one does this, then one can of course say that logical truths are all merely explicative (tautological), whereas mathematical reasoning is normally informative, provided of course that the terms 'explicative', 'tautological', and 'informative' are assumed to refer to surface information.

We have to realize, however, that the ideas on which this view is based are a far cry from the customary modern senses I (b)–(d) of analyticity. The apparent similarity between Kant's view and the modern ones is due to the fact that in both of them the notion of analyticity is related very closely to logical truth. What is not always realized, however, is that Kant means by logic something quite different from what modern philosophers are likely to mean by it. There is something to Peirce's claim that Kant would have had to revise his ideas about the relation of mathematics to logic if he had been familiar with the systematic theory of the logic of relations.[22]

7. *Philosophical consequences*

The notion of surface tautology is also important because it necessitates corrections to certain frequently held doctrines. Recently, many philosophers have been impressed by the fact that logical reasoning, and also many important types of mathematical reasoning, do not give us any new information concerning the reality of which our sentences speak. They have perceived, in other words, that logical reasoning is analytic in sense IV, i.e., tautological in the sense of depth tautology. They have often formulated their insight, however, in a way which is incorrect, because it implies that logical reasoning is analytic in other senses of analyticity too, e.g., that it is also tautological in the sense of surface tautology. Frequently this is also the case with philosophers' remarks on the nature of mathematical truth. Thus one of the foremost contemporary methodologists of mathematics and of science writes:

Since all mathematical proofs rest exclusively on logical deductions from certain postulates, it follows that a mathematical theorem, such as the Pythagorean theorem in geometry, asserts nothing that is *objectively* or *theoretically new* as compared with the postulates from

[22] C. S. Peirce, *Collected Papers* (note 22 to Chapter II above), vol. 3, sections 559–60, vol. 4, section 232, and vol. 2, section 361.

which it is derived, although its content may well be *psychologically new* in the sense that we were not aware of its being implicitly contained in the postulates.[23]

Similar views have been expressed in other terms. For instance, it has been said that if y logically follows from x then 'in saying x ... I have already asserted y'.[24]

Now these statements may perhaps be understood so indulgently as to make them true. As they are naturally understood, however, they are far too sweeping. It is not true that a logical inference gives us nothing new in any objective and non-psychological sense of the word. The notion of surface information is a perfectly objective and non-psychological notion, and a logical inference frequently adds to this kind of information. Likewise, speaking of what we *assert* or *say* in a statement is ambiguous, for it may refer either to surface information or to depth information. As I have indicated already, surface information is in fact usually a better candidate for this role. But if the quoted sentence is understood as referring to surface information, it is incorrect. In this sense, it is not true to say that in asserting x we already assert everything that is asserted by its logical consequences, for the logical consequences of x may have more surface information than x and therefore may assert more than x.

Perhaps the clearest formulation of the view that a logical inference does not really give us anything objectively new is found in the writings of Ernst Mach. Speaking of geometrical proofs, he writes: 'But if we carefully remove from our idea [of the conclusion] everything that enters into it merely as a contribution to the construction or through specialization, and not through the inference [*Syllogismus*], we find in it nothing more than the proposition we started from. . . .'[25] The fact that we do not at once see the conclusion in the premisses is, according to this view, a merely psychological limitation. If we could, so to speak, look at the premisses from the right point of view, we

[23] Carl G. Hempel, 'Geometry and Empirical Science', *American Mathematical Monthly*, vol. 52 (1946), pp. 7–17; reprinted in *Readings in Philosophical Analysis*, ed. by Herbert Feigl and Wilfrid Sellars (Appleton-Century-Crofts, New York, 1949), pp. 238–49; see p. 241.

[24] A. J. Ayer, *Language, Truth and Logic* (note 38 to Chapter VI above), p. 80.

[25] Ernst Mach, *Erkenntnis und Irrtum, Skizzen zur Psychologie der Forschung* (Johann Ambrosius Barth, Leipzig, 1905), p. 300; cf. p. 302.

could see the conclusion at once, right there in the premisses.[26] This view is sometimes dramatized by saying that God has no need of logic. Since He is presumably free from the mental blocks with which we humans are burdened, He can at once see all the conclusions in the premisses.

This view is shown to be wrong by the discovery that logical inference is synthetic in the sense that in going from the premisses to the conclusion we often have to consider individuals which are mentioned neither in the premisses nor in the conclusion. It does not suffice simply to view the premisses in a suitable light in order to perceive the conclusion there, for the transition from the premisses to the conclusion cannot be accomplished without the help of individuals which are not considered in the premisses. It may be the case that God has no need of logic, that He can move from the premisses to the conclusion instantaneously. But this is not due simply to His freedom from psychological obstacles. It is due, rather, to His omnipotence by means of which He can instantaneously introduce all the auxiliary individuals needed in the proof.

Thus group III of the senses of analyticity serves to bring out at least one good reason why logical and mathematical inferences may in a perfectly natural sense be said to 'go beyond the premisses' and to 'give us new information' in spite of being tautological in the sense of being depth tautologies. The question I asked at the end of Chapter VII above thus receives an answer.

8. *Further explanations*

It may be in order to return to our several senses of analyticity and to comment on them briefly in the light of what we have found. Sense III (c) might seem as explicit as you may wish (at least in quantification theory). There is a pitfall hidden here,

---

[26] Thus Mach writes (op. cit., p. 302): 'Indem die syllogistische Deduktion von allgemeinern (selten in ihrer Spezialisierung explizit vorgestellten) Sätzen ausgehend, durch mehrere vermittelnde Glieder, unter Wechsel und Kombination verschiedener Gesichtspunkte, zu spezielleren Sätzen vorschreitet, kann sich hier die Täuschung einer ganz neuen, scheinbar in den Prämissen nicht enthaltenen Einsicht ergeben. Dieselbe hätte aber auch direkt erschaut werden können.' Here Mach thinks that a logical deduction is essentially a transition from a general truth to one of its special cases. This view is misleading, for when new individuals are introduced into our considerations, their properties and relations cannot be conceived as special cases of what is already said in the premisses, and could not 'direkt erschaut werden', as Mach claims.

however. Even though an argument step does not explicitly add to the degree of our sentences, this may be merely because it is a compressed form of a longer chain of arguments, some intermediate stages of which are of a very high degree indeed. In order to avoid this pitfall we may propose to identify an analytic argument step with one which does not turn on the elimination of non-trivially inconsistent constituents. (The distributive normal forms of the premiss must be a part of the normal form of the conclusion, except for trivially inconsistent constituents.) This has the effect of equating senses III (c) and III (a) to all practical purposes. It results in what I called the explicit form of sense III as applied to argument steps. The name of this sense receives in this way an explanation and a justification.[27]

On the basis of this modification of III (c) we can define two senses of analyticity as applied to chains of arguments in analogy with III (d) and (e). We shall refer to these modified senses as explicit forms of the old ones. They give rise to corresponding senses of analytic logical truth and analytic inconsistency.

The relation of III (d) and (e) deserves, and needs, a few further comments. The latter is the more interesting and important of the two. In this sense, almost all the truths and proofs one is likely to find in a logic text are analytic, or can easily be reconstructed so as to become analytic. The main exception is perhaps constituted by the rules for exchanging adjacent quantifiers:

$$(Ex)(Ey)F \supset (Ey)(Ex)F \quad \text{and} \quad (Ex)(Uy)F \supset (Uy)(Ex)F.$$

These logical truths are synthetic to degree one (according to the explicit form of sense III). Logical truths synthetic to a degree higher than one are apt to be more complicated.

A satisfactory feature of sense III (e) is that there is a close connection between the possibility of proving an implication $(F_1 \supset F_2)$ analytically in this sense from propositional tautologies of its own degree on the one hand and the possibility of proving

---

[27] In order to give a complete explanation of the explicit form of sense III we should have to specify more fully the procedure used in converting a sentence into its distributive normal form. The difference between the different ways in which the notion of depth can be understood will then be relevant. I shall not discuss the rules for converting sentences into their distributive normal forms here, however. They can be set up in a fairly obvious way, and their details do not affect my discussion.

F_2 from F_1 analytically in the same sense on the other. A connection of this kind will be missing if we use sense III (d). Various completely trivial arguments become synthetic. For instance, an inference from 'everyone is mortal' to 'Socrates is mortal' will be synthetic. In spite of this, there is no reason to think that the implication 'If everyone is mortal, then Socrates is mortal' should not be provable analytically. For these reasons, sense III (d) appears rather unsatisfactory.

9. *Kant explicated*

It is by no means worthless, however. On the contrary, it seems to have certain interesting uses. It is important to realize, for instance, that the inference from 'everyone is mortal' to 'Socrates is mortal' might very well be conceived of as being synthetic in the sense Kant had in mind. For him, a logical inference dealt with general concepts only. The introduction of an intuition made an argument synthetic. Now the term 'Socrates' is presumably a representative of an individual, and hence an intuition in Kant's sense. Therefore the inference, however trivial it may be, might very well be classifiable as a synthetic inference in Kant's sense of the term.

In any case, one may argue that in his famous example $7+5 = 12$ (which goes back all the way to Plato's *Theaetetus* and probably to Pythagorean arithmetic) Kant was thinking along the lines of III (d) and not along the lines of III (e).[28] He was not asking whether in thinking of the number 12 distinctly we already are in some sense thinking of the numbers 7 and 5, as Descartes asked in the case of a similar example.[29] Kant asked, rather, whether from the concept of the sum of 7 and 5 we can analytically arrive at the concept of twelve.

[28] *Critique of Pure Reason*, B 15–16 (pp. 52–3 of the Kemp Smith translation); *Prolegomena* § 2 (c) (p. 269 of the Academy Edition). Cf. Hans Vaihinger's comments in his *Commentar zu Kants Kritik der reinen Vernunft* (W. Spemann, Stuttgart, 1881–92), vol. 1, pp. 295–300, and my paper, 'Kant in oppi matematiikasta', in *Ajatus*, vol. 22 (1959), pp. 5–85, especially pp. 66–70.

[29] See Descartes, *Regulae*, rule XII (first edition, Amsterdam, 1701, pp. 38–9), where Descartes writes: 'Similarly, if I say that 4 and 3 are 7, this combination is a necessary combination. For we do not conceive the number 7 distinctly, unless we include in it in some inexplicit manner the numbers 3 and 4' (translation by Kemp Smith). This may be contrasted to Kant's formulation: 'That 5 should be added to 7, I have indeed already thought in the concept of a sum = $7+5$, but not that this sum is equivalent to the number 12' (B 16; tr. by Kemp Smith).

In order to see that this difference may in fact be taken to be an instance of the difference of our senses III (d) and (e), we may recall that there is a way of proving such simple arithmetical equations as $7+5 = 12$ in quantification theory (with identity). What we have to do is to take two monadic predicate symbols P and Q, and to set up four sentences S_1, S_2, S_3, and S_4. The first says that exactly seven individuals have the predicate for which P stands. The second says that exactly five individuals have the predicate for which Q stands. The sentence S_3 says that these two predicates are mutually exclusive. The last one says that exactly twelve individuals have one of the two predicates.

All this can be expressed by means of quantifiers, propositional connectives, and identity. For instance, S_2 might be the following sentence

$$(Ex_1)(Ex_2)(Ex_3)(Ex_4)(Ex_5)[x_1 \neq x_2 \ \& \ x_1 \neq x_3 \ \& \ ... \ \& \ x_4 \neq x_5 \ \&$$
$$\& \ Q(x_1) \ \& \ Q(x_2) \ \& \ Q(x_3) \ \& \ Q(x_4) \ \& \ Q(x_5) \ \&$$
$$\& \ (Uy)(Q(y) \supset (y = x_1 \lor y = x_2 \lor ... \lor y = x_5))].$$

The depth (degree) of this sentence is $5+1 = 6$. Likewise, the depth of S_1 is $7+1 = 8$, and the depth of S_4 is $12+1 = 13$, while the depth of S_3 is 1.

Proving $7+5 = 12$ now means proving that S_1, S_2, and S_3 logically imply S_4. Since the depth of S_4 is larger than that of the others, the argument has to be synthetic in sense III (d).

An argument by means of which the implication

$$(S_1 \ \& \ S_2 \ \& \ S_3) \supset S_4$$

can be proved may be compared with Kant's description of the process of verifying the equation $7+5 = 12$. The initial chains of seven and five existential quantifiers in S_1 and S_2, respectively, invite us to consider respective sets of seven and five individuals. This is comparable with what Kant says about the necessity of going outside the concepts of 7 and 5 and of resorting to the use of intuitions which correspond to these concepts, i.e., resorting to considering particular sets of seven and five individuals, whether these be fingers or points or individuals of some other sort. A main part of the formal proof consists in letting the two strings of initial existential quantifiers of S_1 and S_2 coalesce into a longer chain of twelve existential quantifiers. This may be accomplished, e.g., by extending the scope of the five initial quantifiers of S_2 one by one so as to include the sentences S_1 and S_3 too. This is comparable with what Kant says about adding 'one by one' the five units by means of which the concept of 5 was illustrated to the units by means of which the concept of 7 was illustrated. What remains to be done in the proof is to verify that the resulting sentence can be transformed into S_4 by certain trivial transformations that hinge on the properties of identity. This simple process of verification may be compared with what Kant says about 'seeing the number 12 come into being' as a result of adding the two sets of units to each other.

Thus there is a fairly close parallelism between the two processes. The parallelism extends to the philosophical evaluation of the proof. What makes the equation synthetic in Kant's view is the necessity of actually carrying out the addition. It is seen that the counterpart of this addition in the formal proof I sketched, viz. the amalgamation of the two chains of existential quantifiers into one longer chain, is also just what increases the depth of the sentences in question and therefore just what makes the proof synthetic in sense III (d). Kant's reason for the syntheticity of the equation therefore agrees with the reason why it is synthetic in our sense III (d).

10. *Logical truths not laws of thought*

We can bring our concept of analyticity to bear also on the famous example of Langford's and Moore's.[30] On the usual definitions of a cube in ordinary Euclidean geometry, a cube necessarily has twelve edges. Yet someone may know what the word 'cube' means and recognize a cube when he sees one without realizing that a cube has this number of edges.

This possibility is connected with the fact that the argument by means of which one can establish the number of edges of a cube is likely to be synthetic in sense III (d). For instance, if we define cube as a solid which is bounded by three pairs of equidistant planes which are at right angles to each other, we mention a maximum of nine geometrical entities (six planes and three angles). The inference from such a definition to the conclusion that the number of the edges of a cube is twelve must

---

[30] See C. H. Langford, 'Moore's Notion of Analysis', in *The Philosophy of G. E. Moore* (note 6 to Chapter VI), pp. 319–42; cf. Moore's answer, op. cit., pp. 660–7.

therefore increase the number of the geometrical objects we are considering, that is to say, it must be synthetic in sense III (d).

Similarly our observations seem to throw light on other well-known problems in the philosophy of logic. There is a doctrine of venerable antiquity according to which the laws of logic are in some sense laws of thought. Allied with this doctrine is the view that logical inferences are in some sense necessary or unavoidable. Aristotle thought that whenever both the premisses of a syllogism (at least in the case of a perfect syllogism) are present in the human soul 'the soul must . . . affirm the conclusion'.[31] There may be some plausibility in this idea as applied to arguments analytic in sense III (i.e., which are tautologous in the sense of being surface tautologies). The alleged necessity of logical inferences is seen illusory, however, as soon as we consider inferences which are synthetic in sense III. If we have to do something ourselves before we can draw the conclusion, namely, to introduce new auxiliary individuals into the argument, then the drawing of a conclusion cannot be necessary in the sense that one cannot avoid drawing it. Logical inferences which are synthetic in this sense will not be inferences we have to draw, but rather inferences we can draw—if we want to and if we are clever enough.

It is perhaps no accident that the idea of logical truths as laws of thought has fallen into disrepute roughly simultaneously with the development of the modern logic of quantification, most of which has been seen to be synthetic in the relevant sense, viz. sense III. In any case, there seems to be a historical connection between the idea that logical connections are necessary and the idea that they are analytic in sense III. For instance, there is a great deal of similarity between the way Kant explains his notion of an analytic truth and the way Descartes explains his notion of a necessary connection. In both cases, a conclusion follows from a premiss in the desired way if and only if it is implied in the concept of the premiss in such a way that the latter cannot be conceived distinctly without also thinking of the former. Some of Kant's examples are also strikingly reminiscent of Descartes's.[32]

---

[31] *Nicomachean Ethics*, VII, 3, 1147ᵃ27.

[32] Descartes, *Regulae*, rule XII (cf. note 29 above); rule XIV (p. 52 of the first edition). In the former passage, Descartes's example is $3+4 = 7$, which reappears

It has been suggested that the idea of logical truths as laws of thought has been discredited by the discovery that they are analytic (presumably in sense IV of analyticity).[33] It seems to me more illuminating to invert this judgement. The fact that the truths of logic are not laws of thought is best brought out by the realization that they are synthetic in sense III. If we realize this, we realize that the truths of logic do not come to us automatically but require work on our own part. The rules of this work cannot be laid down completely in the sense that its outcome will normally remain unpredictable.

in Kant (letter to Schultz, Academy Edition, vol. 10, pp. 528–31). In the latter passage, Descartes's example is 'body is extended', which is also found in Kant (*Critique of Pure Reason*, A 7 = B 11).

[33] See A. J. Ayer, *Language, Truth and Logic* (note 37 to Chapter VI above), p. 81.

IX

KANT AND THE TRADITION OF ANALYSIS

1. *The directional sense of analysis*

In the preceding chapter it was argued that Kant was right in holding that mathematical arguments are synthetic. He was right if by synthetic we mean synthetic in sense III, i.e., in a sense in which it is the hallmark of a synthetic procedure that it increases the number of individuals we are considering in their relation to each other. Certain ways of making this sense more precise have also been discussed in Chapters VII–VIII. It remains to put this result in a wider perspective by considering it against Kant's historical background.

Like so many other philosophical terms, the terms 'analytic' and 'synthetic' seem to have originated from the mathematical terminology of the ancient Greeks.[1] Although the term 'analysis' was already employed by Aristotle, the fullest statement of the meaning of the terms 'analytic' and 'synthetic' in Greek geometry is found in as late an author as Pappus, who writes:

Now analysis is a method of taking that which is sought as though it were admitted and passing from it through its consequences in order to something which is admitted as a result of synthesis; for in analysis we suppose that which is sought to be already done (ὡς γεγονὸς ὑποθέμενοι), and we inquire what it is from which this comes about, and again what is the antecedent cause of the latter, and so on until, by retracing our steps, we light upon something already known or ranking as a first principle; and such a method we call analysis, as being a solution backwards (ἀνάπαλιν λύσιν).

But in synthesis, proceeding in the opposite way, we suppose to be already done that which was last reached in the analysis, and arranging in their natural order as consequents what were formerly

---

[1] Cf. B. Einarson, 'On Certain Mathematical Terms in Aristotle's Logic', *American Journal of Philology*, vol. 57 (1936), pp. 34–54, 151–72, especially pp. 36–40.

antecedents and linking them one with another, we finally arrive at the construction of what was sought; and this we call synthesis. (Tr. mainly after Ivor Thomas.)[2]

This passage is not without difficulties. One major difficuty concerns the direction of the steps of analysis as compared with the direction of relations of logical consequence. Does one in an analysis draw conclusions, or does one rather try to find antecedents from which conclusions could be drawn? I cannot discuss this problem here in any detail.[3] There is another problem, however, which concerns us directly. Pappus goes on to make a distinction between theoretical and problematic analysis, that is to say, analysis as applied to theorems and analysis as applied to problems. Here we are of course primarily interested in theoretical analysis. 'In the theoretical kind', Pappus writes, 'we suppose what is sought to exist and to be true, and then we pass through its consequences in order, as though they were also true and established by our hypothesis, to something which is admitted.'[4] This statement is not unambiguous, however. Independently of what Pappus himself may have had in mind, his explanations could be developed, and were developed, along

---

[2] Ivor Thomas, ed. and trans., *Greek Mathematics*, vol. 2, *Loeb Classical Library* (William Heinemann and Harvard University Press, London and Cambridge, Mass., 1941), pp. 596–9.

[3] It has been discussed by several scholars recently. See Michael S. Mahoney, 'Another Look at Greek Geometrical Analysis', *Archive for History of Exact Sciences*, vol. 5 (1968–9), pp. 318–48, which may be contrasted with Norman Gulley, 'Greek Geometrical Analysis', *Phronesis*, vol. 3 (1958), pp. 1–14, and F. M. Cornford, 'Mathematics and Dialectic in the *Republic* VI–VII', *Mind*, vol. 41 (1932), pp. 37–52 and 173–90, especially pp. 46–8. For a different line of interpretation, see Harold Cherniss, 'Plato as a Mathematician', *Review of Metaphysics*, vol. 4 (1951), pp. 395–425, especially pp. 414–19, and Richard Robinson, 'Analysis in Greek Geometry', *Mind*, vol. 45 (1936), pp. 464–73. Gulley's interpretation is accepted in the main by R. S. Bluck in the introduction to his edition of Plato's *Meno* (Cambridge University Press, 1961), pp. 76–8. For background, see T. L. Heath, *Euclid's Elements* (Cambridge University Press, 1926), vol. 1, pp. 139–42 and vol. 3, p. 442, and Paul Tannery, 'Du sens des mots analyse et synthèse chez les Grecs', in *Mémoires scientifiques de Paul Tannery*, vols. 1–16 (Toulouse, 1912–43), vol. 3, pp. 162–9. It seems to me that all through this discussion the force of certain crucial terms has been misunderstood, but I cannot pursue this lead here, nor change the translation as I think it ought to be changed. (Cf. note 4 below, however.) This problem is in any case independent of the main line of argument of the present chapter.

[4] It is doubtful, however, whether the 'consequences' of which the translation speaks are intended by Pappus to be logical (deductive) consequences or whether this term merely refers to whatever 'goes together' with, or corresponds to, the desired conclusion in its immediate or distant premises.

two entirely different lines. First, one could emphasize the difference between the directions in which one proceeds when practising analysis and when practising synthesis. This aspect of the distinction had been given a certain prominence by Aristotle when he compared the process of deliberation with geometrical analysis and the process of acting on the deliberation with geometrical synthesis.[5] On this interpretation, one is proceeding analytically when one follows relations of logical consequence (or, in some cases, relations of causal consequence) in a direction opposite to their normal direction, whereas one is proceeding synthetically when one follows them in their natural direction. This interpretation remained the predominant one, or one of the predominant ones, in philosophical literature all through the Middle Ages. We shall call it the *directional* interpretation of the notions of analysis and synthesis.[6] It applies much more generally than merely in geometry. Its connection with geometry was frequently lost altogether in the history of philosophy.

2. *The constructional sense of analysis*

This difference in direction is not, however, what a practising mathematician is likely to find fascinating in the method of

[5] Aristotle, *Nicomachean Ethics*, III, 3, 1112 ᵇ11–24; cf. *Metaphysics* IX, 9, 1051ª21, and T. L. Heath, *Mathematics in Aristotle* (Clarendon Press, Oxford, 1949), pp. 270–2. It should perhaps be mentioned that Aristotle uses the term *analysis* explicitly but usually not the term *synthesis*, speaking instead of 'the order of becoming' or of 'genesis'.

[6] Cf. Neal W. Gilbert, *Renaissance Concepts of Method* (Columbia University Press, New York, 1960), pp. 31–5, 81–3. The philosophical senses of analysis and synthesis had lost their connection with the geometrical usage already at the time of Galen. Gilbert writes: 'Although Galen speaks of synthesis and analysis, he never . . . takes cognizance of the two correlative geometrical methods, but always gives to the terms the meaning they had received in the philosophical tradition' (p. 33). Cf. also A. C. Crombie, *Medieval and Early Modern Science*, vol. 2 (Doubleday & Co., Garden City, N.Y., 1959), pp. 11–17, and A. C. Crombie, *Robert Grosseteste and the Origins of Experimental Science* (Clarendon Press, Oxford, 1953; second printing, 1962), pp. 27–9, 52–90, 193–4, 297–318. Crombie quotes Walter Burley expounding the doctrine of Grosseteste: 'Averroës said that there is a double process in natural science: one is from effect to cause, the other from cause to effect; . . . and this is what Grosseteste . . . means here' (p. 57). This is obviously an instance of what I propose to call the directional sense of analysis and synthesis. It is also interesting to note the frequent contrast between mathematical methods and the methods of natural science in writers like Grosseteste, cf. op. cit., pp. 56–7. The disappearance of this contrast is typical of the methodology of the early modern science. Cf., e.g., Newton's concluding comments in his *Opticks*: 'As in Mathematics, so in Natural Philosophy, the Investigation of difficult things by the Method of Analysis, ought ever to precede the Method of Composition.'

analysis. He is more likely to be interested in the similarities between theoretical and problematic analysis. The reason for this will be appreciated by all who have tried to prove geometrical propositions from axioms and earlier propositions. In proving geometrical theorems, it seldom suffices to consider the given figure, i.e., the figure of which the antecedent of the proposition speaks. In all the interesting cases, we need a 'preparation' or a 'construction' or a 'machinery' (in Greek: κατασκευή) in order to be able to conduct the proof.[7] In other words, we have to complement the given figure by drawing new lines, circles, and other figures. When Pappus says that in a theoretical analysis 'we assume what is sought to exist and to be true', this can be understood as requesting us to assume that the proposition in question is true and that the auxiliary constructions which are needed for the proof have already been carried out. This is in fact what Greek geometers frequently did in their analyses.[8] This interpretation is encouraged also by Pappus' formulation. What can he mean by his invitation to assume (in a theoretical analysis) that which is sought as though it were true, *and existent*, if not that one should assume that sufficient auxiliary constructions have already been made? It may also be pointed out that, in his general definition of an analysis, Pappus says without qualification that in it we assume that which is being sought as if it were already done.

Apart from Pappus' intentions, which are admittedly not very clear, this aspect of the distinction is what is likely to interest a working geometer. He is likely to have learned from his experience that the discovery of suitable auxiliary constructions is frequently not only the most difficult but also the really essential part of proving a geometrical proposition. Nor was this fact lost upon philosophers of mathematics, although they could not always accommodate it within their general theories. The most extreme formulation comes, curiously enough, from Aristotle,

[7] For the division of a proposition into different parts in Euclid, see Heath, *Euclid's Elements* (note 3 above), pp. 129–31.

[8] It may not be entirely irrelevant to recall also the fact that in the famous 'analysis' that was performed by Socrates together with Meno's slave-boy in Plato's *Meno* it was Socrates and not the slave-boy who drew the figures from which they reasoned. They were among the starting-points of the slave-boy's 'analysis', not among its outcomes. Cf. Norman Gulley, *Plato's Theory of Knowledge* (Methuen, London, 1962), pp. 14–15.

who writes that 'it is by activity also that geometrical propositions are discovered; for we find them by dividing. If the figures
had been already divided, the propositions would have been
obvious; but as it is they are present only potentially.'[9] The word
which I have here rendered as 'proposition' can also mean 'construction'. My rendering is justified by the fact that Aristotle's
examples show clearly that he has in mind the fact that when
suitable constructions have been carried out, the truth of a
proposition would be 'evident to anyone as soon as he saw the
figure'.[10] Incidentally, this double meaning illustrates my point
very well. The use of a word which should mean construction
for the whole of a geometrical proposition, bears witness to the
importance of suitable constructions for geometrical theorems in
the Greek mind. There was a similar ambiguity about the word
γράφειν which could mean either 'to draw' or 'to prove'.[11]

Much later, Leibniz wrote in the same vein that in geometry
'the greatest art often consists in finding this preparation' (i.e.,
auxiliary construction).[12] He also complains that 'in ordinary
geometry, we still have no method of determining the *best constructions* when the problems are a little complex'. (The italics
are as in the original.)[13]

Emphasizing this aspect of the distinction between analysis
and synthesis gives rise to a different interpretation of the distinction. On this interpretation, a method or a procedure is
analytic if in it we do not introduce any new geometrical entities,
in brief, if we do not carry out any constructions. A procedure
is synthetic if such constructions are made use of, i.e., if new
geometrical entities are introduced into the argument. This distinction will then apply to problems pretty much in the same

[9] Aristotle, *Metaphysics* IX, 9, 1051ᵃ21–31.

[10] I am following the interpretation of T. L. Heath; see *Mathematics in Aristotle*
(note 5 above), pp. 216–17. Heath refers to *Categories* 14ᵃ39 and *Metaphysics* V, 10,
1014ᵃ36 for further evidence. Cf. also W. D. Ross, *Aristotle's Metaphysics, A Revised
Text with Introduction and Commentary* (Clarendon Press, Oxford, 1924), vol. 2, p. 268,
and Eckhard Niebel, 'Untersuchungen über die Bedeutung der geometrischen
Konstruktionen in der Antike', *Kantstudien*, Supplementary Vol. 76 (Cologne, 1959),
pp. 92–5. Niebel supplies further references to Aristotle and to secondary literature.

[11] Niebel, op. cit. (note 10 above), pp. 97–9.

[12] Leibniz, *Nouveaux Essais*, Book IV, Ch. 17, § 3, where Leibniz expounds the
traditional division of a geometrical proposition into different parts (cf. note 7
above). The translation is taken from Langley's well-known translation (Open
Court, La Salle, Illinois, third ed., 1949).

[13] Leibniz, *Nouveaux Essais*, Book IV, Ch. 3, § 6 (Langley's translation).

way as to theorems. The distinction between problematic and theoretical analysis vanishes. In either sort of analysis, a premium is put on the study of the interrelations of the different parts of a figure.

This meaning of the term 'analysis' was naturally extended from the analysis of geometrical configurations to the 'analysis' of physical or astronomical configurations. This is roughly the sense in which the first great modern scientists speak of analysis.[14]

What they mean is the study of the functional interrelations of a given physical situation. When these interrelations have been discovered and generalized, they can be applied deductively to new configurations of objects which are often more complex than the one from which the general laws were first extracted. This deductive application of the results of analysis and generalization to new cases was often referred to as synthesis. Hence, the relation of the distinction between analysis and synthesis to the distinction between formal and empirical truths was almost the opposite to what it is in present-day philosophy: the empirical element consisted in the analysis while synthesis was performed deductively.[15] When Ernst Cassirer

[14] See A. C. Crombie, *Robert Grosseteste* (note 6 above), pp. 303–19, who supplies further references. The usage of the pioneers of modern science thus marks two important changes as compared with the ideas and the terminology of their medieval predecessors: first, they re-established a connection between the geometrical and the philosophical senses of 'analysis' and 'synthesis', and, secondly, they assimilated the study of the interrelations of the parts of a geometrical configuration to the study of the interrelations of the physical factors in an experimental situation. Both these aspects are strikingly brought out by Newton's terse methodological comments at the end of his *Opticks*, partially quoted in note 6 above. Concerning the rediscovery of the geometrical sense of analysis and synthesis and concerning the switch from the medieval terms *resolutio* and *compositio* to the Greek terms, cf. Gilbert, pp. 81–3. Gilbert writes: 'In fact, the very replacement of these Latin words (sc. *resolutio* and *compositio*) by the Greek in subsequent philosophical and scientific usage is unquestionably due to the fact that the Greek words were now associated very precisely with their geometrical usage, and thus were considered superior to the medieval Latin terms, with their more extensive and vague connotations.' It seems to me that a presupposition of this kind of a change is a degree of mathematical sophistication at which the role of constructions in geometrical proofs is appreciated, for otherwise the geometrical usage is easily assimilated without any change of meaning to the directional sense of analysis and synthesis. For extremely suggestive remarks on the role of the idea of geometrical analysis in Galileo's methodology, see Ernst Cassirer, 'Galileo's Platonism', in *Studies and Essays in the History of Science and Learning Offered in Homage to George Sarton*, ed. by M. F. Ashley Montague (Henry Schuman, New York, 1944), pp. 277–97.

[15] This is in effect observed in connection with Kant's early usage by Hans Vaihinger in his *Commentar zu Kants Kritik der reinen Vernunft* (W. Spemann,

made his illuminating comparison between the geometrical
method of analysis and the methods of the first great modern
scientists,[16] he had in mind just the analogy between the experimental 'analysis' of a given physical configuration and the
'problematic' analysis of the interrelations of the different parts
of a geometrical figure, an analogy which in fact seems to have
been one of the basic methodological ideas of such scientists as
Galileo (who still employed the medieval terms 'composition'
and 'resolution' for 'synthesis' and 'analysis') and Newton.
Where Cassirer erred was in his attempt to find anticipations
of this notion of analysis in certain earlier writers (mainly
Zabarella) whose notions of analysis and synthesis largely
remained in the sphere of the medieval ideas and who mainly
emphasized the relatively trivial directional sense of the notions
of analysis and synthesis.[17]

3. *Kant as an heir to the constructional sense*

It seems to me that Kant's distinction between analytic and
synthetic can be fully understood only against this historical
background. To some extent, Kant was himself aware of it,
although he often tends to stress his own advances over and
above his predecessors. Both the directional sense and the more

Stuttgart, 1881–92), vol. 1, p. 273, but he fails to see how Kant's later usage
developed from this sense of analysis and synthesis.

[16] Cassirer, 'Galileo's Platonism' (note 14 above); see also *Das Erkenntnisproblem*,
vols. 1–2 (Bruno Cassirer, Berlin, 1906), vol. 1, pp. 136–7, and cf. John H. Randall,
Jr., 'Scientific Method in the School of Padua', *Journal of the History of Ideas*, vol. 1
(1940), pp. 177–206, reprinted partly in *The Roots of Scientific Thought*, ed. by P. P.
Wiener and A. Noland (Basic Books, New York, 1957), pp. 139–46, and Randall's
more recent monograph, *The School of Padua and the Emergence of Modern Science* (Saggi
e testi, Padua, 1961).

[17] Gilbert, op. cit. (note 6 above), pp. 172–3. Gilbert apparently has not noticed
Cassirer's own qualifications in 'Galileo's Platonism', however, where Cassirer
writes, in connection with the Padua school to which Zabarella was an heir, as
follows: 'But what Galileo could find here were rather the *terms* in which he
expressed his theory than the theory itself. For even if he read Zabarella's work
De regressu or another work of the same type, he did not read it in the spirit in
which it was written. . . . His thought is, directly and immediately, connected with
Plato, with Eudoxus and Euclid, not with Jean Buridan or Nicholas d'Oresme.
In Euclid he found the first clear and sharp distinction between "analysis" and
"synthesis"' (p. 296). Gilbert ought to have criticized Randall rather than Cassirer,
it seems to me.

On Newton, see Henry Guerlac, 'Newton and the Method of Analysis' (forthcoming).

interesting 'problematic' sense of analysis and synthesis were in
any case current in his time, as one can easily ascertain by
witnessing the way in which these terms were used by Newton,
Leibniz, and others. On two different occasions, Kant states as
clearly as he can (which is not always *very* clearly) that his
distinction between analysis and synthesis is modelled on the
idea of a 'problematic' analysis, not on the directional sense of
analysis and synthesis. In the *Prolegomena*[18] he firmly dissociates
his distinction between analytic and synthetic *sentences* (*Sätze*)
from the distinction between the analytic and the synthetic
method. This difference between the two methods he describes
in terms of the directions in which one proceeds in them essentially in the same way as in the traditional directional sense. In
disclaiming this sense, Kant says that he would rather call it a
distinction between the *regressive* and the *progressive* method. In
his *Dissertation* of the year 1770 (§ 1, footnote) he makes essentially the same distinction in different terms. There he distinguishes two different sorts of synthesis: (1) synthesis in the
sense of a passage from a ground to a consequence (Kant calls
it qualitative synthesis), and (2) synthesis in the sense of a
passage from parts to a whole (quantitative synthesis). In the
same way, according to Kant analysis may mean either (1) transition from a consequence to its grounds (qualitative analysis),
or (2) transition from a whole to its parts (quantitative analysis).
By analysis and synthesis Kant will understand exclusive *quantitative* analysis. It is obvious that this statement assimilates Kant's
notion of analysis once again to the notion of problematic
analysis discussed earlier. Parts of it recall Newton's remarks,
according to which 'by this way of analysis we may proceed
from components to ingredients'.[19]

In earlier chapters of this book it has been suggested that for
Kant the reason why mathematical arguments are synthetic is
that they are constructive. By their constructivity, I suggested
further, Kant meant the fact that new individual mathematical
objects are introduced during these arguments. Now we can see
that Kant was not introducing any novelties here. He was
simply taking the traditional notion of problematic analysis and

[18] *Prolegomena*, § 5 (vol. 4, p. 276, of the Academy Edition of Kant's works),
footnote.
[19] Newton, *Opticks*, many editions, last few paragraphs.

synthesis, and trying to apply it more widely than it had usually been applied. We can also see that the basic idea of Kant's distinction between analytic and synthetic was, at least in contexts similar to geometrical arguments, exactly the same as the basic idea of our sense III of analyticity.

This is borne out by Kant's own explanations. He argued for his claim that mathematical truths are synthetic by in effect trying to show that mathematical arguments are synthetic in our sense III (d) or perhaps (e). (These two were never distinguished from each other by Kant.) The syntheticity of mathematics in our sense III was therefore for Kant a sufficient reason for their being synthetic in his sense of the term. This may be seen as follows: the reason why he thought mathematical truths are synthetic, was that they proceed from the construction of concepts.[20] Kant explains what he means by a construction at the end of the *Critique of Pure Reason*,[21] a passage to which he refers in the *Prolegomena*. 'To *construct* a concept means', he says, 'to exhibit *a priori* the intuition which corresponds to the concept.' It has been noted already that Kant defines an intuition simply as a representative of an individual. For him, an intuition is almost like a 'proper name' in Frege's unnaturally wide sense of the term, except that it did not have to be a linguistic entity, but could also be anything in the human mind which 'stands for' an individual. What made mathematics synthetic was the introduction of such singular terms to represent the individuals to which certain general concepts apply, in the same way that geometrical entities are introduced by geometrical 'constructions' into the figure by means of which we are illustrating the interrelations of the geometrical concepts involved in the proof. Kant's wider notion of a construction is thus nothing but a generalization from the constructions which make geometrical arguments synthetic.[22]

Sometimes Kant seems to say that all mathematical truths turn on the use of 'intuitions' or representatives of individuals whence they are all of them synthetic. Elsewhere he nevertheless admits that some mathematical propositions are 'valid according

[20] *Prolegomena*, § 2, p. 272 of the Academy Edition.

[21] *Critique of Pure Reason*, A 713 ff. = B 741 ff. (p. 576 of the Kemp Smith translation).

[22] Cf. also my paper 'Kantin oppi matematiikasta', *Ajatus*, vol. 22 (1959), pp. 5–85, especially Chs. 3 and 4.

to concepts alone' and hence analytic.[23] What makes the difference is shown by Kant's examples and by the relation of his concepts to the practice of the mathematicians. A mathematical argument is analytic for him, only if it does not require the use of constructions, i.e., only if it does not require the introduction of any *new* intuitions or representatives of individuals. This is obviously the case if and only if the argument in question does not increase the number of individuals we are considering together in their relation to each other. Hence Kant's diagnosis of the reasons why mathematical truths are synthetic comes to telling us that they are synthetic in our sense III. This sense, or a group of senses, is therefore highly important historically.

4. *A current interpretation of Kant is mistaken*

This observation implies, among other things, that a widespread interpretation of Kant's theory of the mathematical method is mistaken. Often it is said or implied that 'Kant, having observed that the geometers of his day could not prove their theorems by unaided argument, but required an appeal to figure, invented a theory of mathematical reasoning according to which the inference is never strictly logical, but always requires the support of what is called "intuition"', to speak with Russell.[24]

This view is mistaken on several counts. I have said already that by an intuition Kant initially meant nothing but a representative of an individual. It is just the introduction of such individual representatives of general concepts that Kant calls a construction; and this construction is what makes mathematical reasoning synthetic. Russell's view amounts to holding that the intuitive and synthetic element of a geometrical argument lies outside the axiomatic and deductive framework, in an appeal to our geometrical imagination. Our observations show, however, that for Kant the synthetic element falls squarely within the familiar distinction between the different parts of a geometrical proposition.[25] The synthetic and intuitive element was located

---

[23] *Prolegomena*, § 2, p. 269 of the Academy Edition.

[24] Bertrand Russell, *Introduction to Mathematical Philosophy* (Allen and Unwin, Ltd., London, 1919), p. 145. Russell's view seems to be shared in these days by a majority of scholars.

[25] Cf. Heath, *Euclid's Elements* (note 3 above), pp. 129–31. The most important parts were: (1) the enunciation (πρότασις), (2) the setting-out (ἔκθεσις), (3) the

mainly in the auxiliary construction or κατασκευή. To some extent, Kant also seems to have thought of another part of the proposition as being synthetic, namely, the setting-out or *ecthesis* (ἔκθεσις) which immediately follows the general enunciation of the proposition in question and in which the geometrical entities with which the general enunciation deals are 'set out' or 'exposed' in the form of a particular figure. By contrast, he considered analytic the proof proper (in Greek: ἀπόδειξις) which follows the auxiliary construction and in which no new geometrical objects are introduced. In this *apodeixis* we merely analyse, in a fairly literal sense of the word, the figure introduced in the *ecthesis* and completed in the 'construction' or 'machinery'.

This is attested to by Kant's examples. His own main example of the contrast between philosophical (analytic) and mathematical (synthetic) modes of reasoning is the familiar theorem according to which the sum of the three angles of a triangle equals two right angles.[26] What makes the difference, Kant says, is that a philosopher is restricted to analysing and clarifying the concepts of straight line, of angle, and of the number three, without being able to make use of constructions. In contrast, a geometer can draw a triangle (Euclid's *ecthesis*), complete it with suitable additional constructions (auxiliary construction or κατασκευή) and 'in this fashion, through a chain of inferences guided throughout by intuition' arrive at 'a fully evident and universally valid solution of the problem'. What Kant describes in this example is nothing but a familiar proof of the theorem in question in elementary geometry. There is not the slightest hint in his description that the basic assumptions of Euclid's system did not suffice to justify all the steps of the argument. There is not the slightest hint of an appeal to anything any axiomatic geometer could not appeal to. In particular, Kant knew perfectly well that the introduction of new geometrical entities in the constructions one performs in geometrical proofs is in Euclid's system governed by the assumptions usually known as postulates. Nevertheless, as the contrast he drew between a geometer and a philosopher clearly shows, Kant saw in these very constructions the essence of the synthetic method of a

construction or 'machinery' (κατασκευή), (4) the proof (proof proper) (ἀπόδειξις), and (5) the conclusion (συμπέρασμα), which followed each other in this order.
[26] *Critique of Pure Reason*, A 716 = B 744; Kemp Smith translation, pp. 578-9.

mathematician. Indeed, in an interesting passage he explicitly enjoins the geometer not to 'ascribe to the figure anything save what necessarily follows from what he has himself set into it in accordance with his concept',[27] that is to say, not to make any use of properties other than those the figure has in virtue of the way it was constructed by means of the postulates. It is the use of constructions (introductions of new geometrical entities) *as such*, and not their use as aids to imagination, that made a geometrical argument synthetic in Kant's eyes.[28]

5. *Kant's distinctions carry over to formalized arguments*

It follows from this that those steps of a geometrical argument that Kant considered synthetic retain their identity even when such an argument is 'formalized' in the sense of being converted into a logical argument. As I have remarked, most arguments of this sort turn out to be quantificational. It has been pointed out against Kant that figures are not needed in geometry, that geometrical proofs can be presented in the form of purely logical deductions.[29] This is beside Kant's point, however, for the distinction he wanted to make largely survives the transformation.

Within quantificational arguments, we may also try to distinguish synthetic steps from analytic ones in the Kantian sense of these terms. Although we cannot perhaps succeed in all cases, the main drift of the distinction is clear enough. Synthetic steps are those in which new individuals are introduced into the argument; analytic ones are those in which we merely discuss the individuals which we have already introduced. In a suitable formulation, arguments of the former kind can be boiled down

---

[27] *Critique of Pure Reason*, B xii; Kemp Smith translation, p. 19.

[28] From this it does not follow, of course, that Kant thought that the use of constructions in geometrical and other mathematical arguments did not in any sense turn on the structure of our sensible perception. It only follows that their use did not turn on it in the trivial sense Russell and others have thought. How Kant came to connect the use of 'intuitions' (representatives of individuals) in mathematics with the structure of our sensibility is discussed briefly in Chapter V above. This discussion rounds up my sketchy interpretation of Kant's theory of mathematics. It is to be noted here that Kant tends to emphasize the fact that mathematical constructions are man-made ('selbsttätig'), and not their possible uses in appealing to mathematical imagination.

[29] This was in fact part of the philosophical motivation of Russell's work in the foundations of mathematics.

to existential instantiation. We thus fall back on sense III of analytic and synthetic. More generally, the old problematic sense of analysis and synthesis in geometry is in this way seen to be little more than a special case of our sense III.

Hence, when Kant saw the essence of mathematical methods in their constructivity he was merely making a point which had been stressed by many earlier philosophers of mathematics. What distinguishes him from his predecessors is primarily the fact that he bases almost his entire theory of the mathematical method on the point, which for most of the earlier philosophers of mathematics had remained merely an incidental *aperçu*.[30]

The possibility of reconstructing Kant's distinction between analysis and synthesis within modern logic is relevant to the evaluation of the one-time grand programme of Frege and Russell.[31] They wanted to disprove Kant's doctrine of the synthetic character of mathematical truths by reducing mathematics to logic. Apart from the question of the success or failure of this attempted reduction, we can now see that a mere reduction to logic is, in any case, not enough to show the analyticity of mathematical truths in every relevant sense of analyticity. In particular, it is not enough to demonstrate their analyticity in the most relevant sense of the word, namely, in Kant's own sense. This sense has been seen to be very close to our sense III. Under some of the most important further developments of this group of sense many quantificational truths turn out to be synthetic. Hence even a reduction of all mathematical truths to the truths of quantification theory would not *ipso facto* prove their analyticity in anything like Kant's sense of the concept.

[30.] I am not saying here anything about the question whether synthetic modes of argument in our sense III (e) are indispensable in the particular mathematical theories Kant was familiar with (e.g., in elementary geometry). It may turn out that in a suitable formulation all the arguments that we have to carry out in them can be made analytic. This would not invalidate Kant's general point, however, for we saw in effect in the preceding chapter that in other mathematical theories (formalizable in a quantificational language) the synthetic element is indispensable (provided we restrict our rules of inference to 'natural' ones in the sense explained last time).

[31] Gottlob Frege, *Die Grundlagen der Arithmetik* (Wilhelm Koebner, Breslau, 1884); reprinted, with English translation (Basil Blackwell, Oxford, 1950); Gottlob Frege, *Die Grundgesetze der Arithmetik*, I–II (Hermann Pohle, Jena, 1893–1903, reprinted in one volume, Georg Olms, Hildesheim, 1962); A. N. Whitehead and Bertrand Russell, *Principia Mathematica*, I–III (Cambridge University Press, 1910–13; second edition 1925–7).

6. *Analogy between geometry and algebra*

When Kant extended the old idea that constructions make geometrical arguments synthetic to other parts of mathematics, he was helped by certain ideas current in his time. The most important of them was probably the idea of a close connection between geometrical and arithmetical operations. This was the basic idea of Descartes's new 'analytic' geometry. A modern reader is likely to think in the first place of the use of co-ordinates when he thinks of analytic geometry. This, however, was not Descartes's starting-point. He was, rather, slowly forced to introduce them in the course of his inquiry. Descartes's basic idea is a thoroughgoing analogy between the basic arithmetical operations and certain geometrical operations. The analogy between arithmetical and geometrical addition (of lines) is obvious enough. One of Descartes's main ideas was to apply an interpretation consistently, on which the multiplication of lines also yields a line. Hence he could interpret all polynomial expressions within ordinary plane geometry. Descartes's approach is stated with his customary vigour in the opening sentences of *La Géométrie*:

Any problem in geometry can easily be reduced to such terms that the knowledge of certain straight lines is sufficient for its construction. Just as arithmetic consists of only four or five operations, namely, addition, subtraction, multiplication, division, and the extraction of roots . . ., so in geometry, to find required lines it is merely necessary to add or subtract other lines; or else, taking one line which I shall call unity in order to relate it as closely as possible to numbers . . ., and having given two lines, to find a fourth line which shall be to one of the given lines as the other is to unity (which is the same as multiplication), or . . . as unity is to the other (which is equivalent to division); or finally, to find one, two, or several mean proportionals (*proportionnelles moyennes*) between unity and some other line (which is the same as extracting the square root, cube root, etc.) . . .

Kant's statements show that he was perfectly well aware of the connection between the basic arithmetical operations and certain geometrical constructions.[32] Descartes had said that he did not hesitate to introduce arithmetical terms into geometry 'for the sake of greater clearness'. It seems to me Kant did not hesitate to generalize to other parts of mathematics, and even

[32] See the Academy Edition of his works, vol. 11, p. 196, and vol. 14, pp. 55–8.

beyond mathematics, the distinction between analysis and synthesis in the old geometrical sense of the distinction.

This explains why Kant seems to have thought it is the necessity of actually carrying out arithmetical and algebraic operations that makes the resulting equations or statements synthetic. An arithmetical or algebraic equation is analytically true according to this view, only if it can be verified without performing any operations. Kant's examples of such analytic truths of mathematics are $a = a$ and $a+b \geqslant a$.

From this point of view we can understand certain statements of Kant's which otherwise remain very puzzling. An analogy between geometrical constructions and the basic arithmetical operations enabled him to extend his distinction to elementary arithmetic and algebra. Keeping this in mind, we can now understand, among other things, the reason why he called simple arithmetical equations like $7+5 = 12$ 'immediately certain' or 'indemonstrable'.[33] This is usually taken to mean that after the numbers in question are 'made intuitive' in a suitable way by means of fingers or points, we can at once perceive the truth of the equation. This interpretation is refuted, however, by the fact that Kant says that his point is seen more clearly if we consider somewhat greater numbers.[34] It is also disproved by the fact that Kant describes in some detail a procedure by means of which the intuitive representatives of the two numbers 7 and 5 are combined. He even insists that this process is not momentary but gradual and that it takes place in time (it is 'der Zeitbedingung unterworfen').[35]

Kant's purpose is seen if the process by means of which the equation $7+5 = 12$ is established is compared with the structure typical of a proposition in Euclid's *Elements*. The preliminary representation of the numbers 7 and 5 by means of groups of five and seven individuals corresponds to the setting-out or *ecthesis*. The gradual process of combining the two groups into a single group of twelve individuals corresponds to the preparatory construction, to the κατασκευή. But what happens to the proof proper, to the ἀπόδειξις? It falls out of the picture or,

---

[33] *Critique of Pure Reason*, A 164 = B 204; Kemp Smith translation, p. 199.
[34] *Critique of Pure Reason*, B 15–16; Kemp Smith translation, p. 53.
[35] See *Prolegomena*, penultimate paragraph, p. 370 of the Academy Edition; and the same edition, vol. 10, p. 530.

speaking more precisely, it reduces to a minimum, to the mere observation that the result of the auxiliary construction equals the desired result, 12. When Kant says that simple arithmetical equations are immediate and indemonstrable, he simply means that no proof proper, no *apodeixis* is required to establish them. That this really was Kant's meaning is verified by his own remarks in a letter to Johann Schultz on 25 November 1788. They show that the reason why Kant thought of such equations as 7+5 = 12 as being 'immediately certain practical judgements' or, as Kant called them, 'postulates' is that they need no 'resolution' and no 'proof'; i.e., they need none of the deductive parts of a proposition or a problem, in the sense in which these parts are distinguished from one another in traditional texts of geometry.[36]

In the same vein, we may perhaps understand another puzzling statement of Kant's. Immediately after having stated in the *Critique of Pure Reason* that all mathematical judgements are synthetic he goes on to say that 'all mathematical inferences (*Schlüsse*) proceed in accordance with the principle of contradiction (which the nature of all apodeictic certainty requires) . . . .'.[37]

One possibility of interpretation scholars seem generally to have overlooked is to understand Kant's remark about proceeding in accordance with the principle of contradiction as pertaining only to the 'proof proper' part of a geometrical proposition, as well as to the analogous parts of other mathematical arguments. After all, this was according to the Greek terminology exactly the 'apodeictic' part of a proposition; and it is exactly the one and only part in which *inferences* are drawn (as opposed to steps of construction).

Otherwise, it is difficult to understand what Kant means by saying that the nature of all apodeictic certainty requires that inferences must be drawn in accordance with the principle of contradiction. He says elsewhere that a sentence which turns solely on the principle of contradiction is analytic. Nevertheless, he often recognizes truths which are apodeictic and yet syn-

---

[36] For the division of a problem (as distinguished from a theorem) into parts in Greek geometry, and for the terms used in these several parts, cf. Heath, *Euclid's Elements* (note 3 above), pp. 140–2.

[37] *Critique of Pure Reason*, B 14; Kemp Smith translation, p. 52. This passage was lifted to the second edition of the first *Critique* from the *Prolegomena*, § 2 (c), ii (p. 268 of the Academy Edition).

thetic.[38] He cannot therefore require that the whole proof of an apodeictic truth in mathematics depends only on the principle of contradiction, for this would make all of mathematics analytic. What is more natural than to take him to be referring to the 'apodeictic' part of a mathematical proposition only? It is obvious that this 'proof proper' must, according to his doctrine, be conducted strictly analytically.

I suspect that some scholars who have understood the quoted passage differently have been misled by the context. A few lines later Kant writes: 'Though a synthetic proposition can indeed be discerned in accordance with the principle of contradiction, this can only be if another synthetic proposition is presupposed, and if it can be apprehended as following from this other proposition.' This statement has often been connected with the passage I quoted. It is not intended, however, as an explanation of how mathematical inferences may be analytic although the propositions proved by means of these inferences are synthetic. The answer to this question is simply that the other parts of the proposition, viz. the *ecthesis* and the auxiliary construction, make it synthetic. Kant's statement is calculated to expose an error in the view that principles of mathematics could be proved 'in accordance with the principle of contradiction', i.e., analytically. He is saying simply that those who have attempted to prove these principles ('die Zergliederer der menschlichen Vernunft') have tacitly presupposed in their proofs some synthetic principle. The mistake he is criticizing cannot very well be that earlier thinkers had overlooked the fact that the syntheticity of postulates make the arguments on which they depend synthetic. Rather, Kant is suggesting that the earlier philosophers were so much impressed with the analytic parts which are there in most mathematical proofs that they wanted to prove the postulates themselves by purely analytic means.

7. Ecthesis *and existential instantiation. Geometrical constructions as examples of synthetic procedures*

There is in the historical material also a partial generalization of the geometrical notion of a construction, which is closely

---

[38] *Critique of Pure Reason*, B 17 (Kemp Smith tr., p. 53); *Prolegomena*, § 12, pp. 284–5 of the Academy Edition.

related to the sense of analytic and synthetic we are studying. If it did not influence Kant's distinction between analysis and synthesis in mathematics, it anticipated it in any case. This generalization is implicit in the term *ecthesis*, which we found applied to the setting-out of a geometrical proposition. This term had other uses. It was applied by Aristotle to a procedure in his syllogistic logic which closely approximates to the rule of existential instantiation.[39] Whether Aristotle himself understood it in this way is not very important. It has been argued that in his syllogistic theory it should be construed in a different way, but I have not been fully convinced by these arguments.[40] Be this as it may, it was understood by many later logicians in the spirit of existential instantiation, i.e., as an 'exposition' of a particular individual among all the individuals in a certain class which we know, or assume, not to be empty. It is not impossible that Aristotle connected this logical procedure with the *ecthesis* of the geometers which he also knew and commented on.[41] If the two are connected in one and the same notion, the result is bound to be something very much like the rule of existential instantiation. Although this possibility of generalization was apparently never developed systematically before Kant, more than one earlier philosopher of mathematics must have been at least vaguely aware of it.

In a way, both Kant's general notion of a construction as the introduction of a new 'intuition', and the rule of existential instantiation, are thus further developments of this old notion of *ecthesis*.[42] The importance of the 'constructive' procedures of

[39] A typical instance of *ecthesis* is found in *Analytica Priora* I, 2, 25^{a}14–17. For further examples and for discussion, see 'Kantin oppi matematiikasta' (note 22 above), Ch. 5; W. D. Ross, *Aristotle's Prior and Posterior Analytics: A Revised Text with Introduction and Commentary* (Clarendon Press, Oxford, 1949), pp. 32–3, 412–14; Jan Łukasiewicz, *Aristotle's Syllogistic* (Clarendon Press, Oxford, 1951; second edn., 1957), pp. 59–67; Günther Patzig, *Aristotle's Theory of the Syllogism* (D. Reidel Publishing Company, Dordrecht, 1968), pp. 156–68.

[40] Patzig, loc. cit. It may be the case that a clear-cut decision between the different interpretations is impossible.

[41] Cf. Einarson, op. cit. (note 1 above), p. 161; 'Kantin oppi matematiikasta' (note 22 above), pp. 55–6.

[42] Concerning the relation of *ecthesis* to the procedures of modern logic, cf. E. W. Beth, 'Semantical Entailment and Formal Derivability', *Mededelingen der Koninklijke Nederlandse Akademie van Wetenschappen*, Afd. Letterkunde, N. R. vol. 18, no. 13, pp. 309–42 (North-Holland Publishing Company, Amsterdam, 1955); E. W. Beth, *La Crise de la raison et la logique* (Gauthier-Villars, Paris, 1957). I do not fully agree with Beth's philosophical views of the matter, however, which do not seem to me

which the rule of existential instantiation is a simple example in modern quantification theory is a tribute to the acumen of those earlier philosophers of mathematics who considered the constructions (the 'machinery' part of a Euclidean proposition) as the essence of geometrical proofs.

The mistakes of some of Kant's critics can also be effectively illustrated by applying their remarks to the special case of the quantificational proofs of elementary axiomatic geometry. I mean the critics who have explicitly or by implication denied that mathematical or logical truths are synthetic in our sense III. Consider, e.g., the statement I made in Chapter VIII, to the effect that our failure directly to perceive the conclusions of a logical argument in the premises is not due simply to whatever blocks there may be clouding our mental vision. This may be illustrated by saying that our inability to perceive the conclusion of each geometrical argument directly in the figure in which the premises of the argument are 'set out' is not due simply to our failure to look at the figure from the right point of view. This failure may be due to the perfectly objective fact that the argument can only be carried out in terms of further geometrical objects which simply are not there in the given figure, but which have to be introduced by a preparatory construction. Aristotle may have been unduly optimistic when he claimed that geometrical propositions are obvious as soon as the right constructions have been made.[43] He displayed his usual shrewdness, however, in refraining from making any claim of this sort *before* the appropriate constructions had been discovered and executed.

That candid positivist, Ernst Mach, did believe in the analyticity of logical arguments, as explained in the preceding chapter. He even formulated his point so widely as to claim in effect analyticity in our sense III. As it happened, he argued in terms of geometrical proofs. He could do this, however, only by implicitly disparaging the role of constructions in these proofs. His words are interesting enough to be quoted again: 'But if we carefully remove from our idea [of the conclusion] everything that enters into it merely as a *contribution to the construction* or through specialization, and not through the inference

---

to do full justice to the interest of the idea that *ecthesis* or something like it is an essential feature of mathematical reasoning.

[43] See the works referred to in notes 9 and 10 above.

[*Syllogismus*], we find in it nothing than the proposition we started from. . . .'[44] Of course, if the introduction of new geometrical objects by constructions is disregarded, then the rest of a geometrical argument is completely analytic or, if you prefer, tautological. But this point is entirely traditional. It does not contradict Kant or Aristotle in the.least. For Kant, the proof proper was obviously analytic. I suspect he thought it could in principle be accomplished by means of syllogisms, just as some of his predecessors had maintained that all geometrical proofs can be accomplished in this way.[45] For Aristotle the proof proper was accomplished by something like direct inspection.

As far as the point which really distinguishes Mach from Aristotle and Kant is concerned, Mach seems to be mistaken. He has it in mind that he can simply look away from 'contributions to the construction'. But if one does so, one has no hope of claiming, as he does, that it is always possible in principle to perceive the conclusion directly in the premises. This is possible, in so far as it is possible, only after suitable constructions have been made.

To adapt one of Kant's examples for our purposes: no amount of variation and combination of different points of view enables one to see from the mere examination of a triangle that the sum of its angles is equal to two right angles. Make a suitable construction, however, and this conclusion becomes obvious.

Thus Mach failed to appreciate a fact which was already seen more or less clearly by Aristotle, Leibniz, and Kant (*inter alios*), namely, the central importance of constructions in mathematical arguments.[46]

8. *Kantian intuitions and their justification*

So far, I have sought to show that Kant's concepts of analytic and synthetic may be reconstructed in modern terms. My

[44] Ernst Mach, *Erkenntnis und Irrtum* (note 25 to the preceding chapter), p. 300, cf. p. 302. The italics here are different from those in the original. It is also interesting to observe that Mach assimilates geometrical reasoning to syllogistic reasoning. Syllogistic reasoning is, as was pointed out in the preceding chapter, tautological not only in the sense of depth tautology but also in the sense of surface tautology, as mathematical (quantificational) reasoning in general is not.

[45] e.g., Leibniz and Wolff. Cf. Christian von Wolff, *Anfangsgründe aller mathematischen Wissenschaften*, Neue Aufl. (Halle, 1775), Erster Teil, §§ 45–6. (Kant used this work in connection with his lectures.)

[46] Cf. the qualifications mentioned in note 30 above, however.

argument to this effect is based on Kant's definition of an intuition as a representative of an individual. I have already given some reasons to think that this is what Kant primarily meant by the term 'intuition' (*Anschauung, intuitus*). It may be added that this is also how Kant's contemporaries understood his concept. For instance, in E. Schmid's *Wörterbuch zum leichteren Gebrauch der Kantischen Schriften* (fourth edn., Cröker, Jena, 1798), we read (p. 54): 'Anschauung. . . . Im engern, eigentlichen Sinne: nicht bloss eine Gesichtsvorstellung, sondern eine jede unmittelbare Vorstellung von dem Einzelnen; eine einzelne Vorstellung, die sich unmittelbar auf einen Gegenstand bezieht; Vorstellung eines Individuum. . . .' But of course this is not the whole story. Although Kant did not want to put more into his concept of an intuition than that it stands for an individual, he wanted to prove that all the intuitions so defined are due to sensibility, at least in the case of us human beings. Although intuitions in the Kantian sense of the word are not intuitive by definition, we might perhaps say, they can, according to Kant, be shown to be intuitive, that is to say, connected with our faculty of sensibility.

Showing this falls into two parts. Kant took it for granted that, to man at least, the only way of having *a posteriori* ideas of the existence of individuals or, as Kant puts it, of being given objects, is through human sensibility. 'Objects are *given* to us by means of sensibility, and it alone yields *intuitions*.'[47] In making this assumption, Kant was merely following an ancient tradition. Aristotle already held that 'it is sense-perception alone which is adequate for grasping the particulars'.[48] This Aristotelian assumption was echoed by Kant's German predecessors.

It is even more intriguing to see how Kant sought to establish a connection between *a priori* intuitions and sensibility. The 'intuitions' or representatives of individuals we make use of in mathematical (quantificational) reasoning are clearly *a priori* in some sense of the word. Kant tried to show that the use of such *a priori* intuitions is made possible by the structure of our sensibility. One may wonder whether my reconstruction of Kant's idea that mathematical reasoning is based on the use of intuitions (and that it is therefore synthetic) will help us in understanding the arguments by means of which Kant tried to

[47] *Critique of Pure Reason*, A 19 = B 33, Kemp Smith translation, p. 65.
[48] *Analytica Posteriora*, I, 18, 81ᵇ7.

establish this connection between the use of intuitions in mathematics and the structure of our sensible perception. One may admit that Kant's concepts of intuition and of construction can be extended so as to apply also to mathematical arguments formalized by means of quantification theory, and yet perhaps want to deny that one can make sense of the further arguments Kant carried out in terms of these concepts. The most important arguments of this kind are of course those by means of which Kant sought to prove in the 'Transcendental Aesthetic' of the *Critique of Pure Reason*, and in the corresponding part of the *Prolegomena*, that space and time, on which Kant thought that all use of mathematical intuitions is based, are really only forms of our sensibility.

It seems to me that these doubts are unfounded. As far as I can see, we can perfectly well understand Kant's line of argument even though we generalize his concepts so as to extend them to modern quantification theory. This is especially true of what Kant calls the transcendental expositions of the basic mathematical concepts (and of the corresponding parts of the *Prolegomena*). Of course, making sense of an argument is not the same thing as recognizing it as a valid argument. For this reason, our attempted extension of Kant's transcendental expositions may have the additional virtue of showing exactly where Kant went wrong.

In fact, this is what was done in Chapter V above. There it was shown that Kant's 'transcendental' question concerning the justification of the mathematical methods (as it was understood by Kant) can be understood as a question concerning the legitimacy of the rule of existential instantiation (A. E). It was also seen in Chapter V precisely where Kant went wrong in his attempt to provide a justification for the use of constructions (introductions of new intuitions) in what he called mathematics but what for us is quantification theory.

In doing this, we gave no more content to Kant's notion of individual than a representative of an individual. An introduction of an intuition will thus mean only an application of the rule of existential instantiation. More justification for this procedure has been provided since in the intervening chapters than was done in Chapter V itself. Conversely, the possibility of accounting for Kant's arguments in 'Transcendental Aesthetic' along the lines followed in Chapter V lends further support to what has lately been found out about Kant's notion of intuition and about his theories of mathematics and logic.

Here I shall only point out that Kant was perhaps not the first philosopher to worry about the problem of justifying the use of constructive (synthetic) methods in mathematics or in logic. Alexander the Commentator already discussed the justification of the process of *ecthesis* in logic—a process which was seen to be a close anticipation of Kant's concept of construction. Alexander held that the singular term introduced in the *ecthesis* is given by perception, and that a proof by *ecthesis* therefore consists in a sort of perceptual evidence.[49] He thus came to anticipate very closely Kant's fundamental doctrine, viz. that the use of *ecthesis*-like constructions in mathematics is based on the way our sensible perception works. In the Middle Ages the scholastics discussed certain modes of reasoning they called syllogisms by exposition (*syllogismi expositori*).[50] The notion of 'exposition' in question is closely related to the Greek idea of *ecthesis*, and is probably only a further development of it. The scholastics also debated whether these syllogisms by exposition are formally true or only materially true. Kant's treatment of his general notion of construction would have been classified by these schoolmen as a form of the view that they are only materially true.

[49] Alexander of Aphrodisias, *Alexandri in Aristotelis Analyticorum Priorum Librum I Commentarium*, ed. by M. Wallies, [*Commentaria in Aristotelem Graeca*, vol. 2 (a)], Berlin, 1883, p. 32, cf. pp. 33, 99–100, 104.

[50] See, e.g., William Kneale and Martha Kneale, *The Development of Logic* (Clarendon Press, Oxford, 1962), p. 273; C. Prantl, *Geschichte der Logik im Abendlande*, I–III (Leipzig, 1850–67, reprinted, Akademische Druck- u. Verlagsanstalt, Graz, 1955), vol. 3, p. 142; I. M. Bochenski, *A History of Formal Logic* (University of Notre Dame Press, Notre Dame, Indiana, 1961), 34.04–06.

X

INFORMATION, DEDUCTION, AND
THE *A PRIORI*

1. *A scandal of deduction*

C. D. BROAD has called the unsolved problems concerning
induction a scandal of philosophy.[1] It seems to me that in addition to this scandal of induction there is an equally disquieting
scandal of deduction. Its urgency can be brought home to each
of us by any clever freshman who asks, upon being told that
deductive reasoning is 'tautological' or 'analytical' and that
logical truths have no 'empirical content' and cannot be used to
make 'factual assertions': in what other sense, then, does deductive reasoning give us new information? Is it not perfectly
obvious that there is some such sense, for what point would there
otherwise be to logic and mathematics?[2] This question is apt to
cause acute embarrassment, for no such sense has so far been
defined in the literature. The only honest answer to our imaginary freshman's question is given by those few unregenerate
logical positivists who are bold enough to deny the existence of
any objective (non-psychological) sense in which deductive
inference yields new information.[3] This is a straightforward

---

[1] C. D. Broad, *The Philosophy of Francis Bacon* (Cambridge University Press, 1926).
Reprinted in C. D. Broad, *Ethics and the History of Philosophy* (Routledge and Kegan
Paul, London, 1952).

[2] An amusing instance of the difficulty of answering such a question is recorded
in *The Nature of Physical Knowledge*, ed. by L. W. Friedrich, S.J. (Indiana University
Press, Bloomington, Indiana, 1960), pp. 139–42.

[3] For different variants of this view, see Hans Hahn, *Logik, Mathematik und Naturerkennen* (Springer, Vienna, 1933) partly translated in *Logical Positivism*, ed. by A. J.
Ayer (Free Press, Glencoe, Illinois, 1959), pp. 147–61; A. J. Ayer, *Language, Truth
and Logic*, 2nd edn. (Gollancz, London, 1946), Ch. IV; Carl G. Hempel, 'Geometry
and Empirical Science', *American Mathematical Monthly*, vol. 52 (1946), pp. 7–17,
reprinted in *Readings in Philosophical Analysis*, ed. by Herbert Feigl and Wilfrid
Sellars (Appleton-Century-Crofts, New York, 1949), pp. 238–49 (see p. 241).

The doctrine that logical truths are tautologies of course figured prominently in
Wittgenstein's *Tractatus* (Ludwig Wittgenstein, *Tractatus Logico-Philosophicus* (Kegan
Paul, London, 1922)). It was no novelty on the Continent, however. Both Ernst
Mach and Moritz Schlick held the same view before Wittgenstein; see Ernst Mach,

answer, although its consequences (which are not always spelt out fully) are somewhat implausible. If no objective, non-psychological increase of information takes place in deduction, all that is involved is merely psychological conditioning, some sort of intellectual psychoanalysis, calculated to bring us to see better and without inhibitions what objectively speaking is already before our eyes.[4] Now most philosophers have not taken to the idea that philosophical activity is a species of brain-washing. They are scarcely any more favourably disposed towards the much more far-fetched idea that all the multifarious activities of a contemporary logician or mathematician that hinge on deductive inference are as many therapeutic exercises calculated to ease the psychological blocks and mental cramps that initially prevented us from being, in the words of one of these candid positivists,[5] 'aware of all that we implicitly asserted' already in the premisses of the deductive inference in question.[6] Unconvinced though many philosophers have

Erkenntnis und Irrtum, Skizzen zur Psychologie der Forschung (Johann Ambrosius Barth, Leipzig, 1905) (chapter on 'Deduktion und Induktion in psychologischer Beleuchtung') and Moritz Schlick, *Allgemeine Erkenntnislehre*, Naturwissenschaftliche Monographien und Lehrbücher (Springer, Berlin, 1918) (Chapter 14, 'Die analytische Natur des strengen Schließens').

[4] Lest it be suspected that I am fighting windmills here, let me quote again the crucial passage from Ernst Mach: 'Indem die syllogistische Deduktion von allgemeinern . . . Sätze ausgehend, durch mehrere vermittelnde Glieder, unter Wechsel und Kombinationen verschiedener Gesichtspunkte, zu spezielleren Sätzen vorschreitet, kann sich hier die Täuschung einer ganz neuen, scheinbar in den Prämissen nicht enthaltenen Einsicht ergeben. *Dieselbe hätte aber auch direkt erschaut werden können*' (op. cit., p. 302; my italics).

[5] Hahn, op. cit., sec. 2 (English translation, p. 157).

[6] It is not quite true to say that the positivistic view commits one to this interpretation of the merely subjective novelty provided by deductive arguments. In fact, a much more commonly attempted way out is to say that deductive reasoning provides us with information concerning our conceptual system or concerning our language. If this reasoning turns on certain logical particles, it serves to 'illustrate the rules which govern our usage of these logical particles', to quote A. J. Ayer's *Language, Truth and Logic* (second edn., p. 80). Now it is not clear that this kind of linguistic and conceptual information cannot be perfectly objective and non-psychological. (I shall later argue myself that the information in question, though objective and non-psychological, can be thought of as conceptual in character, when viewed from a suitable point of view, though this point of view does only partial justice to the facts of the case.) The only way of arguing that it cannot be is (it seems to me) to say that the 'information' involved is about the rules governing those very concepts that are used in making the inferences in question. These rules can be *illustrated* by means of such inferences but not *described* by means of the same 'logical particles' on which these inferences hinge. But this reduces the interpretation *ad absurdum*. For obviously the true state of affairs is the opposite to what the

remained by these implications of the positivistic doctrines, they have totally failed to produce any viable alternative to these honestly and lucidly argued views of the logical positivists.

2. *Defining deductive information*

The purpose of this chapter is to sketch such an alternative by outlining a sense of information in which non-trivial deductive reasoning does increase our information. It will be called *surface information*. This sense of information was already mentioned briefly in Chapter VIII. Some of its characteristic properties were also indicated there. It nevertheless remains to bring together the ideas that go into this concept and to mention some of the further philosophical problems which the existence of such a sense of information brings to the fore.

In the present chapter, it will be indicated how surface information can be defined for all the sentences of some given applied first-order language (quantificational language, language whose logic is that of lower predicate calculus). This sense of information is perfectly objective, and hence provides us with a counter-example to the positivistic dogma. Its nature gives rise to some further reflections of considerable philosophical interest, not unrelated to the views of those earlier philosophers who emphasized the *a priori* character of certain parts of human knowledge.

The inevitable gaps in this sketch are partly filled by what was said in earlier chapters, partly by Chapter XI below, and partly by what is found in my other writings.[7]

The measures of information we shall consider are defined in terms of a system of probability-like weights that are assigned to the sentences of our applied first-order language.[8] If p is the function that gives us these weights, any one of the usual

---

interpretation prescribes: the simpler a deduction, the more efficiently it illustrates the rules involved; and the more complicated and interesting a deduction is, the poorer it is in just illustrating the concepts on which its validity depends. Hence the allegedly non-objective information that deductive reasoning provides us with cannot be linguistic or conceptual.

[7] For the last of these three, see especially 'Surface Information and Depth Information', in *Information and Inference*, ed. by Jaakko Hintikka and Patrick Suppes (D. Reidel Publishing Company, Dordrecht, 1970), pp. 263-97, and 'Surface Semantics: Definition and its Motivation' (forthcoming).

[8] A somewhat longer discussion is given in my essay 'Surface Information and Depth Information' (note 7 above).

definitions[9] of information (informative content) gives us what
we want, e.g., one of the following:

(1) $\inf(F) = -\log p(F);$
(2) $\mathrm{cont}(F) = 1 - p(F).$

How, then, are the weights $\dot{p}(F)$ to be assigned to the different
sentences F? They may be thought of as degrees of belief (of
some sort) that one can rationally assign (*a priori*) to the several
sentences F of our language.

3. *The structure of first-order languages*

In order to explain how $p(F)$ is defined, we must first consider
the structure of our first-order language. For simplicity, we shall
restrict our attention to closed sentences (i.e., general sentences,
sentences without free singular terms). The account that will be
given of them is easily extended to other kinds of sentences.

The structure of the totality of such sentences in a given first-
order language (with a fixed finite list of non-logical predicates)
can be described in terms of a certain (inverted) tree structure
(in the precise mathematical sense of tree). Its branches are normally infinite. Its nodes are certain sentences called *constituents*.
Each constituent belongs to a definite *depth*. Each of them covers
a finite number of constituents of the next greater depth. Our
(inverted) tree thus looks somewhat like this:[10]

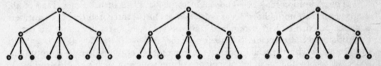

If a constituent can be reached from a given one by going downwards along some branch or other, the former is said to be
subordinate to the latter.

---

[9] For a discussion of some senses of information, see my paper 'The Varieties
of Information and Scientific Explanation', in *Logic, Methodology and Philosophy of
Science, Proceedings of the 1967 International Congress*, ed. by B. van Rootselaar and
J. F. Staal (North-Holland Publishing Company, Amsterdam, 1968), pp. 151–71.

[10] In practice, the branches are much more numerous—so numerous, indeed,
that apart from the simplest cases it is impossible to write out explicitly any of the
expressions involved. However, at each node only a *finite* number of branches
diverge. Hence the familiar 'tree theorem' (König's Lemma) applies: either the
whole tree is of finite length (there is a finite upper bound to the lengths of
branches) or there exists an infinite branch.

Each closed sentence F of our language is characterized by the number of layers of quantifiers it contains at its deepest. This parameter will be called the *depth* of F.[11] The constituents that are located at depth d in our tree structure all turn out to have the very same depth d according to this definition. Our two concepts of depth are thus essentially equivalent. Moreover, each sentence F of depth d can be effectively transformed into an equivalent sentence which has the form of a disjunction of constituents of the same depth d. This general transformability is what gives our tree structure its general significance for the whole of our language. The representation of F as a disjunction of constituents of the same depth is called the (complete disjunctive) *distributive normal form* of F. Its representation as a disjunction of constituents of some greater depth $d+e$ is called its *expansion* at this depth. These several normal forms and expansions are closely related, for each constituent is equivalent to all its subordinate constituents of a fixed given greater depth. Any two constituents of the same depth are mutually incompatible.[12] Hence all the constituents compatible with a given one belong to branches passing through it.

Virtually all logical problems concerning our language could be solved if we could locate all inconsistent constituents in the tree structure.[13] Usually, this cannot be done effectively (mechanically), however, in view of the undecidability of

---

[11] This definition may be—and ought to be—made a little stricter. First of all, it applies in this unqualified form only if an exclusive interpretation of quantifiers is presupposed, i.e., if it is required that the values of variables bound to nested quantifiers do not coincide. (Cf. next chapter, sec. 7.) If the definition is applied to statements with the usual inclusive interpretation of quantifiers, an adjustment is occasioned by the possible coincidence of the values of such nested variables.

Secondly, the notion of depth must be sharpened in the way (and for the reasons) explained in note 32 to Chapter VI above.

These qualifications do not affect at all what is said in the present chapter, however. If our domain is numerical, we can in the usual way replace existential quantifiers by Skolem functions. Then the depth of a sentence will equal the maximum of the number of nestings of functions in it, i.e., the maximum length of sequences of operations it involves. In this case, our notion becomes virtually a special case of what John von Neumann seems to have meant by his notion of arithmetical depth. (See *The Computer and the Brain*, [Yale University Press, New Haven, Conn., 1958], pp. 27, 78–9.)

[12] In the sense that for any two such constituents, C_1, C_2, we have $\vdash C_1 \supset \sim C_2$. Of course it may still happen that $\vdash C_1 \equiv C_2$, viz. when C_1 and C_2 are both inconsistent.

[13] For this would obviously provide us with a decision method for first-order logic, which is known to be impossible.

first-order logic. What we can do is locate effectively certain blatantly self-contradictory constituents which I have called *trivially inconsistent*. (We may think of the black dots in our diagram as representing such constituents.) Moreover, it can be proved that in the long run this partial method of weeding out inconsistent constituents will give us all that we want.[14] A constituent may be inconsistent without being trivially inconsistent, but if we move deeper and deeper into the diagram, eventually its inconsistency will be betrayed by the *trivial* inconsistency of all its subordinate constituents of some fixed depth. (If we cut a branch off as soon as we hit a black mark, then this means that all the branches going through an inconsistent constituent will terminate at some finite depth.[15]) The undecidability of first-order logic is due to the fact that this depth cannot be effectively predicted in advance.

It is easily seen that the decision problem for the theory whose sole non-logical axiom is a given constituent C (say of depth d) amounts to telling which constituents subordinate to C are inconsistent.[16] This is readily extended to finite disjunctions of constituents.

It is worth observing that in order to solve the decision problem just mentioned, it suffices to tell, as a function of e, *how many* inconsistent constituents of depth $d+e$ subordinate to C there are. If we know this number, we can decide *which* subordinate constituents of depth $d+e$ are inconsistent simply by taking any complete axiom system of first-order logic and grinding out theorems until precisely the right number of subordinate constituents of depth $d+e$ occur among the negations of our theorems. Then we know that the remaining ones are all consistent.

4. *Defining depth information. Its defects*

In terms of our tree structure, the problem of defining p can be described very easily. We start from the whole probability-mass

---

[14] Next chapter, sections 15–17.

[15] This depends of course on König's lemma mentioned in note 10 above.

[16] In order to decide whether $\vdash (C \supset F)$, all we need to do is to bring F to its distributive normal form at its own depth or at the depth of C, whichever is greater. If the expansion of C at this depth is $C_1 \vee C_2 \vee \ldots \vee C_w$, the question is whether those constituents C_i ($1 \leqslant i \leqslant w$) which do not occur in the normal form of F are all inconsistent. If they are (or if there are no such constituents), $\vdash (C \supset F)$. If not, the implication is invalid.

of one unit, and start dividing it up. Every time we move one step downwards in the diagram, the weight (probability) of a given constituent $C^{(d)}$ (of depth d, say) is somehow split up between its subordinate constituents of depth $d+1$. The precise principles of so doing are not at issue in this chapter, only the main problem one encounters here: do we want to assign non-zero weights only to consistent constituents, or also to all constituents that are not trivially inconsistent? If we want to define probabilities in the usual sense of the word or if we want to define the total information we can extract from a sentence concerning the reality to which our language pertains, we must not give non-zero weights to inconsistent constituents. If we give non-zero weights to consistent constituents only, we obtain well-defined senses of information. They may be called measures of *depth* information, in brief $\inf_{\text{depth}}$. They were discussed and used in Chapter VII above.

These measures have even worse shortcomings, however, than those we have already noted. (Cf. Chapter VIII, sec. 5, above.) The shortcomings are connected with the non-recursive character of depth information. On any half-way natural principles governing the distribution of weights, measures of depth information are not effectively calculable. For instance, if we follow the simplest possible rule and always divide the weight $p(C^{(d)})$ of a constituent of depth d evenly among all its consistent subordinate constituents of depth $d+i$, we must know how many such constituents there are in order to know the weight of any one of them. But we have already seen that knowing this number means knowing which of them are inconsistent, which is in general impossible to accomplish effectively.

But measures of information which are not effectively calculable are well-nigh absurd. What realistic use can there be for measures of information which are such that we in principle cannot always know (and cannot have a method of finding out) how much information we possess? One of the purposes the concept of information is calculated to serve is surely to enable us to review what we know (have information about) and what we do not know. Such a review is in principle impossible, however, if our measures of information are non-recursive.

The same point can be made in a somewhat different way by recalling the important old idea that information equals elimination of uncertainty. Because of the undecidability of first-order logic, part of the inevitable uncertainty we have to face is the uncertainty as to which constituents are consistent and which of them are inconsistent. Relief from this sort of uncertainty ought to be reflected by any realistic measure of the information which we actually possess (as distinguished from the information we in some sense have potentially available to us) and with which we can in fact operate.

5. *Defining surface information. Surface information* vis-à-vis *deduction*

Such more realistic measures of information are obtained by assigning a non-zero weight somehow to each constituent which is not trivially inconsistent. This means distributing the weight of each constituent $C^{(d)}$ somehow among its subordinate constituents of the next greater depth $d+1$, excepting only the trivially inconsistent ones. The new situation which we occasionally face here is that all these subordinate constituents are trivially inconsistent while $C^{(d)}$ is not. This means that a branch comes to an end in $C^{(d)}$. Where does its weight go? One natural answer is the following: we trace the branch back to the last node (corresponding, say, to the constituent $C_0^{(e)}$) from which at least one branch reaches down to depth $d+1$.[17] The weight of $C^{(d)}$ is then redistributed somehow between all those branches passing through $C_0^{(e)}$ that reach all the way down to depth $d+1$. (For instance, we may divide the weight of $C^{(d)}$ between them in proportion to their earlier weights.) We cannot let this weight 'come to rest' on constituents of a lesser depth, however, for their weights have already been fixed, but must move it further along the branch to deeper constituents until we reach a constituent of depth $d+1$.

The measures of probability and information which we obtain in this way will be called measures of *surface probability* and *surface information*, in brief p_{surf} and inf_{surf}.

If sufficiently similar methods of distribution are used in defining depth information and surface information (for instance, if completely egalitarian distribution is consistently practised on both occasions), it may be shown that[18]

$$\lim_{e \to \infty} [inf_{surf}(E^{(d+e)}(F))] = inf_{depth}(F).$$

[17] In my paper 'Are Mathematical Truths Synthetic *A Priori*?', *Journal of Philosophy*, vol. 65 (1968), pp. 640–51, this point is mis-stated.
[18] See 'Surface Information and Depth Information' (note 7 above), sec. 12.

Here $E^{(d+e)}(F)$ is the expansion of F at depth $d+e$. In brief, we might say that the surface information of a sentence converges to its depth information when it is expanded into deeper normal forms.

This is interesting because elsewhere it has been shown that all the usual types of logical operations (disproofs, proofs, proofs from premises, equivalence proofs, searches for Craigian interpolation formulas, searches for explicit definitions, etc.) can be carried out by means of such an expansion process.[19] For this reason, it may be said that the depth information of a sentence is its surface information after we have subjected it to the whole treatment logic puts at our disposal. Surface information and depth information might thus be called pre-logical and post-logical information, respectively.

All non-trivial deduction, represented in the form just mentioned, involves expanding a sentence beyond its original depth so as to show that certain constituents not trivially inconsistent are in fact inconsistent. This results, as pointed out above, in the reshuffling of certain weights. If more and weightier possibilities are excluded by F than before, then the surface information of F grows since it turns out to reduce one's uncertainty more than before. In this sense, deduction can increase one's surface information. One can easily define other interesting senses in which this also happens. Here, then, we have an objective sense of information in which deduction can increase one's information —a sense that definitively confutes logical positivists on this point.

6. *What is surface information information about? The nature of constituents*

This does not yet explain sufficiently the nature of surface information. I have not yet faced squarely the question that undoubtedly has already formed in my readers' minds. What on earth is surface information information *about*?

[19] For the first four, this is shown in Chapter XI below. For the interpolation formulas, this is shown in my paper 'Distributive Normal Forms and Deductive Interpolation', *Zeitschrift für mathematische Logik und Grundlagen der Mathematik*, vol. 10 (1964), pp. 185–91. For explicit definitions, the situation is sketched in Jaakko Hintikka and Raimo Tuomela, 'Towards a General Theory of Auxiliary Concepts and Definability in First-Order Theories', in *Information and Inference*, ed. by Jaakko Hintikka and Patrick Suppes (D. Reidel Publishing Company, Dordrecht, 1970), pp. 298–330.

In order to answer this salient question it is advisable to look more carefully into the nature of the constituents and normal forms. The structure of our first-order language was explained above in terms of constituents, but I have not explained fully either the intuitive nature or the formal definition of a constituent. Luckily, a sketch of both of these can be given at one and the same time. (An explicit account of the latter will be given in the next chapter.) A constituent of depth d may be said to be as explicit a description of a possibility concerning the world— of a 'possible world', if you do not object to the term—as can be given in our language without speaking of more than d individuals together in their relation to each other.[20] What do we want such a description to tell us? It must of course tell us what we may expect to find in the world so described. First of all, it must tell us what different kinds of individuals we may expect to come across in such a possible world. Secondly, it must specify, after we have found one of them (say x), what kinds of individuals we perhaps come across in our further examination of the world.[21] Each such individual, say y, will be characterized by its relationships to x. If we are willing to consider as many as three individuals in their relation to one another, we must specify, for each kind of individual x and each kind of further individual y that can be found after it, how the different kinds of still further individuals are related to x and y that the next move in our 'game of exploring the world' may uncover; and so on until we are considering our full quota of d individuals in their relation to each other.

What a constituent does is precisely to provide such a list (or, speaking more precisely, a tree-like system of ramified lists) of the different eventualities that our examination of the inhabitants of the world in question may turn up when they are examined in sequences no longer than d. It is certainly not unexpected that these lists provide us with as explicit general descriptions of different possible worlds as can be given in our language without considering more than d individuals together in their relation to each other.

Some descriptions of this kind are incoherent, however. Some

---

[20] For an explicit definition of a constituent, see next chapter, sec. 3.
[21] Different possibilities as to these further individuals of course create 'invisible' differences concerning the first-choice individuals x.

of them are blatantly self-contradictory and can be dismissed without further ado.[22] Others seem to be all right, and can only be shown to be inconsistent by considering deeper (in more than one sense) constituents. Before we have actually done this to a given inconsistent constituent, we must be prepared for the possibility that it might describe a realizable alternative. If $T^{(d)}$ is a surface tautology of depth d (i.e., disjunction of all constituents of this depth that are not trivially inconsistent), then the conditional surface probabilities $p(F/T^{(d)})$ may be thought of as admissible degrees of belief for a rational agent who thinks of all these events as possible which are described by sentences of depth d or less that are not trivially inconsistent.[23] This illustrates strikingly the import of our concept of surface probability.

What the normal form of a sentence F (say of depth d) accomplishes is thus simply to spell out which of the relevant possibilities concerning the world F admits of and which ones it excludes. The more possibilities it excludes, the more it reduces our uncertainty, and the more informative it is. The relevant possibilities are the ones that can be described by means of those resources of expression which have already been used in F, to wit, by means of the same predicates and by means of the same number of individuals considered (at any one time). In a straightforward sense, in the normal form of F its meaning is simply spelt out in as explicit terms as these resources of expression allow.[24]

[22] These are the trivially inconsistent constituents mentioned above. The crucial role of the notion of trivial inconsistency in my discussion makes it advisable to explain it in some detail. Since this explanation would break the continuity of the argument, I shall relegate it to an appendix.

[23] In view of the usual betting-theoretical motivation of the axioms of probability calculus, this may be demonstrated by showing that these conditional weights satisfy the normal Kolmogorov axioms of probability calculus (with the exception of countable additivity). This betting-theoretical point of view dates from Ramsey and de Finetti, whose fundamental papers are handily reprinted in *Studies in Subjective Probability*, ed. by H. E. Kyburg and H. E. Smokler (John Wiley, New York, 1964).

For modern expositions, see the papers by John C. Kemeny, Abner Shimony, and R. Sherman Lehman in *Journal of Symbolic Logic*, vol. 20 (1955), pp. 263–73, 1–28, and 251–61, respectively.

In view of our observations, it is not surprising that some theorists of subjective (personal) probability have expressed the view that a realistic personal probability should not be invariant with respect to logical equivalence. For such views, see L. J. Savage, 'Difficulties in the Theory of Personal Probability', *Philosophy of Science*, vol. 34 (1967), pp. 305–10, and Ian Hacking, 'Slightly More Realistic Personal Probability', ibid., pp. 311–25.

[24] Thus the notion of sentential meaning (in the usual sense of intended explicit

7. *Surface information as information about reality*

Consider now an inconsistent but not trivially inconsistent constituent $C^{(d)}$. For the sake of illustration, assume that it is one of the alternatives admitted by a sentence F we know to be true. Increasing one's surface information presupposes establishing the inconsistency of some such constituents. As long as we have not actually accomplished this, however, we must be prepared for the kinds of experiences $C^{(d)}$ says can take place—that is to say, prepared to meet certain kinds of individuals related to each other in certain ways.

This preparedness may even be a matter of practical precautions and of considerable urgency. If and when our surface information increases and we come to know the inconsistency of $C^{(d)}$, we are relieved of the need of these preparations and precautions. We are relieved, in the most concrete sense imaginable, of uncertainty concerning the world (or the aspect of the world) our sentence F speaks of.

8. *Surface information as conceptual information*

In this vivid and important sense, surface information is information about the reality. However, if we focus our attention, not on what the practical uses of surface information are, but on the way it is obtained, it is equally clear that this information is also in some important sense conceptual. In order to eliminate an inconsistent but not trivially inconsistent constituent, it does not suffice to put oneself in the right mood or to look at the matter from the right point of view so as to be able to see its inconsistency right there in the given constituent itself. Hard work is usually needed, work the extent of which can be objectively measured. What, however, is *not* required are new observations, experiments, or factual evidence of any other sort. All we have to do is to look deeper into our own language, to carry out further that purely conceptual analysis of the different contingencies one may encounter in examining the world in which a constituent is true. Each constituent itself carries this anticipatory analysis just to the extent of its own depth. The fact

meaning, 'meant' meaning) seems to be much more closely related to the distributive normal form of a sentence F than (say) to the total logical consequences of F or the totality of Carnapian state-descriptions compatible with it.

that there are inconsistent but not trivially inconsistent constituents is a feature of our conceptual system, a feature of the way
in which first-order sentences are related to the reality they are
about. Eliminating such a constituent thus seems to tell us something about our conceptual system but nothing about any mind-
independent reality.

9. *Conceptual and real information inseparable*

This double nature of surface information is at first blush
extremely puzzling. It is not unnatural that something like this
confusing conceptual situation should have prompted (as one
may suggest that it did) Kant's doctrine of the synthetic *a priori*
character of mathematical truth. Surface information seems to
be synthetic in so far as it is about the reality,[25] and *a priori* in
so far as it is conceptual.

I do not think that Kant's formulation is a particularly happy
one, however. The main point that *is* brought out by the puzzling duality of surface information is the inseparability of conceptual information from factual information in first-order
languages. When we use a first-order language to communicate,
to register, or to store information about some aspect of reality,
certain merely apparent alternatives concerning the world are
normally involved. Eliminating some of them at one stroke
enhances *both* our appreciation of the reality *and* our appreciation of our own conceptual system. The deep fact here is that
we are relying on the mediation of a certain conceptual system
in order to 'reach' the reality. The better we know the way this
conceptual system works, the more efficiently we can *ipso facto*
use it to discuss (describe, anticipate, etc.) the reality. In this
sense, it is wrong to ask whether surface information is information 'about' the world or 'about' our concepts: it is inevitably
and inseparably both, for (in the relevant sense of the phrase)
one cannot reduce one's uncertainty concerning the conceptual

[25] There is, however, a second sense in which non-trivial logical truths would
have been synthetic for Kant. This sense even seems to be much closer to Kant's
own formulations. It is brought out by the fact that such non-trivial truths (say,
a non-trivial deduction of *G* from *F*) turn on considering more individuals together
than are considered in their relation to each other in *F* or *G*, and hence turn on
considering new individuals. I have argued for a close relation between this fact
and Kant's theory of the synthetic nature of mathematical truths in Chapter VIII
and IX above.

system without thereby also reducing one's uncertainty concerning the reality.

To quote another exposition of mine:[26] our conceptual system works like a highly complex instrument that connects our knowledge with the reality this knowledge is about. The instrument is so intricate that we do not know which of its registrations are due to the influence of the reality we are interested in and which of them merely reflect the mode of functioning of the instrument itself. The better we know this instrument, the more of the merely apparent registrations we can disregard. This also means that we can use the instrument more efficiently than before for the purpose of coming to know the reality its feelers touch.

The inevitability of this dual nature of surface information is due to the undecidability of first-order logic. What this undecidability shows is that it is impossible to master the conceptual system once and for all so as to be able to concentrate exclusively on purely factual information (depth information).

10. *Inseparability and the* a priori

The insight which we have reached seems to me deeper than any simple answer to the question whether Kant or the logical positivists were 'right' in their views concerning the possibility of synthetic knowledge *a priori*. Many thinkers have held that by its conceptualizing activity the human mind contributes essentially to our knowledge. 'The a priori has its origin in an act of the mind; it . . . bears the stamp of mind's creation', writes C. I. Lewis, echoing a long line of earlier thinkers.[27] However, this emphasis on the active, creative role of the mind's conceptualizing activity will not be particularly important if the contributions of this activity can on any particular occasion be neatly separated from the contributions of the reality. It is the latter that we are normally interested in, and the former is therefore apt to catch our attention only if for some reason it cannot be separated from the 'unadulterated' information about the reality. It is not accidental, it seems to me, that C. I. Lewis apparently emphasized the role of the *a priori* in our knowledge to the same extent he emphasized the impossibility to isolate 'the given'

---

[26] 'Are Mathematical Truths Synthetic *A Priori*?' (note 17 above).
[27] C. I. Lewis, *Mind and the World-Order* (Charles Scribner's Sons, New York, 1929), p. 213.

in our experience and the impossibility to express it in language. (Cf., e.g., op. cit., p. 62.)

An inseparability of this kind has just been discovered, however. This discovery puts in a new perspective many old issues concerning the nature of *a priori* knowledge, it seems to me. It will affect our ideas concerning that interwovenness of reality—especially social reality—with our concepts about reality which has recently been emphasized in a somewhat crude form by Peter Winch[28] and others. It may also throw some light on that negative concept which is the inescapable shadow of the inseparability of the contributions of our conceptual system from the contributions of 'the reality', viz. the concept of *Ding an sich*. This notion marks, according to my lights, the idealization of being able to consider 'things in themselves' as they would be completely independent of our concepts and of the activities which give these concepts their import. In order for this notion to have any point, it does not suffice that our knowledge depends on our conceptualizing activity. If the results of this activity can be effectively separated from the contributions of the mind-independent reality, this reality can without further ado be identified with 'things in themselves' which thus becomes an empty concept. However, if (and in so far as) the inseparability I have discussed really obtains, *Dinge an sich* are to be classified in the way they are typically described: as indescribable and unclassifiable.

At the same time, our discussion shows how such apparent paradoxes can be—and must be—domesticated. For us, speaking of *Dinge an sich* does not mean speaking of some weird class of transcendent entities. It amounts only to a somewhat over-dramatic way of speaking of perfectly ordinary objects in terms which we could only use if we were not bound by the limitations of that particular way in which our conceptual system operates. In the case of first-order languages, these limitations take the form of the presence of merely apparent possibilities in anything we try to say. Speaking of things in themselves therefore means here trying to discuss the world in terms of depth information rather than surface information. There is nothing illegal or absurd in the enterprise—as long as we remember that in general

---

[28] Peter Winch, *The Idea of a Social Science*, Studies in Philosophical Psychology (Routledge and Kegan Paul, London, 1958).

we have no method of doing so and that the concrete realities we face are to be approached in terms of surface information rather than in terms of depth information. But, then, it seems to me that the concept of *Ding an sich* has always been misunderstood whenever it has been interpreted as signalling a special class of entities rather than an inaccessible but self-imposed limit of our knowledge.

In fact, it is even inaccurate to speak of inaccessibility here. In the case of any particular sentence F, it is not only the case that the surface information of its expansion $\inf_{\text{surf}}(E^{(d+e)}(F))$ approaches its depth information $\inf_{\text{depth}}(F)$ as a limit when e grows indefinitely. It will actually reach this limit at some finite depth. Thus whatever we want to say of the objects of our knowledge *qua Dinge an sich* we can also say of them within the limitations of our conceptual system, provided that we carry the analysis of the situation far enough. The only trouble is, as was already indicated, that in general we cannot know what is 'enough' in the requisite sense. *Dinge an sich* are hidden from our view, we may thus say by way of a slogan, not by their inaccessibility, but by the fact that we cannot in general know whether, and when, we have reached them.

The conceptual situation in first-order languages thus offers a clear-cut and handy example in terms of which several important traditional problems concerning *a priori* knowledge can be discussed and, at least in some cases, solved. The ubiquity and the central role of first-order logic in our discourse—Quine has even tried to use it as a 'canonical notation' in which all the vocabulary and syntax that are needed for scientific purposes can be expressed—strongly suggests that the results that can be reached concerning this special case can be generalized.

APPENDIX

The nature of trivially inconsistent constituents

What does a trivially inconsistent constituent look like? In the body of this chapter, it was indicated how each constituent $C_0^{(d)}$ of depth d describes what may happen in one's systematic step-by-step examination of one's domain of individuals down to sequences of d individuals. Now there must obviously be systematic connections between, on the one hand, the set of all the different courses of events (in one's 'game of exploring the world') which $C_0^{(d)}$ says are initially possible and, on the other hand, the set of all the briefer courses of events that are open to us (according to $C_0^{(d)}$) after the discovery of one of the kinds of individuals x that $C_0^{(d)}$ asserts there exist in the world. The only difference between the two sets of possible courses of events is that in the latter case we have already come upon one individual which we may disregard in the sequel, and also that in the latter case we have one move fewer to worry about than in the former. Of course, this holds for each kind of individual x said to exist in $C_0^{d)}$. Furthermore, similar—and equally obvious—requirements may be formulated concerning the congruence of the possible continuations of longer sequences of discoveries of different kinds of individuals asserted to be possible by $C_0^{d)}$. The totality of all these continuations must be the same except for the individuals already discovered and for the different lengths of the different continuations.

These requirements are not automatically satisfied. The constituents which do not satisfy them are precisely the trivially inconsistent ones. The remarks just made show that the inconsistency of such constituents can be seen from the constituent itself in a very straightforward sense: different parts of one and the same constituent claim that different sequences of experiences (discoveries of different kinds of individuals) are possible in the world described by the constituent, which of course is self-contradictory.

It is a most remarkable feature of the conceptual situation we face here that there are inconsistent constituents whose inconsistency is not betrayed in this way by a contradiction between their several parts. No matter how you compare the 'game of exploring the world' that such a constituent describes with the different subgames which are obtained as continuations of its initial moves (down to the number of moves, say d, allowed by the whole constituent) or compare the latter games with each other, you will never discover any discrepancies. The inconsistency of such a constituent can only be discovered by considering the different longer 'games of exploring the world' which are obtained by adding further moves to the game considered in the given constituent. Furthermore, we usually do not know how long are the games we have to consider to bring out possible hidden inconsistencies.

This contrast, which will be explained in formal (but less intuitive) terms in the next chapter, perhaps serves to explain the sense in which trivially inconsistent constituents are (in principle) explicitly self-contradictory while other inconsistent constituents can at most be said to be implicitly self-contradictory. (Even so, it must be added that a contradiction is implicitly contained in them in the sense in which 'plants are contained in their seeds', not in the sense in which 'beams are contained in a house', to use Frege's metaphor.)

The distinction between trivial and non-trivial inconsistency can be extended from constituents to other sentences. A sentence F of depth d is trivially inconsistent if and only if all the constituents in its normal form at depth d are trivially inconsistent. Such sentences may be called surface tautologies; their surface information is zero.

Some further comments may be in order here. First of all, the talk of games which I have so far employed on the level of a metaphor can easily be made precise. This was in fact done in Chapter III above in general terms. Their application to the special case of constituents is straightforward.

The main question one faces here is whether our distinction between trivial and non-trivial inconsistency captures a natural and unique distinction between different kinds of inconsistent first-order sentences. The naturalness of my distinction can be argued for in different ways. The purpose of the explanation just given of the nature of trivial inconsistency is to illustrate the naturalness, not to say the inevitability, of the distinction. Another way of arguing for the same point would be to show that the method of weeding out trivially inconsistent constituents is closely related to virtually all current methods of proof in first-order logic, and perhaps even in a sense equivalent to them.[29] Such observations would further enhance the claims of my distinction to naturalness and hence to philosophical importance.

A minor qualification is nevertheless in order here. In one respect, the difference between trivial and non-trivial inconsistency can equally naturally be drawn at another place. Since both of them are entirely natural, this does not seem to make any essential difference, however. In any case, the situation admits of a simple explanation in the intuitive terms we have already been using.

In fact, it is obvious that, in the same way as we can compare with each other, on the one hand, the totality of those courses of events that $C_0^{(d)}$ says are possible and, on the other hand, the totality ofs uch courses of events we might still be faced with after coming upon one of the kinds of individuals x which $C_0^{(d)}$ says there are, in somewhat the same way we can compare the different courses of events that might materialize if we chanced upon the kinds of individuals $C_0^{(d)}$ says there are *in an order different from* the one envisaged in some part of $C_0^{(d)}$. Such variations of order certainly must not lead away from the courses of events (interrelated sequences of individuals one might

---

[29] This will be argued for in a forthcoming paper of mine, 'On the Surface Semantics of First-Order Proof Procedures'.

meet) asserted to be possible in $C_0^{(d)}$. If they do, $C_0^{(d)}$ is inconsistent. It is perhaps not entirely surprising that the class of inconsistent constituents discoverable in this way equals the class of constituents whose inconsistency can be revealed by just one application of the quantifier-interchange axioms

$$(x)(y)Fxy \equiv (y)(x)Fxy \quad \text{and} \quad (Ex)(y)Fxy \supset (y)(Ex)Fxy.$$

If inconsistencies discoverable in this way are added to the trivially inconsistent constituents described earlier, we obtain what I shall call the new definition of trivial inconsistency. It is captured in an explicit form by the conditions (A)–(C) of section 10 of the next chapter.

It also turns out that the class of trivially inconsistent constituents in the new sense is included in the class of constituents whose inconsistency can be discovered by our earlier methods (i.e., that of comparing the totality of interrelated sequences of individuals admitted by $C_0^{(d)}$ with the totalities that remain after one or more of the allegedly available individuals have been discovered) if we are allowed to go one step deeper, i.e., if we are allowed to consider sequences of $d+1$ individuals over and above the sequences of d individuals already considered in $C_0^{(d)}$. In other words, by means of the new change-of-order criteria we can discover inconsistent constituents which are not trivially inconsistent in the 'old' sense characterized earlier. However, their non-triviality is minimal, if measured by the number of new individuals one has to consider over and above those already considered in $C_0^{(d)}$. In fact, the introduction of just *one* more individual suffices. A combinatorial reason for this fact is also not very difficult to perceive.

Since the new method of locating inconsistent constituents can be characterized so handily in terms of the old one, I have carried out my discussion in terms of the latter instead of the former, and I also tend to think that the old criteria are somewhat more straightforward. However, I am not holding a brief for one set of criteria rather than for the other. What is important to appreciate is the availability of two slightly different criteria here, and also the fact that facing a choice between these two clear-cut alternatives with an intuitively obvious meaning does not detract from the naturalness of either of them.

There are some reasons, however, for preferring the new characterization of trivial inconsistency to the old. I have repeatedly stressed the idea that what is important here is the number of individuals considered together in their relation to each other. In a very natural sense of the term, this number is not changed when we consider the different orders in which different kinds of individuals may come up in the course of those explorations of the world which are envisaged in a constituent. Hence criteria of inconsistency that turn on changes in this order should perhaps be included in our criteria of trivial inconsistency.

XI

DISTRIBUTIVE NORMAL FORMS
IN FIRST-ORDER LOGIC

1. *The purpose of this chapter*

THE distributive normal forms of first-order logic (functional calculus of first order, quantification theory, predicate calculus) were first described and proved to exist in the author's dissertation of 1953.[1] Subsequently, some of the basic ideas of these normal forms have been independently rediscovered and used by others (Hanf, Ehrenfeucht, Dana Scott).[2] In the earlier chapters of the present book, distributive normal forms have been frequently been used, and the ideas on which they are based have been sketched. In this chapter, an attempt will be made to explain, in a form more systematic and more complete than that of earlier chapters and yet more compact and more manageable than that of my original paper, what these normal forms are. We shall also attempt to carry their theory further by studying some of their most important properties. In particular, we shall describe and prove semantically complete a disproof procedure which is connected especially closely with their structure. The properties of the distributive normal forms would seem to repay closer study in several directions. In this book, however, we are trying to survey the basic features of these normal forms rather than to push their applications to the limit in any particular direction.

Our discussion will be restricted to first-order logic, although similar normal forms are easily seen to exist elsewhere, for

[1] Jaakko Hintikka, *Distributive Normal Forms in the Calculus of Predicates*, Acta Philosophica Fennica, vol. 6 (Helsinki, 1953). The notation and terminology used in this work are not identical with those employed in the present chapter.

[2] See, e.g., A. Ehrenfeucht, 'An Application of Games to the Completeness Problem for Formalized Theories', *Fundamenta Mathematicae*, vol. 49 (1961), pp. 129–41. Distributive normal forms have also been employed by Francis C. Oglesby in his monograph, *An Examination of a Decision Procedure*, Memoirs of the American Math. Soc., vol. 44 (Providence, R.I., 1963).

instance in higher-order logics and in modal logics. The reason for the restriction is that the properties of these parallel normal forms are so different as to make a separate treatment advisable.

2. *Special cases*

The distributive normal forms of first-order logic are generalizations of the well-known 'complete' normal forms of propositional logic and of monadic first-order logic. The notation and terminology that will be employed in this chapter can be conveniently explained in terms of these more restricted normal forms.

Consider first propositional logic. Each consistent formula F of propositional logic has a complete disjunctive normal form which is a disjunction of certain conjunctions that will be called *constituents*. If F does not contain any atomic formulae different from $p_1, p_2, ..., p_k$, then a constituent occurring in its normal form contains for each $i = 1, 2, ..., k$ either p_i or $\sim p_i$ (but not both) as a member. An arbitrary conjunction of this kind will be referred to in the sequel as

$$\prod_{i=1}^{k} p_i.$$

Different conjunctions of this kind may be distinguished from each other by attaching subscripts to Π. It will be assumed that these subscripts run from one on so that the same kind of notation can be used repeatedly.

By means of this notation the normal forms of monadic first-order logic (without identity) are easily characterized. They are again disjunctions of certain conjunctions that will be called constituents. A constituent of course depends on the predicates which occur in it. If these are $P_1 x, P_2 x, ..., P_k x$, an arbitrary constituent of monadic first-order logic is of the form

$$(1) \qquad \prod_{j=1}^{j=2^k} (Ex) \prod_{i=1}^{i=k} P_i x.$$

Whenever the limits of our *pi*-operations are inessential or can be gathered from the context, they may be omitted. Thus instead of (1) we may sometimes write

$$\prod_{j=1} (Ex) \prod_{i=1} P_i x$$

or even

$$\prod_{j=1} (Ex)\, \Pi_j\, Px.$$

The intuitive meaning of (1) is worth noting as it is generalizable to the whole of first-order logic. Using the language of an interpreted logical system, one may say that in propositional logic the constituents list all the different possible states of affairs or 'possible worlds' that can be specified by means of the atomic propositions p_i (plus propositional connectives). In monadic first-order logic, the constituents (1) likewise describe all the different kinds of worlds (states of affairs) that can be specified by means of the monadic predicates $P_i x$ (plus quantifiers and propositional connectives). From (1) we see how these descriptions come about. First all the possible kinds of individuals that can be specified by means of the predicates $P_i x$ (plus propositional connectives) are listed. This is what the conjunctions

$$\prod_{i=1}^{k} \Pi_j\, P\, x$$

(where $j = 1, 2,..., 2^k$) accomplish. Then it is indicated, for each such possible kind of individual, whether individuals of that kind exist or not. This is what the rest of (1) does.

On the basis of this intuitive meaning of (1) certain simple observations can be made. For instance, we see that (1) can be written in a different form. Instead of listing all the different kinds of individuals that exist and also all the different kinds of individuals that do not exist, it clearly suffices to list all the existing ones and then to add that they are *all* the existing ones. In other words, (1) can be rewritten as follows:

(2) $\quad (Ex)\Pi_{j_1} Px\ \&\ (Ex)\Pi_{j_2} Px\ \&\ ...\ \&\ (Ex)\Pi_{j_m} Px$
$\qquad\ \&\ (Ux)(\Pi_{j_1} Px\ \vee\ \Pi_{j_2} Px\ \vee\ ...\ \vee\ \Pi_{j_m} Px)$

where $\{\Pi_{j_1} Px,..., \Pi_{j_m} Px\}$ is the set of those conjunctions whose existential closures occur unnegated in (1).

Here it is useful to have a shorthand notation which will save us the trouble of writing out the main conjunction and disjunction of (2) explicitly. Using such a notation, (2) may be written as

(3) $\qquad \pi_r \underset{j=1}{(Ex)} \prod_{i=1} P_i\, x\ \&\ (Ux)\, \sigma_r \underset{=1}{\prod_{i=1}} \Pi_j\, P\, x.$

The conventions on which this more compact version is based may be expressed as follows: given the conjunction $\prod_{i=1}^{r} p_i$,

$$\pi_r \atop i=1 \; p_i$$

is the conjunction of all its unnegated members, and

$$\sigma_r \atop i=1 \; p_i$$

is the disjunction of the same formulae. More generally, given two arbitrary functions f and g whose arguments and values are formulae,

$$\pi_r \atop i=1 \; f(p_i)$$

is the conjunction of all the formulae $f(p_i)$ where p_i ranges over all the unnegated members of $\prod_{i=1}^{r} p_i$; and

$$\sigma_r \atop i=1 \; g(p_i)$$

is the disjunction of all the formulae $g(p_i)$ with the same choice of the arguments p_i. Thus π_r and σ_r essentially express the formation of arbitrary conjunctions and disjunctions. The identity of subscripts merely serves to indicate that the same selection of arguments is involved in the two cases.

The equivalence of (1) to (3), which was found intuitively obvious, is also readily demonstrable. In order to convert (1) to (3), you may proceed as follows: first replace every combination of symbols $\sim(Ex)$ by $(Ux)\sim$; then let all the universal quantifiers thus introduced merge into one (in virtue of the distributivity of universal quantification with respect to conjunction). From propositional logic it follows that the formula which then constitutes the scope of the universal quantifier is equivalent to

$$\sigma_r \atop j=1 \; \prod_{i=1}^{j} P_i x$$

where the subscript of the first $\prod$ in (1) is assumed to be r.

Another observation: in propositional logic, a formula has a (non-empty) normal form if and only if it is consistent. In monadic first-order logic, this remains true, but only with a qualification. This qualification pertains to the 'only if' part of the equivalence. This part remains valid only if all the constituents (1) are consistent (satisfiable). Now there is one constituent (and one only) which is satisfiable only in an empty domain of individuals. It is that constituent (1) all of whose members are negated. On the basis of the intuitive meaning of (1) it is seen to deny that there are individuals of any kind in existence, i.e., that the universe is empty. Admitting empty domains of individuals on a par with non-empty ones thus simplifies our discussion in that it enables us to say that all constituents of monadic first-order logic are consistent. This simplifying assumption will be made throughout our discussion.

3. *The definition of distributive normal forms*

The distributive normal forms of full first-order logic (without identity) are also disjunctions of certain conjunctions which we shall call constituents. In order to define the normal form we therefore have to define a constituent. A constituent depends essentially on the following features which will be called its *parameters*:

(P.1)   The set of all the predicates occurring in it;
(P.2)   The set of all the free individual symbols occurring in it;
(P.3)   The maximal length of sequences of nested quantifiers occurring in it.

The parameter (P.3) will be called the *depth* of the formula in question.[3] More loosely, the depth of a formula is the number of layers of quantifiers it contains. If it is stipulated that the scopes of two quantifiers which contain the same bound variable must not overlap, we can characterize (P.3) in analogy to (P.1)–(P.2): the depth of a formula is the number of all the different bound individual variables it contains when this number is made as small as possible by renaming bound variables.

The definition of a constituent is facilitated by a few shorthand notations. Given a set (P.1) of predicates, let $A_i(a_1, a_2,..., a_k)$ (where $i = 1, 2,...$) be all the atomic formulae that can be formed from the members of (P.1) and from the free individual

---

[3] The concept of depth can also be sharpened as explained above in note 32 to Chapter VI. This change does not necessitate any modifications in our subsequent results, however, and all the arguments given below can easily be amplified so as to take cognizance of the change.

symbols a_1, a_2,..., a_k. Furthermore, let $B_i(a_1, a_2,..., a_k)$ $(i = 1,$ $2,...)$ be all those atomic formulae so defined which contain at least one occurrence of a_k. Then we have, trivially,

$$(4) \qquad \Pi_{\substack{r \\ i=1}} A_i(a_1,..., a_{k-1}, a_k)$$
$$= \Pi_{\substack{s \\ i=1}} A_i(a_1,..., a_{k-1}) \text{ \& } \Pi_{\substack{t \\ i=1}} B_i(a_1,..., a_{k-1}, a_k)$$

for each given r and for suitably chosen (with a view to r) s and t.

Before defining a constituent with given parameters (P. 1)– (P. 3), it is advisable to define a closely related kind of formula which will be called an *attributive constituent* (in short, an *a-constituent*) with the same parameters. An attributive constituent with a given fixed parameter (P. 1) whose depth is d and whose parameter (P. 2) is $\{a_1, a_2,..., a_k\}$ will be referred to as $Ct^d(a_1,..., a_k)$. It may be defined recursively in terms of a-constituents of depth $d-1$ as follows:

$$(5) \qquad Ct^d_r(a_1,..., a_k)$$
$$= \Pi_{\substack{s \\ i=1}} B_i(a_1,..., a_k) \text{ \& } \Pi_{\substack{t \\ i=1}} (Ex)Ct^{d-1}_i(a_1,..., a_{k-1}, a_k, x).$$

We have assumed here that indices are used to distinguish different a-constituents with the same parameters from one another. In (5) the first index r is of course a function of s and t. It does not matter what the dependence is as long as the values r can assume are 1, 2,... up to some finite number.[4]

When $d = 0$, the second member of the right-hand side of (5) vanishes, giving us a basis for recursion.

After an attributive constituent is defined, it is easy to define a constituent:

$$(6) \quad C^d(a_1,..., a_k) = \Pi_{i=1} A_i(a_1,..., a_{k-1}) \text{ \& } Ct^d(a_1,..., a_{k-1}, a_k).$$

For simplicity, the indices of C^d, of Π, and of Ct^d have not been indicated here. The first depends on the other two; it is again assumed that the values it can take run consecutively from 1 on.

What is thus defined will be called the *first* distributive normal

---

[4] One especially simple method of defining this dependence would be to put $r = (s-1)+2^n \cdot (t-1)+1$ where n is the number of different formulae of the form $B_i(a_1,..., a_k)$ (with the appropriate parameters). Analogous definitions may be used elsewhere on similar occasions. We shall not use the details of these definitions, however.

form. The constituents and attributive constituents just defined will be said to be of the *first kind*.

In monadic first-order logic, every constituent (1) may be rewritten as (3). In the same way, constituents and attributive constituents of the first kind may be transformed so as to become constituents and a-constituents of the *second kind*.

Attributive constituents of the second kind may be defined as follows:

$$(7) \qquad Ct_r^d(a_1,..., a_k) = \prod_{i=1}^s B_i(a_1,..., a_k) \ \& $$
$$\pi_{\substack{t \\ i=1}} (Ex)Ct_i^{d-1}(a_1,..., a_k, x) \ \& \ (Ux) \ \sigma_{\substack{t \\ i=1}} Ct_i^{d-1}(a_1,..., a_k, x).$$

Here r depends on s and t as before. The first parameter (**P**. 1) is assumed to be constant throughout (7).

Constituents of the second kind may be defined in terms of a-constituents of the second kind in the same way as before, viz. by (6). Alternatively, this definition may be rewritten as follows:

$$(8) \qquad C_r^d(a_1,..., a_k) = \prod_{i=1}^s A_i(a_1,..., a_k) \ \& $$
$$\pi_{\substack{t \\ i=1}} (Ex)Ct_i^{d-1}(a_1,..., a_k, x) \ \& \ (Ux) \ \sigma_{\substack{t \\ i=1}} Ct_i^{d-1}(a_1,..., a_k, x).$$

4. *The intuitive meaning of constituents and of attributive constituents*

The normal forms of monadic first-order logic are special cases of the more general normal forms just defined. A comparison of (1) with (5) and of (3) with (7) or (8) shows that these special cases are not entirely unrepresentative. The similarity between (1) and (5) or between (3) and (8) can be further heightened by writing (1) as

$$(1)^* \qquad \qquad \prod_{i=1} (Ex)Ct_i^0(x)$$

and (3) as

$$(3)^* \qquad \qquad \pi_{\substack{r \\ i=1}} (Ex)Ct_i^0(x) \ \& \ (Ux) \ \sigma_{\substack{r \\ i=1}} Ct_i^0(x).$$

This similarity helps us to appreciate the nature of the general normal forms in many respects. For one thing, the intuitive meaning of constituents and of attributive constituents can be explained pretty much in the same way as in the monadic case. If we speak as if we were dealing with an interpreted system, we may say that constituents with certain fixed parameters (P. 1)–(P. 3) list all the different kinds of world that can be described by the sole means of these parameters (plus quantifiers and propositional connectives). Attributive constituents do not describe possible worlds (states of affairs) but rather *possible kinds of individuals*. (Hence their name.) If the attributive constituents (5) or (7) are considered as complex attributes of the individual referred to by a_k, they may be said to list all the different kinds of individuals that can be specified by the sole means of (i) a given fixed set of predicates (P. 1); (ii) the 'reference-point' individuals specified by $a_1,..., a_{k-1}$; (iii) at most d layers of quantifiers; (iv) propositional connectives. The recursion equation (5) shows how the list comes about: first we list all the kinds of individuals that can be specified by means of (i) the same set of predicates; (ii)' the reference-point individuals specified by $a_1,..., a_{k-1}$ *as well as* a_k; (iii)' at most $d-1$ layers of quantifiers; (iv) propositional connectives. This is what the a-constituents $Ct^{d-1}(a_1,..., a_{k-1}, a_k, x)$ do. Then we specify, for each such kind of individuals, whether individuals of that particular kind exist or not. This is what the second *pi*-operator and the accompanying quantifier accomplish in (5). This adds one more layer of quantifiers, but it also makes the result something we can attribute to the individual referred to by a_k. Finally, we specify how the individual referred to by a_k is related to those of $a_1,..., a_{k-1}$; this is what the first member of the right-hand side of (5) does.

Intuitively, (7) is obviously related to (5) in the same way as (3) is to (1). The equivalence of (7) to (5) (the same parameters in both cases) can also be proved by an argument closely reminiscent of the proof which was sketched in section 2 for the equivalence of (3) with (1). The former equivalence is most easily proved by induction on d. Both the case $d = 1$ (which gives us a basis for induction) and the inductive step can be dealt with in the same way as the relation of (3) to (1) was dealt with earlier.

From (8) we see what a constituent with given parameters (P. 1), (P. 2) $(= \{a_1,..., a_k\})$, and (P. 3) $(= d)$ says. First, it says which possible kinds of individuals, specifiable with reference to $a_1,..., a_k$ by means of at most $d-1$ layers of quantifiers, there exist; second, it says how the individuals referred to by $a_1,..., a_k$ are related to each other.

5. *The existence of distributive normal forms*

The possibility of converting every formula F (of first-order logic without identity) with given parameters $(P.1)$–$(P.3)$ into the first distributive normal form with the same parameters (or with certain fixed larger ones) can be proved by induction on the depth d of F. A basis for induction is given us by the propositional normal forms $(d = 0)$. In the general case F is a truth-function of formulae of the following two forms: (a) $A_i(a_1,..., a_k)$, where $\{a_1,..., a_k\}$ is the parameter $(P.2)$ of F; (b) $(Ex)G$, where all the predicates of G are among those of F, where the depth of G is at most $d-1$, and where all the free individual symbols of G are among $a_1,..., a_k, x$.

By the inductive hypothesis G is therefore equivalent to a disjunction of formulae of the form

$$\prod_{i=1} A_i(a_1,..., a_k) \ \& \ Ct^{d-1}(a_1,..., a_k, x).$$

By well-known laws of first-order logic (the distributivity of existential quantification with respect to disjunction, the irrelevance of the scope of an existential quantifier as far as members of a conjunction which do not contain the bound variable in question are concerned), $(Ex)G$ is then equivalent to a disjunction of formulae of the form

$$\prod_{i=1} A_i(a_1,..., a_k) \ \& \ (Ex)Ct^{d-1}(a_1,..., a_k, x).$$

But this means that F is equivalent to a truth-function of formulae of the following two kinds:

(a) $\qquad\qquad A_i(a_1,..., a_k)$, as before;

(b) $\qquad\qquad (Ex)Ct^{d-1}(a_1,..., a_k, x).$

The desired normal form is then obtained simply by a transformation into the propositional normal form. This completes the proof of the existence of the first distributive normal form.

From the argument just given we can read a set of directions for actually converting each given formula to the first distributive normal form. The term *distributive* normal form is chosen because of the importance of the distribution of existential quantifiers in this conversion. It is seen that the process by which the distributive normal forms are reached is in a sense opposite to the one by which a formula is converted to the prenex form:

instead of pulling the quantifiers out to the front of the formula in question they are pushed as deep into it as they will go.

The possibility of converting each given formula to the second distributive normal form now follows from the equivalence of the first and the second normal form. In the sequel, we shall consider only the second normal form, usually omitting the word 'second'. Likewise, only constituents and a-constituents of the *second* kind will normally be considered unless the opposite is stated in so many words.

There also exist normal forms and constituents dual to the ones we have defined. They will not be considered here either.

As a special case of the convertibility of every formula into the distributive normal form, we see that each constituent with depth d and with certain given parameters (P.1)–(P.2) can be converted into a disjunction of constituents with the same parameters (P.1)–(P.2) but with a greater depth $d+e$, for each $e = 1, 2, \ldots$. These constituents will be said to be *subordinate* to the constituent in whose normal form they occur.

We see that every a-constituent Ct^d of depth d may be converted into a disjunction of a number of a-constituents of depth $d+e$ with the same parameters (P.1)–(P.2) as Ct^d. These a-constituents are said to be subordinate to Ct^d. Again, this holds for every $e = 1, 2, \ldots$. The procedure by means of which this is accomplished is, *mutatis mutandis*, the same as in the case of constituents.

6. *The structure of distributive normal forms*

The structure of the distributive normal forms of both kinds is very clear-cut. In the constituents of the first kind there are no disjunctions and no universal quantifiers. All negation-signs are prefixed to atomic formulae or to existential quantifiers.

In the constituents and a-constituents of the second kind all negation-signs are prefixed to atomic formulae. Since disjunction, conjunction, and both kinds of quantification are monotonic operations as far as the logical strength of formulae is concerned, it follows that the same is true of constituents and attributive constituents (of the second kind): whenever a subformula S_1 of an arbitrary a-constituent Ct_0 implies another formula S_2, Ct_0 implies the result of replacing S_1 by S_2 in Ct_0. The same obviously holds for the simultaneous replacement of non-overlapping subformulae by weaker formulae. From this the following *omission lemma* immediately follows:

If we omit from an a-constituent any number of subformulae of the following kinds: (i) negated or unnegated atomic formulae; (ii) quantified formulae, then the result is implied by the original a-constituent.

The same result obviously holds also for constituents (of the second kind). Certain qualifications are needed in both cases, however. It has to be understood that not all the members of any conjunction which occurs as a member of a disjunction are omitted, i.e., that no member of a disjunction is allowed to disappear altogether. It has to be understood also that connectives which become idle as a result of the omissions are likewise omitted.

It is readily seen that whenever an a-constituent occurs in another a-constituent or in a constituent (of the second kind), it also occurs there without being a subformula of any disjunction, universally quantified formula, or (trivially) negation. Now the operations of conjunction and of existential quantification cannot remove an inconsistency from a formula. It therefore follows that whenever an a-constituent is inconsistent, every constituent or a-constituent that contains it is likewise inconsistent. This observation will be called the *inconsistency lemma*.

A formula which is like one of the constituents or a-constituents we have defined except for (i) the order of the conjunctions and disjunctions it contains, (ii) the repetitions of some of the members of conjunctions and disjunctions, or (iii) the naming of the bound individual variables it contains will be called its *notational variant*. We shall call two constituents or a-constituents *different* only if they are not notational variants of each other. If this convention is presupposed, we can say that in propositional logic two different constituents with the same atomic formulae are logically incompatible.[5] As a special case, we see that two different constituents or a-constituents of the first kind with the same parameters are logically incompatible. From the equivalence of our two normal forms it follows that the same is true of constituents and of a-constituents of the second kind. (*Incompatibility lemma.*)

---

[5] In the sense that each of them implies the negation of the other. Of course they may still be equivalent in one special case, viz. when they are both inconsistent.

Each a-constituent and constituent of the second kind has the structure of a tree in the mathematical sense of the word. The elements of the tree are the a-constituent in question—let us call it Ct_0^d—and all the a-constituents of lesser depth occurring in Ct_0^d. If one of them is Ct^{d-e}, the elements covering it are all the a-constituents of depth $d-e-1$ occurring in it. Turning the tree upside down, the structure of the a-constituent Ct_0^d can therefore be represented schematically by the following diagram:

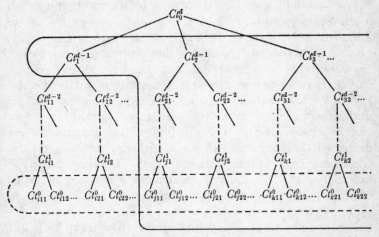

The two dividing lines (solid and dotted) will be given a meaning later.

7. *The effects of identity*

So far, we have been dealing with first-order logic *without* identity. In first-order logic *with* identity, normal forms similar to the ones we have discussed can be defined. In fact, an attributive constituent may still have exactly the same appearance as it had in first-order logic without identity. The only difference is that quantifiers must now be given an exclusive interpretation.[6] That is to say, a formula of the form $(Ex)F$ will now be understood as shorthand for the formula $(Ex)\ (x \neq a_1\ \&\ x \neq a_2\ \&\ ...\ x \neq a_k\ \&\ F)$ where $a_1,\ a_2,...,\ a_k$ are all the free individual symbols of F and where the quantifier is understood in the usual

---

[6] See my paper 'Identity, Variables, and Impredicative Definitions', *Journal of Symbolic Logic*, vol. 21 (1956), pp. 225–45. The difference between the two variants of exclusive interpretation which I distinguish in this earlier paper is immaterial in the case of distributive normal forms. For this reason, I shall in the sequel occasionally resort to the solecism of speaking of *the* exclusive interpretation.

way. The universal quantifier has of course to be reinterpreted in the same way: $(Ux)F$ will now mean the same as the formula $(Ux)\,((x \neq a_1\ \&\ x \neq a_2\ \&\ \dots\ \&\ x \neq a_k) \supset F)$ used to mean on the old interpretation. In (5) and (7) this reinterpretation has to be applied to all quantifiers, but in all other respects these definitions will remain intact. A constituent will still be like (6) except that it will always contain as additional members of the main conjunction all the formulae $a_i \neq a_j$ where $i \neq j$, $i, j \leqslant k$. It may also contain as additional members of the main conjunction a number of formulae of the form $b = a_i$, one for each b, where b is different from all the free individual symbols a_i ($i = 1, 2, \dots, k$). It is obvious that formulae of the latter form cannot affect the consistency or inconsistency of the constituent in question. Hence they may be disregarded for many purposes (cf. section 8).

Any formula (with identity) whose depth is no greater than d and whose free individual symbols are all among the a_i's and b's can be converted into a disjunction of the constituents just described. The argument that was given in section 5 for the corresponding result for formulae without identities can be extended to the case at hand. In fact, the operations by means of which the normal form was reached remain applicable on the exclusive interpretation of quantifiers. Hence essentially the only new thing to do is to transform the given formula first to a form in which the interpretation of quantifiers can be changed. There are no difficulties about this, however.[7]

The three lemmata formulated above (the omission lemma, the inconsistency lemma, and the incompatibility lemma) remain valid in first-order logic with identity. Some qualifications are needed here, however. In the omission lemma the prohibition against omitting members of disjunctions has to be applied also to the disjunction $(Ux)\,(x = a_1 \lor x = a_2 \lor \dots \lor x = a_k \lor F)$ which is implicit in the universally quantified formula $(Ux)F$, exclusively interpreted. The incompatibility lemma applies to a-constituents without change, but not to constituents. It does

---

[7] Suppose, for instance, that a is the only free individual symbol in $(Ex)F$. Then this formula is trivially equivalent to a formula of the form $(Ex)\,(x = a\ \&\ F_1) \lor (Ex)$ $(x \neq a\ \&\ F_2)$ which in turn is equivalent to $F_1(a/x) \lor (Ex)\,(x \neq a\ \&\ F_2)$ where $F_1(a/x)$ is the result of replacing x by a in F_1, subject to the usual precautions concerning variables. By using the exclusive interpretation, this may be written simply $F_1(a/x) \lor (Ex)F_2$. The cases in which we have more than one free individual symbol may be treated similarly, and universally quantified formulae dually.

apply to what we shall call the *main parts* of constituents, i.e., to the constituents just defined minus the identities $b = a_i$. Thus it applies, e.g., to closed constituents.

8. *Distributive normal forms and decision problems*

In propositional logic and in monadic first-order logic distributive normal forms yield a decision method: if a formula has a non-empty normal form, it is satisfiable, and vice versa; it is logically true if and only if its normal form contains all the constituents with the same parameters as it. In view of Church's undecidability result they cannot do this in the full first-order logic (with or without identity). It is easily seen that this failure is possible only if some of our constituents are in this case inconsistent. In fact, the decision problem of first-order logic is seen to be equivalent to the problem of deciding which constituents are inconsistent. More explicitly, the decision problem for formulae with certain fixed parameters is equivalent to the problem of deciding which constituents with these parameters are inconsistent. For instance, the decision problem for formulae of depth $\leqslant 2$ is equivalent to the problem of locating the inconsistent constituents of depth 2. In this case, the problem is known to be solvable.[8] In fact, it can be shown (although we shall not do it here) that the conditions (A)–(C) which we shall formulate in section 9 give us a decision method in this case. In the case of formulae of depth 3 no decision method can be available, for it is known that these formulae constitute a reduction class. In fact, this remains true even though we impose limitations on the other parameters of these formulae; for instance, we may require that they contain only one fixed dyadic predicate plus an indefinite number of monadic predicates, and that they contain no free individual symbols.[9] (It is assumed here that no identities are present.)

---

[8] See G. H. von Wright, 'On Double Quantification', *Societas Scientiarum Fennica, Commentationes physico-mathematicae*, vol. 16, No. 3 (Helsinki, 1952). As pointed out by Wilhelm Ackermann in his review of von Wright's paper (*Journal of Symbolic Logic*, vol. 17 (1952), pp. 201–3), this case can be reduced to cases which have been proved soluble by Gödel, Kalmar, and Schütte. A generalization of Ackermann's point was put forward by Dana Scott in a paper read at the January 1963 meeting of the Association for Symbolic Logic in Berkeley, California.

[9] See János Surányi, *Reduktionstheorie des Entscheidungsproblems im Prädikatenkalkül der ersten Stufe* (Verlag der ungarischen Akademie der Wissenschaften, Budapest, 1959).

In addition to obtaining reduction classes for the decision problem of the whole first-order logic (without or with identity) we obtain formulations for a number of more specific decision problems. For instance, consider a finitely axiomatizable first-order theory the conjunction of whose non-logical axioms is F. Then it is easily seen that the theory in question is decidable if and only if the set of all inconsistent constituents which have the same parameters as F and which are subordinate to one of the constituents C_1, C_2,..., C_f occurring in the normal form of F is recursive. For a decision method it even suffices to have a recursive function which for each d indicates *how many* inconsistent constituents (with the appropriate other parameters) there are subordinate to one of the C_i ($i = 1, 2,..., f$). For if we know this number, we can for each d enumerate recursively all the inconsistent formulae until this number of constituents of depth d (with the appropriate other parameters) has appeared in the enumeration; then we know that the rest are all consistent. The same service would of course be performed by the function $r_F(d)$ which gives us the number of consistent subordinates of the constituents (of depth d) in the normal form of F.

Such a function $r_F(d)$ of course always exists, although it is not always recursive. It will be called the *range function* of F. Even when it is not recursive, it can be seen to be of the same degree of unsolvability as the theory axiomatized by F. A theory of range functions might be of considerable interest. For instance, from a result of Hanf's it follows that every recursively enumerable degree of unsolvability contains the range function of some formula.[10] Here we shall only list some of the most obvious properties of range functions:

(i) The range function of each F is the sum of the range functions of the constituents occurring in its normal form. The range functions of constituents thus constitute a base for all range functions.

(ii) In particular, the range function of a constituent C^d of depth d

---

[10] William Hanf has proved that every recursively enumerable degree of unsolvability contains the class of Gödel numbers of the theorems of some finitely axiomatizable theory; see 'Degrees of Finitely Axiomatizable Theories', *Notices of the American Mathematical Society*, vol. 9 (1962), pp. 127–8 (abstract). By the degree of unsolvability of a theory we of course mean the degree of the set of the Gödel numbers of its theorems.

is for every $e = 1, 2,...$ equal to the sum of the range functions of all the constituents of depth $d+e$ which have the same parameters (P.1)–(P.2) as C^d and which are subordinate to C^d. When a constituent is split into a disjunction of deeper constituents, its range function is thus split into the sum of their range functions.

(iii) The range function of any constituent subordinate to C^d is Turing reducible to that of C^d. The higher up we climb along a branch of the tree which is constituted by all the constituents subordinate to C^d, the easier our decision problems thus become—in so far as they change at all.

(iv) Given two constituents C_1 and C_2 with the same parameters (P.1)–(P.2) neither of which is subordinate to the other, the sum $r_{C_1}(d) + r_{C_2}(d)$ of their range functions belongs to the join of the degrees to which $r_{C_1}(d)$ and $r_{C_2}(d)$ belong in the semi-lattice of degrees of unsolvability.

(v) A formula axiomatizes a complete theory if and only if its range function is everywhere $= 1$.

9. *Conditions of consistency*

The theory of range functions will not be developed any further here. It has been mentioned mainly as an illustration of the interest of the problem of locating the inconsistent constituents—or at least some of them. As far as the general form of this problem is concerned, we know that the set of all inconsistent constituents is not recursive (Church's undecidability theorem). It is, however, recursively enumerable. One thing we may thus hope to accomplish is to find as natural methods of recursive enumeration as possible (i.e., as natural disproof procedures as possible). What we shall do in the next few sections is just to provide such methods of recursive enumeration —methods which are especially closely connected with the structure of our constituents and attributive constituents.

This will be done in two stages. First, certain sufficient (but not necessary) conditions of inconsistency for constituents and a-constituents will be formulated. Then it will be proved that these conditions, when used in a certain systematic fashion, really provide us with a method of recursively enumerating all the inconsistent constituents and a-constituents. In other words, it will be proved that every inconsistent constituent and a-constituent has a disproof of a certain simple structure. This structure can be compared with the structure of the disproofs which are in the simple normal forms of first-order proofs that have been established by Herbrand and by Gentzen. Prima facie, the relation of our disproofs to the Herbrand and Gentzen normal forms is not very close. As far as the propositional structure of our disproofs is concerned, they embody the ideals of Herbrand and Gentzen well enough; no applications of *modus ponens* or of the cut rule are needed. As far as quantifiers are concerned, however, our procedure may seem to be diametrically opposed to that of Herbrand: instead of eliminating quantifiers in our disproofs, as Herbrand does, we introduce new ones all the time. There is a closely related normal form of first-order disproofs, however, which is much more obviously comparable with the Herbrand-type proofs and disproofs. It will be explained briefly in section 18. We shall not examine its relation to the Herbrand proofs and disproofs, however.

The sufficient conditions of inconsistency (necessary conditions of consistency) which we shall formulate will be given in two different forms. The first set of conditions makes fuller use of the structure of the constituents and attributive constituents than the second. On the other hand, the second set of conditions seems even simpler than the first. Either of them serves the purpose of recursive enumeration; hence there does not seem to be much to choose between them on the level of general considerations. The first will be described and shown really to establish inconsistency in section 10, the second in section 12.

10. *Conditions based on the compatibility of different partitions*

In order to find suitable necessary criteria of consistency for attributive constituents, let us assume that we are given an a-constituent (7). Each a-constituent of depth $d-1$ occurring in (7)—say $Ct_u^{d-1}(a_1,..., a_k, x)$—is again of the form

$$(9) \quad \prod_{i=1}^{v} B_i(a_1,..., a_k, x) \ \& \ \pi_{i=1}^{w} (Ey)Ct_i^{d-2}(a_1,..., a_k, x, y)$$
$$\& \ (Uy) \ \sigma_{i=1}^{w} \ Ct_i^{d-2}(a_1,..., a_k, x, y).$$

Consider the simplest case $k = 0$ as an example. Switching over to the language of an interpreted system once again, we may say that (7) then gives us a list of all the different kinds of individuals that can be specified by means of the parameters of (7) and that are exemplified in the world in case (7) is true. In (9) all the different kinds of individuals that there are in the world are listed again; this time kinds of individuals specifiable by means of the same parameters *plus* the 'random' reference-point individual which is the value of x. Since (9) occurs in (7), at least one such reference-point individual will exist if (7) is true. Hence the two lists have to be compatible in order for (7) to be consistent: every individual mentioned in the 'relative' list (9) has to find a place in the 'absolute' list (7), and vice versa. Moreover, the individual referred to by x will have to find a place in its own 'relative' list (9).

It is obvious that similar considerations apply to the general case. In every case, the partitions effected by (7) and by (9) have to be compatible in a similar way in order for (7) to be consistent.

The three intuitive conditions of consistency which were just explained can be converted into explicit formal conditions, formulated in terms of the structure of the a-constituent in question. Let us consider the intuitive conditions one by one.

(A) Assume that we are given (7), (9), and furthermore some a-constituent $Ct_p^{d-2}(a_1,\ldots, a_k, x, y)$ which occurs in (9). We shall call the following formula the *bough* of (9) determined by $Ct_p^{d-2}(a_1,\ldots, a_k, x, y)$:

$$(10) \qquad \prod_{i=1}^{v} B_i(a_1,\ldots, a_k, x) \ \& \ Ct_p^{d-2}(a_1,\ldots, a_k, x, y).$$

The reason for the choice of the term 'bough' should be obvious in view of the tree structure of a-constituents. Notice that the first conjunction of (10) is the same as that of (9).

We shall apply to boughs criteria of identity similar to the ones we have been applying to constituents and attributive constituents: notational variation does not constitute a reason for calling two boughs different. Hence we may say, in the same way as in the case of a-constituents and for the same reason, that any two different boughs with the same parameters are logically incompatible. Whenever a bough (or one of its notational variants) is determined by one of the a-constituents of depth $d-2$ occurring in (9) or in (7) we shall say that this bough is *contained* in (9) or in (7), respectively.

If the roles of x and y are interchanged in (10), we obtain a formula which is again a bough with the same parameters (up to notational variation, which we are here disregarding). This bough will be called the *inverse* of (10). The operation of forming the inverse will be expressed by 'inv'.

After these preparations, we may argue as follows: by the omission lemma, (7) implies

$$(Ex)(Ey) \left(\prod_{\substack{v \\ i=1}} B_i(a_1,..., a_k, x) \ \& \ Ct_p^{d-2}(a_1,..., a_k, x, y) \right),$$

for this formula can be obtained from (7) by omitting quantified formulae and by extending the scope of the quantifier (Ey). In virtue of the permutability of the two existential quantifiers, (7) also implies

$$(11) \qquad (Ex)(Ey) \left(\text{inv} \left(\prod_{\substack{v \\ i=1}} B_i(a_1,..., a_k, x) \ \& \ Ct_p^{d-2}(a_1,..., a_k, x, y) \right) \right).$$

On the other hand, (7) implies by the omission lemma the formula

$$(12) \qquad (Ux)(Uy)(Bg_1(x,y) \ \lor \ Bg_2(x,y) \ \lor \ ...)$$

where the members of the disjunction are all the boughs of depth $d-2$ that are contained in (7). Because of the incompatibility lemma (as applied to boughs), (11) and (12) are compatible only if the inverse of (10) is among the members of the disjunction in (12). But this means that *an a-constituent of depth d is inconsistent unless it contains the inverse of each bough of depth d—2 contained in it.*

This condition is the formal counterpart to the intuitive requirement that each individual mentioned in the relative list (9) has to find a place in the absolute list (7).

(B) Assume again that we are given (7) and (9) in (7) and that we are also given another a-constituent $Ct_q^{d-1}(a_1,..., a_k, x)$ which likewise occurs in (7). Then by the omission lemma (7) implies

$$(Ex)(Uy)(Bg_{u_1}(x,y) \ \lor \ Bg_{u_2}(x,y) \ \lor \ ...)$$

where the members of the disjunction are now all the boughs of depth $d-2$ that are contained in (9). In virtue of the well-known exchange rule for quantifiers of different kinds (7) also implies

$$(13) \qquad (Ux)(Ey)(\text{inv}(Bg_{u_1}(x,y)) \ \lor \ \text{inv}(Bg_{u_2}(x,y)) \ \lor \ ...).$$

On the other hand, by the omission lemma (7) also implies

$$(14) \qquad (Ex)(Uy)(Bg_{q_1}(x,y) \ \lor \ Bg_{q_2}(x,y) \ \lor \ ...),$$

where the members of the disjunction are all the boughs of depth $d-2$ that are contained in $Ct_q^{d-1}(a_1,..., a_k, x)$. In virtue of the incompatibility lemma, (13) and (14) are incompatible unless the two disjunctions share at least one member. But this means that *of two attributive constituents of depth $d-1$ occurring in the same consistent a-constituent of depth d one has to contain the inverse of at least one of the boughs of depth $d-2$ which the other contains.*

This condition is the formal counterpart to the intuitive requirement that every individual mentioned in the absolute list (7) must find a place in the relative list (9).

(C) By universal instantiation the a-constituent (9) implies

$$\prod_{i=1}^{v} B_i(a_1,..., a_k, x) \,\&\, \sigma_w \, Ct_i^{d-2}(a_1,..., a_k, x, x).$$

This formula is inconsistent unless

(15) $$\prod_{i=1}^{v} B_i(a_1,..., a_k, x) \,\&\, Ct_p^{d-2}(a_1,..., a_k, x, x)$$

is consistent for at least one a-constituent $Ct_p^{d-2}(a_1,..., a_k, x, y)$ occurring in (9). In order for (15) to be consistent, it must not contain any conjunction one of whose members is the negation of another. (This is so for the same reason for which the inconsistency lemma is valid.) Whenever this is the case, we say that the corresponding bough (10) is *strongly symmetric* with respect to x and y.

By the same token, in order for (7) to be consistent it must contain at least one bough of depth $d-1$ which is strongly symmetric with respect to a_k and x. Furthermore, by the very same token (7) must for each a_i (where $i = 1, 2,..., k$) contain at least one bough of depth $d-1$ which is strongly symmetric with respect to a_i and x. In general, it may be said that *every consistent a-constituent of depth d whose outermost bound variable is x must, for every free individual symbol b occurring in it, contain at least one bough of depth $d-1$ which is strongly symmetric with respect to x and b.*

This is the general, exact form of the intuitive requirement that the individual referred to by x in (9) must find a place in its own list.

It is not difficult to see that in a given a-constituent (9) there can be contained at most one bough of depth $d-2$ (say (10)) which is strongly symmetric with respect to x and y, provided that the conditions (A) and (B) of consistency are satisfied. (There cannot be more than one place, we may thus say, which the 'random' individual specified by x may assume in its own 'relative' list.)

This suffices to explain what the three conditions (A)–(C) of consistency are. When they are said to be applied to a constituent or an a-constituent, it is understood that they are applied to this constituent or a-constituent as well as to all the a-constituents of lesser depth occurring in it. If one of these a-constituents is inconsistent, then so is the given constituent or a-constituent by the inconsistency lemma. Even in this extended sense, the question whether a given constituent or a-constituent fulfills the conditions (A)–(C) (or any single one of them) can always be decided in a finite number of steps.

The three sufficient conditions of inconsistency (A)–(C) were the main content of Chapter 5 of the author's dissertation.[11] Here they have been reformulated in a different terminology and notation, and derived from one and the same intuitive principle.

11. *The effects of an exclusive interpretation of quantifiers*

What happens to the conditions (A)–(C) in first-order logic *with* identity? As was pointed out earlier, a change in the interpretation of quantifiers is the only modification which we have to make here. How, then, do the conditions (A)–(C) fare on the exclusive interpretation of quantifiers? It is easily seen that (A) carries over without any changes. The condition (B) is also seen to apply without major changes. Its applicability has to be restricted to the cases in which the a-constituents (9) and $Ct_q^{d-1}(a_1,..., a_k, x)$ which were assumed to occur in (7) are really *different* a-constituents. Since two different a-constituents with the same parameters are logically incompatible (by the incompatibility lemma), the individuals satisfying them must be different from each other. And this may be seen to suffice to restore the condition (B).

In fact, we shall assume that this restriction is built into the condition (B) itself. This does not make any difference for our purposes. It is true that in the original formulation of (B) we did not exclude the case $u = q$. However, the force of (B) in this

---

[11] See the first footnote of this chapter.

special case is also obtained from (C), as you may easily verify. Hence we may exclude this case from (B), and say that it remains unchanged on the exclusive interpretation.

In contrast to (A) and (B), the condition (C) is based entirely on modes of reasoning that are incompatible with the exclusive interpretation of quantifiers. It therefore becomes inapplicable in first-order logic with identity.

12. *Omitting layers of quantifiers*

Here the conditions (A)–(C) will not be discussed as much as certain consequences of theirs. These consequences may also be derived independently in a rather simple manner. They are found by asking: what happens to a constituent or a-constituent when a layer of quantifiers is omitted from it? There are two cases to be considered here: (a) the omission of the innermost layer of quantifiers and (b) the omission of the outermost layer of quantifiers. The other cases in effect reduce to these. In order to eliminate an intermediate layer of quantifiers from an a-constituent (7)—say to eliminate the eth layer of them—it suffices to omit the outermost layer of quantifiers from every a-constituent Ct^{d-e+1} of depth $d-e+1$ occurring in (7).

(a) What happens to (7) when all the subformulae of the form

$$(Ex_d)Ct^0(a_1,..., a_k, x_1,..., x_{d-1}, x_d)$$

or

$$(Ux_d) \; \sigma \; Ct^0(a_1,..., a_k, x_1,..., x_{d-1}, x_d)$$

are omitted? An answer is obtained by examining what happens to the subformulae of the form $Ct^1(a_1,..., a_k, x_1,..., x_{d-1})$ of (7), i.e., by considering the special case $d = 1$. In this case, the result is seen to be of the form $Ct^0(a_1,..., a_k, x_1,..., x_{d-1})$ with the possible exception of notational variation. From the way deeper a-constituents depend on shallower ones, it is seen that in the general case (7) becomes a formula of the form $Ct^{d-1}(a_1,..., a_k)$, i.e., becomes an a-constituent with the same parameters (P.1)–(P.2) but with depth $d-1$, with the possible and inessential exception of notational variation. From the omission lemma it follows that the resulting a-constituent is implied by (7).

(b) Assume that we are given (7) and (9) in (7). A part of (7) is then $(Ex)Ct_u^{d-1}(a_1,..., a_k, x)$. What happens to this part of (7) if all the atomic formulae containing x (and the quantifier (Ex)) are omitted from it? The result is obviously of the form

$$(16) \qquad \pi_p \ (Ey)Ct_i^{d-2}(a_1,...,a_k,y) \ \& \ (Uy) \ \sigma_p \ Ct_i^{d-2}(a_1,...,a_k,y)$$
$$ i=1 \phantom{(Ey)Ct_i^{d-2}(a_1,...,a_k,y) \ \& \ (Uy) \ } i=1$$

except, perhaps, for notational variation. If we add to (16) as an additional member of the conjunction the unquantified part

$$\Pi_s \ B_i(a_1,...,a_k)$$
$$i=1$$

of (7), we obtain a formula which is of the form $Ct^{d-1}(a_1,...,a_k)$, again up to notational variation. In virtue of the omission lemma, this formula is implied by (7). It will be said to be obtained from (7) by *reduction* with respect to (9).

When (7) is reduced with respect to the different a-constituents of depth $d-1$ occurring in it, we obtain a number of formulae of the form $Ct^{d-1}(a_1,...,a_k)$. If there are two formulae among them which are different (apart from notational variation), then (7) is inconsistent, for it implies both of these formulae which are mutually incompatible by the incompatibility lemma. In order for (7) to be consistent, the results of reducing it with respect to the different a-constituents of depth $d-1$ occurring in it must all coincide. This gives us a necessary condition of consistency for an a-constituent (7). It will be called condition (D). When in the sequel it will be said to be applied to a given constituent or a-constituent, this will be understood to mean that it is also applied to the a-constituents of lesser depth occurring therein.

In the diagram of section 6 the reduction of the constituent illustrated there (with respect to one of the a-constituents of depth $d-1$ occurring in it) is represented schematically by the solid line. As we just saw, the result should be independent of the choice of Ct_1^{d-1}.

Further conditions of consistency are obtained by comparing the results of eliminating the different layers of quantifiers which occur in an a-constituent, say in (7). If (7) is to be consistent, the result is in the case of each layer an a-constituent of depth $d-1$, as we just saw. It may now be added that all these resulting a-constituents of depth $d-1$ must be identical (up to notational variation); otherwise they would be incompatible, though they are all implied by (7). Hence the omission of a layer of quantifiers must yield the same result, no matter which layer is omitted,

if a constituent or a-constituent is to be consistent. This requirement will be called condition (E).

In our diagram (section 6) the omission of the last layer of
quantifiers is indicated by the dotted line. Notice that the two
omissions that are represented schematically in the diagram
must yield the same result if the attributive constituent represented by the diagram is to be consistent.

Since the result of omitting one layer of quantifiers from a
given a-constituent $Ct_r^d(a_1,..., a_k)$ is unique if this a-constituent is
consistent, we can refer to all these results in one and the same
way: each of them will be called $Ct_r^{d[-1]}(a_1,..., a_k)$. In case
$Ct_r^d(a_1,..., a_k)$ does not yield a unique result when a layer of
quantifiers is omitted, or if the result is not an a-constituent, we
shall say that $Ct_r^{d[-1]}(a_1,..., a_k)$ disappears. If it does not disappear,
it is easily seen to satisfy the conditions (D)–(E) of consistency
and hence to yield a unique result when another layer of quantifiers is omitted.

The result of applying the same operation to $Ct_r^d(a_1,..., a_k)$
e times will be called $Ct_r^{d[-e]}(a_1,..., a_k)$.

Notice that there is an operation which in a certain sense is
the inverse of the operation of omitting a layer of quantifiers. It
is the operation of expanding a constituent or a-constituent C^d
of depth d to a disjunction of a number of subordinate constituents or a-constituents of depth $d+1$. The procedure which
was mentioned earlier in section 5 for converting formulae into
the normal form may be assumed to be such that each of the
subordinate constituents (or a-constituents) of depth $d+1$ again
yields C^d when the innermost layer of quantifiers is omitted. We
may also require that this is the case no matter which layer of
quantifiers is omitted from the subordinate constituent or
a-constituent in question, for if the result is not C^d, the subordinate constituent is inconsistent and hence may be omitted from
the normal form of C^d with depth $d+1$.

A constituent which fails to satisfy (C)–(E) will be called
trivially inconsistent. The other, competing sense of trivial inconsistency which was discussed above in the appendix to Chapter
X is similarly captured by the conditions (A)–(C).

The relation of the two sets of conditions (A)–(C) and (D)–(E)
(conceived of as conditions of consistency) is straightforward. It
may be proved that whenever a constituent or a-constituent

satisfies (A)–(C) it also satisfies (D)–(E). In fact, it may be proved that it satisfies (D)–(E) whenever it satisfies (A) plus (B) in its original, strong form.

Conversely, it may be shown that a constituent or a-constituent C^d satisfies the conditions (A)–(B) if at least one of its subordinate constituents or a-constituents of depth $d+1$ satisfies the conditions (C)–(E). In a sense, the two sets of conditions (A)–(C) and (C)–(E) are thus equally powerful for the purpose of discovering inconsistent constituents and a-constituents. In order to apply the latter ones successfully to a constituent, however, we must first explicate its content by expanding it into a disjunction of constituents of depth $d+1$, and apply the conditions (C)–(E) to each of these.

These results may be proved rather simply by means of the diagrams of constituents and a-constituents which have been explained in section 6. For reasons of space the proofs are not given here. Suffice it to say that the implication from the satisfaction of (A)–(C) to that of (D)–(E) is proved conveniently by induction on d. That this should be the case is not surprising in view of the intuitive meaning of the conditions (A)–(C), for from the intuitive meaning they have it is rather easy to gather that they require (among other things) that the omission of two *adjacent* layers of quantifiers has to give us the same result.

13. *The effects of identity again*

So far, we have considered the process of omitting a layer of quantifiers only in first-order logic without identity. What changes are occasioned by the exclusive interpretation in this respect?

The omission of the last (innermost) layer of quantifiers can be accomplished as before. The omission of an intermediate layer of quantifiers also reduces to the omission of the outermost quantifier in the same way as before. What cannot be done in the same way as above is the process of relative reduction. Applied to (7) with respect to (9), it no longer gives us a formula which is implied (in all cases) by (7). The reason why the omission lemma fails in this case is the following: in order to get rid of the outermost quantifiers (Ex) and (Ux) we have to omit from (9) not only all the atomic formulae containing x but also all the identities involving x which on the exclusive interpretation are implicit in the quantifiers (Ex) and (Ux) themselves as well as in all the inner quantifiers (Ez) and (Uz) of (9). Simply omitting all these identities does not always fall within the scope of the omission lemma. In some cases it does; thus the part of (7) beginning with (Ux) is omitted altogether in the reduction, eliminating all problems concerning identities occurring in it. Furthermore, all identities implicit in existential quantifiers are easily seen to fall within the scope of the omission lemma. Thus there only remains the problem of dealing with a universal quantifier (Uz) occurring in the inner layers of (7). On the exclusive interpretation, this quantifier really means (Uz) $(z \neq x \supset ...)$. Intuitively, it is easy to see whence the trouble comes here. We are trying to omit x, that is, we are trying to convert a statement about all individuals different from the value of x into a statement about *all* individuals without restrictions. Clearly this is possible only if we add a new clause which takes care of the case in which one of these 'all' individuals is the value of x. The way to do this is as follows.

Assume that we are reducing (7) with respect to (9). Then at the same time as we omit all the atomic formulae which contain x from (9), we add as a new member of the main conjunction of (9) the following formula:

$$(17) \qquad (Ey)Ct_u^{d-1[-1]}(a_1,..., a_k, y)$$

and as a new member of the outermost disjunction

$$\sigma_w Ct^{d-2}(a_1,..., a_k, x, y)$$

the following formula:

$$(18) \qquad Ct_u^{d-1[-1]}(a_1,..., a_k, y).$$

The same operation has to be applied to every a-constituent $Ct_p^{d-e}(a_1,..., a_k, x, y,...)$ which occurs in (9), and whose outermost quantifiers are (let us say) (Ez) and (Uz). At the same time as we omit from it all the atomic formulae which contain x, we add as a new member of the main conjunction the formula

$$(17)^* \qquad (Ez)(Ct_p^{d-e[-1]}(a_1,..., a_k, z, y,...) \,\&\, G)$$

and as a new member of the outermost disjunction the same formula without '(Ez)'. Here G is the conjunction of all negated or unnegated atomic formulae containing x which occur in (9) within the scope of some (or all) of the same quantifiers as $Ct_p^{d-e}(a_1,..., a_k, x, y,...)$ (but not within the scope of any others) with x replaced by z.

The result of carrying out this operation in all the a-constituents which occur in (9) as well as in (9) itself, at the same time as we omit all the atomic formulae containing x from (9) and add as a new member of the main conjunction of (9) the unquantified part

$$\Pi_s \underset{i=1}{B_i(a_1,..., a_k)}$$

of (7), will be called the result of reducing (7) with respect to (9) in first-order logic with identity.

This result is implied by (7) (on the exclusive interpretation of quantifiers, of course). This implication will not be proved formally here. No proof is probably needed to convince the reader, for on the basis of the intuitive considerations which led us to modify the process of relative reduction it should be obvious (at least on a moment's reflection) that the modification is just what is needed to reinstate the implication.

After the reduction of an a-constituent with respect to another has thus been redefined so as to restore the crucial implication, everything else may be done in the same way as in first-order logic without identity. We can define what it means to omit a layer of quantifiers, and we can reformulate the necessary conditions of consistency (D)–(E) for first-order logic with identity.

The relation of these conditions to (A)–(B) (the latter in the weak form) is even more clear-cut than before. A constituent or a-constituent C^d satisfies (D)–(E) if it satisfies (A)–(B); and it satisfies (A)–(B) if at least one of its subordinate constituents or a-constituents of depth $d+1$ satisfies (D)–(E).

14. *A disproof procedure defined*

The conditions (A)–(E) are connected in an intimate and intuitive way with the structure of constituents and a-constituents. It will now be shown that they provide us with a disproof procedure for inconsistent constituents and a-constituents, a procedure which is semantically complete in that every inconsistent constituent is subject to this disproof procedure.

The procedure can be described very simply. Given a constituent C^d of depth d, how can we try to find out whether it is consistent or inconsistent? It may be the case that our conditions (A)–(E) suffice to establish its inconsistency. If not, we do not yet know whether C^d is consistent or not. What we can do, however, is to expand C^d into a disjunction of a number of subordinate constituents of depth $d+1$ (with the same parameters (P.1)–(P.2)), to which we may apply our conditions. If all of them are inconsistent by our sufficient conditions, their disjunction and therefore C^d itself is likewise inconsistent, and we have an answer to our question. If not, we have to keep on expanding C^d into a disjunction of subordinate constituents of greater and greater depth $d+e$. If during this procedure some constituents are inconsistent by our conditions, they may be omitted in the sequel. If for some e all the subordinate constituents of depth $d+e$ turn out to be inconsistent by (A)–(E)—that is, trivially inconsistent in one of the two alternative senses of this notion—then so is C^d. What we want to show is that for each *inconsistent* constituent C^d there is an e such that this happens at depth $d+e$. In other words, whatever inconsistencies there may be in a constituent can be brought to light by adding to its depth. And since every formula can be brought to a distributive normal form, this likewise gives us a method of disproving every inconsistent formula. This method consists of the rules for converting a formula to the (second) distributive normal form (they also give us rules for expanding a constituent to a disjunction of a number of deeper constituents) plus our sufficient conditions (A)–(E) of inconsistency. The statement that this method really can be used to disprove every inconsistent formula will be called the *completeness theorem* of our theory of distributive normal forms.

Because of the connection between the two sets of conditions (A)–(C) and (C)–(E) either of these combinations of conditions may be used in the disproof procedure just described (in first-order logic without identity). The only difference between the two sets of conditions is that if we use the former we may be able to see inconsistencies one step earlier than if we used the latter; i.e., if using the former we have to go down to depth $d+e$ (in the case of some given formula), then using the latter we may have to go down to depth $d+e+1$. The same relationship holds in first-order logic with identity between the two sets of conditions (A)–(B) and (D)–(E) (modified).

In proving the completeness theorem either set of conditions may be used. Because of the greater simplicity of (D)–(E) they will be used in what follows instead of (A)–(B).

15. *Completeness proof (first part)*

The disproofs described in the preceding section have the structure of a tree. Since each constituent of depth d has only a finite number of subordinate constituents of depth $d+1$, at each point of this tree only a finite number of branches can diverge. Hence the tree theorem (König's lemma) applies, showing that the completeness theorem can be proved by proving the following result:

A constituent is consistent (satisfiable) if it can occur in a sequence of constituents which satisfies the following conditions:

(i) each member of the sequence is subordinate to its immediate predecessor;

(ii) each member satisfies the conditions (C)–(E) of consistency (in first-order logic with identity, the conditions (D)–(E)).

We may also assume, for simplicity, that the depth of each member of the sequence is $d+1$ when the depth of its immediate predecessor is d. It clearly suffices to prove that the first member of each sequence which satisfies (i)–(ii) is consistent.

Let us assume that we are given a sequence S_0 of deeper and deeper constituents which satisfies all the conditions just mentioned. We shall show that the first member of S_0 is satisfiable. For this purpose, we shall first construct a sequence of attributive constituents S_1. This will be done in such a way that instead of adding to the depth of constituents (as in S_0) we introduce new free individual symbols. In fact, the depth of all the members of S_1 will be the same as that of the first member of S_0 (say d); however, each of them will have one free individual symbol more than its immediate predecessor. Each member of S_1 will be chosen in such a way that it occurs in the corresponding member of S_0, i.e., occurs there with appropriate bound variables substituted for some of its free individual symbols, of course. For the first member of S_1 we may take the attributive constituent of depth d which occurs in the first member of S_0.

The main question which remains to be answered is therefore: How is a member of S_1 obtained from its immediate predecessor? In order to answer this question, let us assume that (7) is an arbitrary member of S_1. Let us also assume that of the free individual symbols of (7) $a_1, a_2,..., a_j$ $(1 \leqslant j \leqslant k)$ occur already in the first member of S_0 while $a_{j+1}, a_{j+2},..., a_k$ do not occur there. Then an a-constituent of the form $Ct_r^d(a_1,..., a_j, x_{j+1},..., x_k)$ occurs in the corresponding member of S_0. Since the next member of S_0 is obtained (as was pointed out in section 12) by adding one more layer of quantifiers, there must be in the next member of S_0 at least one attributive constituent (usually there are several) which is subordinate to the one just mentioned and which is of the form $Ct_q^{d+1}(a_1,..., a_j, x_{j+1},..., x_k)$ or, more explicitly,

$$(19) \qquad \prod_{i=1}^s B_i(a_1,..., a_j, x_{j+1},..., x_k)$$

$$\& \; \pi_{i=1}^{t'} (Ex_{k+1}) Ct_i^d(a_1,..., a_j, x_{j+1},..., x_k, x_{k+1})$$

$$\& \; (Ux_{k+1}) \; \sigma_{i=1}^{t'} \; Ct_i^d(a_1,..., a_j, x_{j+1},..., x_k, x_{k+1}).$$

In order to obtain the next member of S_1, we choose one of the a-constituents of depth d occurring in (19). The principle of selection will be explained later. If the attributive constituent chosen is

$$(20) \qquad Ct_p^d(a_1,..., a_j, x_{j+1},..., x_k, x_{k+1}),$$

the next member of S_1 is simply

$$(20)^* \qquad Ct_p^d(a_1,..., a_j, a_{j+1},..., a_k, a_{k+1}),$$

where a_{k+1} is a new free individual symbol.

This a-constituent satisfies by construction the requirement that the corresponding bound-variable formula (20) occurs in the corresponding member of S_0.

How is (20) to be selected? We shall first explain one particular method of making the choice. Subsequently, it will be pointed out that this method can be considerably generalized.

Let T_k be the set of all the a-constituents of depth $d-1$ which occur in (7), and let T_k' be the set of all the similar a-constituents which contain $x_{j+1}, x_{j+2},..., x_k$ instead of $a_{j+1}, a_{j+2},..., a_k$. Each of the a-constituents from among which (20) is chosen arises from a member of T_k' through the addition of a new layer of quantifiers. For the members of T_k' we shall shortly establish a certain *seniority ranking*. After this has been accomplished, (20) may be chosen to be any of the a-constituents which arise from members of T_k' *of the highest rank*.

Because of the similarity of T_k and T_k', a similar ranking will be automatically induced for the members of T_k, too.

The only thing that remains in order to define S_1 is therefore to explain how the seniority ranking is established. This ranking will be a linear quasi-ordering, i.e., it will be a linear ordering of the different ranks into which the members of T_k' (and of T_k) will be partitioned. The ranking of the a-constituents of depth $d-1$ occurring in the first member of S_1 does not matter. Hence the only thing we have to do is to explain how this ranking is carried over from one member of S_1 to the next one. (In each case, we have a ranking of the a-constituents of depth $d-1$ occurring in a member of S_1.)

In order to explain this, notice that one and the same result is obtained from (19) in two different ways:

(a) By omitting the last layer of quantifiers;

(b) By reducing it with respect to (20).

This identity follows from the fact that (19) satisfies the conditions (D)–(E). The result of (a) is simply $Ct_r^d(a_1,..., a_j, x_{j+1},..., x_k)$, which is therefore also obtainable through the operation (b), i.e., whose quantified part is obtainable by omitting all reference to x_{k+1} from (20). This fact establishes a one-to-many correlation between the members of T_k' and the members of the set T_{k+1}' of all a-constituents of depth $d-1$ which occur in (20): each of the former arises from one of the latter by omitting all mention of x_{k+1}. This correlation will be called the *weak* correlation between the members of the two sets and conceived of as a symmetric relation. A similar relation, which will be referred to in the same way, obtains between the members of T_k and the members of the set T_{k+1} of all the a-constituents of depth $d-1$ which occur in (20)*. It is to be observed that this relation is determined as soon as the sequence S_1 is given; its definition does not in any way turn on the definition of our seniority ranking.

The weak correlation can be strengthened (artificially, so to speak) into a one-to-one correlation between *all* the members of T_k (or of T_k') and *some* of the members of T_{k+1} (or of T_{k+1}' respectively). All we have to do for the purpose is to choose one of the weak correlates of each member of T_k and assign it to this member as its strong correlate. This can of course be done in a variety of ways in most cases; in the sequel we shall assume some arbitrary but fixed way of doing so.

One important exception will be made here, however. That member of T_k which gave rise to (20)* (i.e. which is identical with $Ct_p^{d[-1]}(a_1,..., a_k, x_{k+1})$) will not be assigned any strong correlate in T_{k+1}; instead, we shall say that it is *associated with* (20)*. The same will of course apply to T'_k, T'_{k+1}, and (20).

When the strong correlation has been established, the seniority ranking may be carried over from T_k to T_{k+1} by stipulating that strong correlation preserves relative rank, and that members of T_{k+1} which do not have any strong correlate in T_k rank lower than one which has such a correlate.

The net effect of the transition from (7) to (20)* (i.e., from a member of S_1 to the next one) on the seniority ranking is thus that the ranking is preserved except that (i) one member of the highest rank gets lost and that (ii) a new rank will be created which is lower than all the old ones.

From this we can gather what happens in the long run in the sequence S_1. Every rank will become empty while lower and lower new ranks will (usually) be created. Every chain of strong correlations will come to an end with an a-constituent which does not have a strong correlate any more but which is associated with the next member of S_1. Conversely, every member of S_1 is associated with an a-constituent of depth $d-1$ which occurs in its predecessor. Notice also that if we move backwards in S_1 no chain of weak correlations comes to an end until it reaches the first member of S_1.

What has been said so far applies in the first place to first-order logic *without* identity. In first-order logic *with* identity, the situation is slightly complicated by complications that were needed in the definition of relative reduction in section 13. They enter the present discussion through the operation (b) which was applied to (19) earlier in this section. The net effect of the complications here is that one of the members of T_k may become weakly correlated, not with any member of T_{k+1}, but rather with $Ct_p^{d[-1]}(a_1,..., a_k, x_{k+1})$. This member of T_k will, however, be the one which is not going to have any strong correlate anyway. The fact that it may now also lack a weak correlate does not interfere with the way the seniority ordering is carried forward in S_1. Nor does it interfere with the statements made in the preceding paragraph.

This completes our explanation of how the sequence S_1 may be obtained from the given sequence S_0. We can see that such a sequence can always be obtained. It only remains to show that all the members of S_1 are simultaneously satisfiable. If we can do this, then we have shown that the first member of S_1 is satisfiable. In first-order logic with identity, the satisfiability of the first member of S_0 is thereby made obvious. In first-order logic without identity, the satisfiability of the first member of S_0 can be established by an argument similar to the one we shall give at the end of section 17.

16. *Attributive constituents and model sets*

The simultaneous satisfiability of all the members of S_1 may be proved by embedding them into one and the same *model set*.[12] If no negation-signs are allowed except those which immediately precede an atomic formula, if no identities are admitted, and if the only propositional connectives are $\sim$, &, and v, then a model set may be defined as a set of formulae—say μ—which satisfies the following conditions:

(C . $\sim$)   If $F \in \mu$, then not $\sim F \in \mu$.
(C . &)   If $(F \& G) \in \mu$, then $F \in \mu$ and $G \in \mu$.
(C . v)   If $(F \vee G) \in \mu$, then $F \in \mu$ or $G \in \mu$ (or both).
(C . E)   If $(Ex)F \in \mu$, then $F(a/x) \in \mu$ for at least one free individual symbol a.

Here $F(a/x)$ is the result of replacing x everywhere by a in F, subject to the usual precautions against the conflict of variables. The same notation will be used in what follows.

(C . U)   If $(Ux)F \in \mu$ and if b is a free individual symbol occurring in at least one formula of μ, then $F(b/x) \in \mu$.

Satisfiability has to be interpreted here as satisfiability in an empty or non-empty domain of individuals.

For the exclusive interpretation of quantifiers, the definition

---

12 For model sets and for a proof of the fact that embeddability in a model set equals satisfiability (consistency), see Chapter I above and the literature mentioned there in note 14. Cf. also 'Modality and Quantification', *Theoria*, vol. 27 (1961), pp. 119–28. It is convenient to assume here that (C. &) and (C. v) have been generalized so as to apply also to conjunctions and disjunctions with more than two members.

of a model set can obviously be modified by changing (C . E) and (C . U) as follows:[13]

(C . E$_{ex}$)   If $(Ex)F \in \mu$, then $F(a/x) \in \mu$ for at least one free individual symbol a which does not occur in F.

(C . U$_{ex}$)   If $(Ux)F \in \mu$ and if the free individual symbol b occurs in the formulae of μ but not in F, then $F(b/x) \in \mu$.

These conditions can be geared more closely to the structure of constituents and attributive constituents. It is easily seen that an a-constituent is embeddable in a model set and therefore satisfiable if it can be embedded in a set λ of attributive constituents which satisfies the following conditions (in these conditions (7) is thought of as an arbitrary a-constituent):

(C . ct $\sim$)   If an atomic formula all of whose individual symbols are free occurs unnegated in a member of λ, then it never occurs negated in any member of λ.

(C . ct E)   If (7) occurs in λ, then for every a-constituent (9) of depth $d-1$ which occurs in (7) there is a free individual symbol b such that $Ct_u^{d-1}(a_1,..., a_k, b) \in \lambda$.

(C . ct U)   If (7) occurs in λ, then for every free individual symbol b which occurs in at least one member of λ there is an a-constituent (9) of depth $d-1$ which occurs in (7) and which is such that
$$Ct_u^{d-1}(a_1,..., a_k, b) \in \lambda.$$

A set λ of a-constituents which satisfies these conditions will be called a constitutive model set.[14] For the exclusive interpretation of quantifiers, the conditions (C . ct E) and (C . ct U) have of course to be modified in the same way as in (C . E$_{ex}$) and in (C . U$_{ex}$), respectively, by requiring that b does not occur in

---

[13] In the terminology of the paper referred to in note 6 above, these conditions formulate the *weakly* exclusive interpretation of quantifiers.

[14] Given a constitutive model set λ, an ordinary model set μ is easily obtained as the closure of λ with respect to the following operations:

(i) Whenever a conjunction occurs in λ, adjoin to λ all its members.

(ii) Whenever (7) occurs in λ and b occurs in the formulae of λ, adjoin the disjunction
$$\sigma_{i=1}^t Ct_i^{d-1}(a_1,..., a_k, b)$$
to λ.

This μ contains λ as a part and has exactly the same free individual symbols as λ.

(9)—or in (7), which is the same thing. The resulting conditions will be called $(C . ct E_{ex})$ and $(C . ct U_{ex})$.

17. *Completeness proof (concluded)*

The simultaneous satisfiability of all the members of the sequence S_1 which was defined earlier will be proved first for first-order logic with identity. Subsequently, the modifications needed for the ordinary interpretation of quantifiers will be explained briefly.

On the exclusive interpretation of quantifiers, all we have to do in order to embed S_1 in a constitutive model set is to form its closure with respect to the following operations:

(a) The operation of omitting a layer of quantifiers.

(b) The operation of omitting a free individual symbol (i.e., of omitting all the atomic formulae which contain this symbol, together with all the connectives which hence become idle).

The operation (b) requires a few comments. First, we shall restrict it by requiring that the free individual symbol omitted is not the distinguished (last) free individual symbol of an a-constituent. For instance, the symbol a_k must not be omitted from (7). Otherwise (b) might not give an a-constituent as a result when applied to an a-constituent.

Furthermore, in first-order logic with identity the operation (b) has to be modified in the same way and for the same reason as the operation (a). Suppose, for instance, that we are omitting the free individual symbol a_i ($1 \leqslant i \leqslant k$) from (7); and suppose that $Ct_p^{d-e}(a_1,..., a_k, x, y,...)$ is an arbitrary a-constituent which occurs in (7) and whose outermost quantifiers are (Ez) and (Uz) (exclusively interpreted). When we omit the atomic formulae which contain a_i we must add to the main conjunction the formula

$$(Ez)(Ct_p^{d-e[-1]}(a_1,..., a_{i-1}, z, a_{i+1},..., a_k, x, y,...) \ \& \ G),$$

where G specifies the relation of

$$z = a_i \text{ to } a_1, a_2,..., a_{i-1}, a_{i+1},..., a_k, x, y,...,$$

and to the outmost disjunction the same without '(Ez)'.

Let the closure of S_1 with respect to the operations (a) and (b), so qualified, be λ. Then it is easy to see that λ satisfies $(C . ct \sim)$. For the purpose, consider an arbitrary atomic formula which occurs in the formulae of λ with all its individual symbols free.

If it occurs (in this way) in a member of λ, negated or unnegated, it must likewise occur, in view of the way λ was obtained from S_1, in a member of S_1. Hence it suffices to verify (C . ct $\sim$) for S_1 alone. Now all the free individual symbols of S_1 are $a_1, a_2, \ldots$; we assume for simplicity that they are different from all the bound individual variables we are dealing with. If the last member of this sequence which occurs in F is a_k, then F occurs (negated or unnegated but not both) in exactly one member of S_1, viz. in (7) provided of course that $k > j$. But if $k \leqslant j$, F cannot occur in any member of S_1 at all. Hence F cannot occur both negated and unnegated in the members of S_1 nor therefore in the member of λ.

It is also easy to see that all the members of λ satisfy the other two defining conditions of a constitutive model set provided that all the members of S_1 do so in λ. Indeed, the relation between (7) and (9) which is mentioned in (C . ct E) and (C . ct U) and hence also in (C . ct E_{ex}) and (C . ct U_{ex}) continues to obtain if one of the operations (a) and (b) is applied to both of them. From this it follows in first-order logic without identity that the other (new) members of λ satisfy (C . ct E) and (C . ct U) if the members of S_1 do so. In first-order logic with identity, there are two additional cases we have to worry about. They are caused by the fact that in omitting a free individual symbol on the exclusive interpretation a new attributive constituent of depth $d-1$ is added to each attributive constituent of depth d from which a free individual symbol is omitted. Let the latter be (7) and the former therefore

$$(21) \qquad Ct_r^{d[-1]}(a_1, \ldots, a_{i-1}, x, a_{i+1}, \ldots, a_k).$$

Now λ might prima facie fail to satisfy (C . ct E_{ex}) because of the presence of this new a-constituent of depth $d-1$ in the modified form of (7), and it might prima facie fail to satisfy (C . ct U_{ex}) because a free individual symbol (viz. a_i) which formerly did occur in (7) does not do so any more and hence seems to open a new possibility of applying (C . ct U_{ex}). In both cases the violation of one of the two conditions is avoided because λ is closed under (a) and hence contains the formula (cf. (21)):

$$Ct_r^{d[-1]}(a_1, \ldots, a_{i-1}, a_i, a_{i+1}, \ldots, a_k).$$

Hence the only thing that remains for us to do in order to

show that λ is a constitutive model set is to prove that the members of S_1 satisfy the conditions (C . ct E) and (C . ct U) or (C . ct E_{ex}) and (C . ct U_{ex}), as the case may be, when they are considered as members of λ. This may be proved by means of certain lemmata concerning S_1. These lemmata follow directly from the way in which S_1 was constructed.

LEMMA I: *Whenever* $Ct_m^{d-1}(a_1,..., a_k, x) \in T_k$ *is weakly correlated with* $Ct_n^{d-1}(a_1,..., a_k, a_{k+1}, x) \in T_{k+1}$, *the former results from the latter (up to notational variation, as usual) by omitting the free individual symbol* a_{k+1} *in the sense of operation* (b) *defined earlier in this section.*

This is, on reflection, just what being weakly correlated means. Lemma I can be generalized:

LEMMA I*: *Whenever* $Ct_m^{d-1}(a_1,..., a_k, x) \in T_k$ *is connected by the ancestral of the weak correlation with* $Ct_n^{d-1}(a_1,..., a_k, a_{k+1},..., a_{k+l}, x) \in T_{k+l}$, *the former results from the latter by omitting the free individual symbols* $a_{k+1}, a_{k+2},..., a_{k+l}$.

Another useful lemma is the following:

LEMMA 2: *Whenever* $Ct_m^{d-1}(a_1,..., a_k, x) \in T_k$ *is associated with the next member* (20)* *of* S_1, *it results from the latter by omitting one layer of quantifiers.*

This is just what being associated means. By means of Lemmata I* and 2 we can show that the members of S_1 satisfy (C . ct E_{ex}) and (C . ct U_{ex}) in λ. For this purpose, assume that (7) is a member of S_1 and that

$$(22) \qquad Ct_m^{d-1}(a_1,..., a_k, x)$$

occurs in (7). As pointed out in section 15, the chain of strong correlations which passes through (22) will always come to an end at some a-constituent which is not strongly correlated with any further a-constituent but which is instead associated with the next member of S_1—say with

$$(23) \qquad Ct_n^{d}(a_1,..., a_k, a_{k+1},..., a_{k+l}).$$

Then by Lemmata I* and 2 it follows that

$$(22)* \qquad Ct_m^{d-1}(a_1,..., a_k, a_{k+l})$$

results from (23) by first omitting one layer of quantifiers and by then omitting the free individual symbols $a_{k+1}, a_{k+2},..., a_{k+l}$. But since λ is closed under the operations (a) and (b), this implies that (22)* belongs to λ. This means that (C . ct E) is satisfied by (7). Moreover, since a_{k+l} does not occur in (7) or (22), it also means that (C . ct E_{ex}) is satisfied.

In order to verify (C . ct U_{ex}), assume that (7) occurs in S_1. Then every free individual symbol of λ which does not occur in (7) (nor in the less deep a-constituents which occur in (7)) is of the form a_{k+l}. Consider now the first member of S_1 which contains a_{k+l}; let it be (23). Then (23) is associated with some member of T_{k+l-1} which is in turn connected by a chain of weak correlations with some member of T_k, i.e., with some a-constituent of depth $d-1$ occurring in (7). Let this a-constituent be (22). Then from Lemmata 1* and 2 it follows in the same way as in the case of (C . ct E_{ex}) that (22)* results from (23) by means of the operations (a) and (b) and hence belongs to λ. This suffices to verify (C . ct U_{ex}) for (7).

This completes our argument to the effect that all the members of S_1 are simultaneously satisfiable for a system *with* identity. For a system *without* identity, an additional argument is needed to take care of those cases of (C . ct U) in which b occurs in (7), i.e., in which b is an a_i where $1 \leqslant i \leqslant k$. In the special case of S_1 we know that each member (7) of S_1 satisfies the condition (C) of consistency. Hence there must be in (7) an a-constituent (9) of depth $d-1$ such that the bough of (7) determined by (9) is strongly symmetric with respect to x and a_i. Consider, then, the formula $Ct_u^{d-1}(a_1,..., a_{k-1}, a_k, a_i)$ obtained from (9) by replacing x by a_i. By a straightforward argument whose details are here omitted, it can be shown that because of strong symmetry this formula is identical with the result of reducing (7) with respect to (9) and therefore also identical with the result of omitting one layer of quantifiers from (7). (Identity here means, as usual, identity except for the naming of bound variables and the order of conjunctions and disjunctions, and in this case also for the vacuous repetition of some members of conjunctions and disjunctions.) Since λ is closed with respect to the operation (a), this implies that $C_u^{d-1}(a_1,..., a_{k-1}, a_k, a_i) \in \lambda$ and shows that the condition (C . ct U) is satisfied also in the cases which do not fall within the scope of (C . ct U_{ex}).

18. *General considerations*

This brings to an end our completeness proof for the disproof procedure described in section 14, both in first-order logic without identity and in one with it. As a dual of the disproof procedure we obtain a complete proof procedure for first-order logic. Proofs of this form have an easily surveyable structure, and most of their steps are quite innocent-looking. They may be taken to be linear, i.e., each line of the proof is a single formula which is obtained from its immediate predecessor. Most of these formulae are conjunctions; hence we may, if we want, split the proof into branches (*Beweisfäden*) which are tied together into the form of a tree by the simple inference rule $F, G \vdash (F \& G)$. It may be worth while to list, by way of summary, the different kinds of step which will occur in these proofs (with the optional exception of the inference rule just mentioned). In listing these steps, we are looking at the proofs not in the direction from the axioms to the formula to be proved but in the opposite direction.

The following operations are needed to convert a formula into the dual of its distributive normal form:

(1) Transformation into propositional normal form without affecting the parameters (P.1)–(P.3) of the formula in question.

(2) The distributivity of the universal quantifier with respect to conjunction.

(3) The possibility of reducing the scope of a universal quantifier by omitting from it members of disjunctions which do not contain the variable which is bound to the quantifier in question.

We must be able to carry out these operations also within a formula (i.e., to apply them to a subformula of a larger formula). Furthermore, we must of course assume the usual interrelation between the two quantifiers and the possibility of renaming bound variables.

These operations also enable us to reach the dual of the second distributive normal form.

In adding to the depth of the dual of a constituent we must assume something further:

(4) One may add to the depth of a formula by introducing propositionally redundant parts which do not change the other parameters (P.1)–(P.2).

Finally, in each branch of the proof or in each conjunct of the first line of the rest of the proof (looking at it now in the direction from axioms to the formula to be proved) we need exactly one initial operation which is the dual of the argument by means of which attributive constituents not satisfying (A)–(C) (or, in first-order logic with identity, (A)–(B)) were shown to be inconsistent. From section 10 it is seen that in the case of (A) and (B) these operations are, apart from certain inessential preparatory steps, essentially applications of the well-known exchange laws for adjacent quantifiers:

$(5)_1$ $\qquad\qquad \vdash (Ux)(Uy)\,F \equiv (Uy)(Ux)\,F.$

$(5)_2$ $\qquad\qquad \vdash (Ex)(Uy)\,F \supset (Uy)(Ex)\,F.$

In the case of (C) this initial step is essentially an application of the law

$(5)_3$ $\qquad\qquad \vdash (Ux)\,F \supset F(a/x)$

where a occurs in F.

The application of these laws may seem to be the only non-trivial step of the argument. In each initial conjunct, only one application of one of them is needed.

In reality, however, the sole non-trivial element lies in the increase in depth. This fact can be illustrated by using here the conditions (C)–(E) instead of (A)–(C). Then $(5)_1$–$(5)_2$ are dispensable, and their place is taken by whatever laws are needed to guarantee the validity of our Omission Lemma. Unlike $(5)_1$–$(5)_2$ these are fairly clearly monadic principles, such as

$$\vdash (Ux)(Fx \supset Gx) \supset ((Ux)Fx \supset (Ux)\,Gx),$$

which do not involve any changes in depth or in the order of quantifiers. This impression is in fact confirmed by a closer analysis of the situation, which also shows the sense in which all the other inferences (besides the innocent-looking increase in depth) are all trivial. (For instance, they do not affect depth on our sharpened definition of this notion.) Hence in a sense *all* the novelty in an argument of the kind described is due to the increase in depth which takes place in it.

In first-order logic with identity, a few unimportant complications arise because of the presence of identity. We shall not discuss them in detail here.

We also obtain two dual methods of proofs from assumptions.

These proofs are interesting because they are linear; each line of the proof consists of a single formula.[15] We may consider that method which turns on our original (second) distributive normal form. In order to prove G from F by means of this method, we may proceed as follows: first, we pool together the parameters (P.1)–(P.2) of F and G, take the maximum (say d) of their depths, and convert F and G into their respective normal forms F^d and G^d in terms of the parameters so obtained. Then we expand the normal forms F^d and G^d by splitting their constituents into disjunctions of deeper and deeper constituents while their other parameters are unchanged. At each depth we test all the constituents for consistency by means of (A)–(C) or (C)–(E) (or, if identities are present, by means of (A)–(B) or (D)–(E)) and omit all the ones which fail the test. Let us call the disjunction of the remaining ones of depth $d+e$, F^{d+e} and G^{d+e}, respectively. Then if G really follows from F there will be an e such that all the members of F^{d+e} are among the members of G^{d+e}. A proof of G from F will then proceed from F to F^d to F^{d+1} to ... to F^{d+e} to G^{d+e} to G^{d+e-1} to ... to G^{d+1} to G^d to G. All the steps of this proof except the one from F^{d+e} to G^{d+e} are equivalences.

The same procedure gives us a complete method of equivalence proofs. If F and G are equivalent, then for some e the disjunctions F^{d+e} and G^{d+e} will have the same members and therefore be equivalent. In this case, all the steps of the proof from F to G will be equivalences.

In both cases, the argument is in a certain sense trivial ('analytic') if no increase in depth is needed, that is to say, if the elimination of trivially inconsistent constituents of depth d already suffices to bring out the desired relationship between F and G. The philosophical implications of this sense have already been studied in several earlier chapters of this book.

In all non-trivial disproofs, proofs, proofs from premisses, and equivalence proofs, we thus have to add to the depth of the formulae we are dealing with. Consider disproofs as an example. In order to disprove F, we bring it to its distributive normal form F^d (where d is the depth of F) and keep adding to the depth of the constituents of F^d until at some depth $d+e$ all the subordi-

[15] For an interesting discussion of a different standard form of linear proofs from assumptions, see William Craig, 'Linear Reasoning, A New Form of the Herbrand–Gentzen Theorem', *Journal of Symbolic Logic*, vol. 22 (1957), pp. 250–68.

nate constituents are inconsistent by our conditions. Here the difference e between the depth of F and the depth at which the inconsistency of F becomes explicit may be considered as a kind of (rough) measure as to how deeply hidden the inconsistency of F is and therefore also as a measure of the amount of 'development' or 'synthesis' required to bring this inconsistency into the open. This idea seems to have some philosophical interest. It also applies to the other kinds of proofs we have mentioned. For instance, in the method of equivalence proofs just described the difference between $d+e$ and the depth of F perhaps serves as a numerical measure of the amount of 'synthesis' which has to be performed on F in order to bring out its equivalence with G.[16]

It may be objected here that these suggested measures are all relative to the particular conditions of consistency which are being used in the proof in question, and hence not likely to have much general significance. That they depend on the conditions employed is true; but on the other hand it seems to me that in some rather elusive sense our conditions (A)–(E) of inconsistency are as strong as we can possibly hope natural conditions to be. Further work is needed here to clear up the situation.

From the way we proved the completeness theorem we can also read directions for a different standard form for first-order proofs which is much closer than the ones we have just mentioned to the earlier standard forms of Herbrand and Gentzen. Consider disproofs first. In this new standard form, each stage of the proof is again a disjunction of constituents, preceded by a transformation to the distributive normal form. Again, each disjunction is obtained from its immediate predecessor. The way in which this happens is now different, however. Instead of adding to the depth of our constituents we add new free individual symbols to them. In order to describe the procedure in more detail, assume that (8) occurs in one of the disjunctions. We choose one of the a-constituents of depth $d-1$ occurring in (8), say (9); the principles of selection will be commented on later. We drop the existential quantifier (Ex) which precedes an occurrence of (9) in (8), and replace x everywhere in this occurrence of (9) by a new free individual symbol a_{k+1}. This leaves

---

[16] If the depths of F and G are identical, exactly the same amount of 'synthesis' is required to convert F into G by the method just described as is required to disprove $\sim (F \equiv G)$, if these amounts are measured in the suggested way.

the parameter (P. 1) of (8) and its depth unchanged, but adds a new member to the set (P. 2). Hence we may transform the formula we have obtained into a disjunction of constituents with the same (P. 1) and the same depth as (8) but with one more free individual symbol a_k. This procedure corresponds to the expansion of a constituent of depth d into a disjunction of subordinate constituents of depth $d+1$.

To each of the new constituents we may apply the conditions (A)–(E) and eliminate those which turn out to be inconsistent. Each of the remaining ones is related to (8) in the same way as each member of S_1 was related to its predecessor. We can set up strong and weak correlations as well as associations in the same way as before and also define a seniority ranking among the a-constituents which occur in (8) and which have depth $d-1$ in the same way as in the completeness proof. For the particular a-constituent of depth $d-1$ in (8) into which the new free individual symbol was first introduced we may simply choose one of the highest ranking ones.

This disproof procedure is complete in the same way as the earlier one: either at some stage of the procedure all the constituents are inconsistent by our conditions (A)–(E) or else we have a sequence of constituents which is just like the sequence S_1 of a-constituents and which can be shown to be satisfiable in the same way as S_1. The only new feature is that there is not just one way of going from one stage to the next one, for there usually is some choice in the selection of that a-constituent of depth $d-1$ in (8) into which the new free individual symbol is first introduced.

In fact, both here and in the completeness proof there may even be more choice than we have allowed so far. The situation is the same in the two cases; hence we may consider S_1 by way of example. Suppose that we construct S_1 without any regard to the selection of (20) in (19) (section 15). Then we can define weak correlation and association as before. We can also define strong correlation in a variety of ways in most cases. From section 17 (from the argument which follows the lemmata) we can see that there is only one further thing which is needed in order for us to be able to carry out the completeness proof. This is that every chain of strong correlations eventually comes to an end when we proceed further and further in S_1. The use of the seniority ranking was simply an artifice for securing this end. If it can be obtained by other means, so much the better. In any case, the conventions concerning the seniority ranking need only be adhered to from some (arbitrarily late) stage on.

This suffices to describe the new disproof procedure. Similar procedures for proofs from premises and for equivalence proofs are obtained as a consequence, and a similar proof procedure as its dual.

The number of new free individual symbols which are introduced in one of these proofs may be said to indicate the amount of synthesis performed in it. The situation is now more complicated than before in that a given formula F may now have different disproofs with different numbers of free individual symbols introduced in them. The smallest of these numbers may be taken, however, to indicate the amount of synthesis needed to bring out the hidden inconsistency of F. It may be shown that this measure of the amount of synthesis required to disprove F coincides with the measure suggested earlier. Similar considerations apply to the other types of proofs.

We have described a proof procedure in which the free individual symbols remain unchanged but in which the depth of our formulae grows steadily, and one in which the depth of our formulae remains intact while new free individuals are introduced. These are really the two ends of a long spectrum of mixed proofs in which our two methods are employed together.

The method by means of which the completeness theorem was proved is now seen to be tied to the second type of disproof (introduction of new free individual symbols) much more closely than with the first (adding to the depth of constituents) although it is the first one which was initially considered in the completeness proof. In fact, in the completeness proof we first transformed the increase in depth into an increase in the number of free individual symbols. This may seem a rather roundabout way of proving the completeness of the first main method of disproof. In fact, we could have avoided this complication, but only at the expense of complicating the proof considerably in other respects. For this reason, the 'direct' proof will not be attempted here. It would be of interest to construct a model for a sequence S_0 of deeper and deeper constituents which satisfy (A)–(E) and which are subordinate to their predecessors directly without going by way of the auxiliary sequence S_1, for such a construction promises us a survey of the different kinds of model which S_0 (essentially, an arbitrary consistent and complete theory) can have. An interesting line of development seems to open here, a line in which the important results of Vaught's on models of complete theories (which entail the Ryll-Nardzewski $\aleph_0$-categoricity theorem) appear to assume a natural place.[17]

[17] For Vaught's results see 'Denumerable Models of Complete Theories', in *Infinitistic Methods, Proceedings of the Symposium on Foundations of Mathematics, Warsaw, 2–9 September 1959* (Pergamon Press, Oxford and London, 1961), pp. 303–21.

INDEX OF NAMES

SUBJECT INDEX